THE
CONSISTENT ETHIC OF LIFE

THE CONSISTENT ETHIC OF LIFE

Assessing Its Reception and Relevance

Thomas A. Nairn
Editor

The Bernardin Center
Catholic Theological Union, Chicago

ORBIS BOOKS

Maryknoll, New York 10545

Founded in 1970, Orbis Books endeavors to publish works that enlighten the mind, nourish the spirit, and challenge the conscience. The publishing arm of the Maryknoll Fathers and Brothers, Orbis seeks to explore the global dimensions of the Christian faith and mission, to invite dialogue with diverse cultures and religious traditions, and to serve the cause of reconciliation and peace. The books published reflect the opinions of their authors and are not meant to represent the official position of the Maryknoll Society. To obtain more information about Maryknoll and Orbis Books, please visit our website at www.maryknoll.org.

Library of Congress Cataloging-in-Publication Data

The consistent ethic of life : assessing its reception and relevance / Thomas A. Nairn, editor.
    p. cm.
    Includes index.
    ISBN-13: 978-1-57075-792-1
1. Ethics. 2. Christian ethics. 3. Christian ethics—Catholic authors. 4. Catholic Church and philosophy. 5. Consistent ethic of life. I. Nairn, Thomas A., 1948-
    BJ1249.C486 2008
    241'.697—dc22
                                                        2008018050

CONTENTS

CONTRIBUTORS

Elisabeth Brinkmann, R.S.C.J., is assistant professor of religious studies at the College of New Rochelle, New Rochelle, New York.

Ronald P. Hamel is senior director, ethics, at the Catholic Health Association, St. Louis, Missouri.

Patricia Beattie Jung is professor of Christian ethics and Oubri A. Poppele Professor of Health and Welfare Ministries at St. Paul School of Theology, Kansas City, Missouri.

James F. Keenan, S.J., is Founders Professor of Theology at Boston College, Chestnut Hill, Massachusetts.

M. Therese Lysaught is associate professor of theology at Marquette University, Milwaukee, Wisconsin.

Thomas A. Nairn, O.F.M., is the Erica and Harry John Family Professor of Catholic Ethics and the director of the Health Care Mission Leadership Program at Catholic Theological Union, Chicago, Illinois.

Dawn M. Nothwehr, O.S.F., is associate professor of Christian ethics at the Catholic Theological Union, Chicago, Illinois.

Thomas A. Shannon is Professor Emeritus of Religion and Social Ethics at Worcester Polytechnic Institute, Worcester, Massachusetts.

James J. Walter is the Austin and Ann O'Malley Professor of Bioethics and chair of The Bioethics Institute at Loyola Marymount University, Los Angeles, California.

Regina Wentzel Wolfe is Wicklander Senior Fellow at the Institute for Business and Professional Ethics at DePaul University, Chicago, Illinois.

A NOTE ON DOCUMENTATION

Throughout this volume the reader will find the abbreviation "SG" followed by a page number. This abbreviation plus page number identifies the source in the collection of Cardinal Bernardin's speeches gathered in *The Seamless Garment: Writings on the Consistent Ethic of Life* (Maryknoll, NY: Orbis Books, 2008).

The collection of Cardinal Bernardin's works made by Alphonse Spilly, C.Pp.S., is referred to often. In most cases the reference will cite the collection as follows: "Spilly, vol. 1, 44-49 (with "44-49" meaning "pages 44-49"). The full bibliographic information for these two volumes is Alphonse Spilly, ed., *Selected Works of Joseph Cardinal Bernardin*, 2 vols. (Collegeville, MN: Liturgical Press, 2000).

INTRODUCTION

THOMAS A. NAIRN, O.F.M.

Although December 2008 marks the twenty-fifth anniversary of the first of Cardinal Joseph Bernardin's consistent ethic of life lectures, the origin of this volume can properly be traced to 1996, during the last months of the cardinal's life. Catholic Theological Union (CTU) discussed with him its dream to establish a center to carry on his legacy. Shortly before his death, the cardinal gave permission for CTU to found the Bernardin Center for Theology and Ministry. In his letter to the school, he recommended that "the prospectus of the Bernardin Center make explicit mention of the Consistent Ethic of Life." He added, "It would be a source of great consolation to me to know that theologians will continue to develop the concept and continue that dimension of my legacy." Attentive to this responsibility, the contributors of this volume hope that this work will be seen as part of a larger undertaking by theologians and others to continue developing the consistent ethic of life and extending this dimension of Cardinal Joseph Bernardin's legacy.

The Development of the Consistent Ethic of Life

In January 1981, Archbishop John Roach of St. Paul–Minneapolis, who at the time was president of the National Conference of Catholic Bishops (NCCB, now the United States Conference of Catholic Bishops [USCCB]), created an ad hoc committee on war and peace and charged it with the task of writing a pastoral letter on the subject. He named Archbishop Joseph Bernardin of Cincinnati to chair the committee.[1] Fr. J. Bryan Hehir, then an associate secretary for international peace and justice of the United States Catholic Conference, became a staff member to the committee. The committee's work reached its conclusion in May 1983 when the conference voted 238-9 to approve the pastoral letter *The Challenge of Peace: God's Promise and Our Response.*[2] Fordham University invited Cardinal Bernardin to give the Gannon Lecture[3] the following December in order to discuss further the issue of the Catholic Church's stand on war and peace.

The autumn of 1983 was a busy one for Cardinal Bernardin. Not only was he a member of the World Synod of Bishops, which met from September 29 to October 28, but he was also a member of the Council of the General Secretariat of the Synod that prepared for the synod itself. Soon after returning to the United States, he was part of the national meeting of the NCCB from November 14 through November 17. At this meeting he was named chair of the NCCB's Pro-Life Committee.

It was only a few weeks before the lecture that Cardinal Bernardin con-
tacted Fr. Hehir and asked him to collaborate in writing the Gannon Lecture.
The final section of the pastoral letter had linked the issue of war with that
of reverence for life.[4] Now, as the former chair of the ad hoc committee that
wrote the pastoral letter and current chair of the bishops' Pro-Life Committee, the cardinal wanted to use the lecture to expand on this understanding
of linkage among a variety of life and justice issues, including both war and
abortion, under the rubric of reverence for life.

Years earlier, Hehir had collaborated with then Archbishop Humberto
Medeiros on a statement called "A Call to a Consistent Ethic of Life and the
Law."[5] He revived the term "consistent ethic of life" to describe the linkage
that Cardinal Bernardin wanted to articulate. In fact, as the earlier document proposed an ethic that was "comprehensive in scope and consistent in
substance,"[6] the Gannon Lecture likewise emphasized the need for an ethic
that is both comprehensive and consistent in nature.

The Gannon Lecture might have been the only lecture of the cardinal's
dedicated to the consistent ethic of life, were there not present in the audience
at Fordham University Kenneth Briggs, a reporter for *The New York Times.*
The next day, that newspaper carried a front-page article under the headline
"Bernardin Asks Catholics to Fight Both Nuclear Arms and Abortion." In
the article, Briggs described the talk as opening "a broad attack on a cluster
of issues related to the 'sanctity of life,' among them nuclear arms, abortion
and capital punishment." Briggs added that "the Cardinal said the various
issues made a 'seamless garment' that deserved the utmost attention of the
American Catholic Church."[7]

The article occasioned intense reactions. Letters were written by those
associated with pro-life issues and those associated with justice issues, many
criticizing the consistent ethic of life, but some praising the cardinal's stance.
The consistent ethic of life had captured people's imagination, both positively
and negatively. Needing to clarify his position in light of these criticisms, the
cardinal again enlisted the help of Fr. Hehir. Three months after the Gannon
Lecture, Cardinal Bernardin delivered his second lecture on the consistent ethic
of life at St. Louis University as part of the William Wade Lecture Series. He
introduced his talk by commenting that his Gannon Lecture had "generated
a substantial discussion both inside and outside the Church" (SG, 15) and
concluded the talk with a plea:

> The pastoral on war and peace speaks of a "new moment" in the
> nuclear age. . . . I am convinced that there is an "open moment"
> before us on the agenda of life issues. . . . I submit that a clear
> witness to a consistent ethic of life will allow us to grasp the op-
> portunity of this "open moment" and serve both the sacredness
> of every human life and the God of Life who is the origin and
> support of our common humanity. (SG, 20)

As it became evident to Cardinal Bernardin that the consistent ethic of life would become a regular theme among his lectures, he entrusted the development of these lectures to members of his staff in the Archdiocese of Chicago. In 1984, Fr. Alphonse Spilly, C.Pp.S., became special assistant to the cardinal, and among his tasks was that of writing the lectures on the consistent ethic of life. The following year he was joined by Fr. Michael Place, who became the cardinal's theological consultant. Both priests continued to work with the cardinal on developing the consistent ethic of life. Fr. Spilly describes the collaborative manner in which all of Cardinal Bernardin's talks were developed:

> A "resource group" helped Cardinal Bernardin draft his talks and writings on a regular basis. This anonymous group numbered from three to ten persons over the years. In addition, many others—within the archdiocese and across the country—helped with specific talks and writings. At times, the cardinal prepared an initial draft himself. Drafts prepared by others were usually routed through my office where they were entered into a computer and edited in accord with the cardinal's thought and style. Then he himself edited the drafts, sometimes several times. If he were not a bishop, he would have made an excellent editor or publisher. He was very concerned that, even though others often helped him prepare his talks and writings, he always made the texts his own. He did not say anything he did not want to say. It usually seemed clear to his listeners and readers that he spoke from his heart even if others had helped him find the right words to convey his message.[8]

The Scholars' Seminar

When the Erica and Harry John Family Chair of Catholic Ethics was established at CTU in 2002, part of the task entrusted to the holder of the chair was to abide by Cardinal Bernardin's wish in his giving permission for the establishment of the Bernardin Center—developing the concept of the consistent ethic of life and continuing that dimension of the cardinal's legacy.

Eventually, the ten scholars whose essays are part of this volume committed themselves to meet annually over a three-year period to examine the consistent ethic of life. During our first meeting, we agreed that two major questions would guide our discussions: (1) What do the different areas of life ethics and social justice bring to the consistent ethic of life? and (2) What does the consistent ethic of life still bring to these areas? The seminar then brainstormed regarding the content of the essays that would eventually become part of this volume.

The second meeting was spent critically analyzing the ten essays and offering suggestions for improvement. Again the participants agreed that the task at hand was not merely to repeat what Cardinal Bernardin had already done. Rather, the seminar looked at the trajectory of the consistent ethic of life and asked what it might look like in the present context. The members agreed to meet a third and final time to discuss the revised essays. At that meeting, the participants again engaged in a critical analysis of the ten essays and discussed the ordering of the essays and the section headings used in this volume. By this time, the authors had become so familiar with one another's works that it was suggested that, when appropriate, authors should refer to the other essays that comprise this volume.

The Essays

The ten essays are presented in four sections. The first section, "Exploring the Perspectives," raises some general questions concerning the nature of the consistent ethic of life. In the first chapter, James Walter uses Bernard Lonergan's understanding of horizon analysis to probe Cardinal Bernardin's project. Referring to the metaphor of a visual horizon, he suggests that "there are also horizons to our knowledge and desires, and they too can change on the basis of what we care to know and love." He concludes that the challenge that the consistent ethic of life continues to offer is its "placing into dialogue both the legitimate secularity of society with its values and the authenticity of the Christian tradition and its values." In the next chapter, Ronald Hamel describes the perspective of the consistent ethic of life as a "corrective vision," which he describes as "a way of seeing the world that is characterized by a particular set of beliefs and values." He then analyzes this vision to investigate more traditional issues of medical ethics and the issue of health-care reform. Hamel concludes that, in spite of the unfinished nature of the consistent ethic, there is nevertheless "a richness and a power in the fundamental vision it offers that is capable of guiding and motivating even … medicine and health care."

The second section, "Engaging Moral Reasoning," looks to particular methodological issues that are part of Cardinal Bernardin's consistent ethic of life. Thomas Nairn notes that the cardinal understood analogical reasoning as part of the "very character of Catholic moral thought" (SG, 103). His chapter suggests that in the consistent ethic of life there are three ways to understand moral analogy, the first being a sense of "family resemblance," the second that form of reasoning most often associated with casuistry, and the third, that which the philosopher David Burrell describes as a breaking open of language. He concludes that in its "moving to this third sense of analogy, the consistent ethic may finally contribute substantially to the development of moral theology." In chapter 4, James Keenan compares the consistent ethic of life to virtue ethics. He analyzes Cardinal Bernardin's statement that "ultimately ethics is about principles to guide the actions of individuals and of institutions" (SG, 12). Keenan concludes that what is needed is not necessarily an ethic of principles but rather a way to "develop those dispositions desirable to appreciate the sanctity of life and the practices appropriate for those dispositions." In the final chapter of this section, Patricia Beattie Jung looks at certain methodological inconsistencies in Cardinal Bernardin's ethic, especially in its "public-realm" vs. "private-realm" divide, and uses feminist ethics as a way to ensure that the consistent ethic of life becomes more consistent, concluding that, although the church must continue to illuminate the sanctity of life, it must also acknowledge life's ambiguities.

The third section of this volume, "Forming the Ecclesial Voice," looks at two areas of Catholic life in the United States and questions the "reception" of Cardinal Bernardin's project. In chapter 6, Elisabeth Brinkmann considers the rhetoric of the consistent ethic of life and uses her undergraduate students as a case study to explore how this ethic might be understood and accepted today. In doing so, she illustrates some of the social needs that must continue to be addressed by any development of the consistent ethic of life. Regina Wentzel Wolfe then addresses pastoral ministry. She takes as her starting point the document "Forming Consciences for Faithful Citizenship," written by the USCCB in 2007, and suggests that, although it might appear in this document that the consistent ethic of life has reached maturity in the U.S. Catholic Church, political debate among Catholics actually seems to have devolved into single-issue discussions that foster further division in the church, the exact opposite of Cardinal Bernardin's project. She notes that "establishing a moral stance grounded in the consistent ethic of life as a hallmark of ongoing faith formation is one way to respond to Cardinal Bernardin's request for ongoing examination of and dialogue on the concept 'in the quest for a comprehensive and consistent ethic of life.'"

The final section of this volume, "Expanding Contexts," looks beyond the cardinal's consistent ethic of life lectures themselves. In chapter 8, M. Therese Lysaught looks to two other works by the cardinal and describes them as the bookends that define the consistent ethic of life, the first being *The Challenge of Peace* and the other being his final book, *The Gift of Peace.*[9] Lysaught maintains that in order for the consistent ethic of life to fulfill its function, Catholics must attend to the substantive theological vision out of which the project arose and which must continuously inform it: a theology and spirituality of peace. Next, Dawn Nothwehr discusses ecology, an issue that Cardinal Bernardin did not address in his lectures. Using Denis Edwards's ecological theology, she demonstrates that for a consistent ethic of life to take ecology seriously it must posit a radically relational Triune God creating "a world that is relational to its core." She then uses her understanding of mutuality to move the consistent ethic forward and concludes that, while numerous distinctions continue to exist, "The ontological reality of mutuality provides a sobering attitude and principle from which to discern moral action." Finally, Thomas Shannon considers the emerging issue of genetics and calls for a consistent methodology across the range of life and justice cases, "one which will be more attentive to the social and political context of the choices, the nuanced way in which one's moral principles helps negotiate a resolution of the moral landscape, and a more coherent vision of the moral life."

A Word of Thanks

The Consistent Ethic of Life Scholars' Seminar at the Bernardin Center was able to begin its work because of grants from the Catholic Health Association; from its then president, Rev. Michael Place; and from the Menard Family Foundation. Further grants from the Menard Family Foundation and the ongoing interest of Barbara Menard allowed the seminar to continue and this volume to be printed. The Scholars' Seminar is especially grateful to her. At the same time, the Bernardin Center is indebted to the Archdiocese of Chicago and the Joseph Cardinal Bernardin Archives and Records Center for making all of Cardinal Bernardin's lectures on the consistent ethic of life available to the seminar. These thirty-five lectures have now been published in the book, *The Seamless Garment: Writings on the Consistent Ethic of Life.*

Where Do We Go from Here?

During the last meeting of the scholars' seminar, the participants raised among themselves questions such as: what is still unresolved in the consistent ethic of life, and where do we need to go from here? At one time the seminar considered writing an epilogue to this volume that would try to answer these questions. Yet, such an epilogue could never fulfill its stated purpose. The members of the seminar wrestled with the consistent ethic and offer the readers of this volume the results of the struggle of ten Catholic moral theologians. The authors do not all agree in our assessment of the relevance of the consistent ethic of life. Neither do we agree on what developments of the consistent ethic would ensure its reception by Catholics in the United States today. Readers of this volume—and its companion volume, *The Seamless Garment: Writings on the Consistent Ethic of Life* by Cardinal Joseph Bernardin—will most likely write the most important epilogue by their continued wrestling with these texts and by their own assessment and developing reception of the consistent ethic of life. We believe that such wrestling is well worth the effort.

PART 1

EXPLORING THE PERSPECTIVES

1.
WHAT DOES HORIZON ANALYSIS BRING TO THE CONSISTENT ETHIC OF LIFE?

James J. Walter

Cardinal Bernardin's speeches on the consistent ethic of life that occupied much of his attention before his death have definitely challenged much of the Catholic moral theology that has developed before and since Vatican II. My interest in his speeches is to apply a specific type of analysis to his notion of a consistent ethic in order to interpret what his intentions were in developing this provocative challenge. The particular type of analysis I rely on is horizon analysis or intentionality analysis, which has been used by such scholars as Edmund Husserl, Martin Heidegger, Maurice Merleau-Ponty, Paul Ricoeur, Karl Rahner, and Bernard Lonergan.[1] My own interpretation of this type of analysis draws principally from the thought of Lonergan.

Let me begin with the central thesis of this chapter. My focus in discussing Cardinal Bernardin's consistent ethic of life is primarily descriptive and analytic, not evaluative. To use a metaphor, I seek to use a hermeneutic key to unlock the inner intentionality of what I think Bernardin meant by the "consistent ethic of life." I do not seek to appraise and evaluate its validity or adequacy; that is a task for another time or for others in this volume to undertake. The argument of this chapter is that what Bernardin intended by his consistent ethic was essentially to develop a "moral stance." In other words, the cardinal most often described what he meant by a "consistent ethic of life" by reference to a "vision"[2] or a "framework"[3] that could be used across a wide range of concrete issues affecting the dignity or sacredness of human life, especially innocent human life. He believed that all the moral issues from "womb to tomb"—that is, issues from abortion to capital punishment to policies on health care and warfare—should be placed within a comprehensive "framework" or "vision" to formulate a normative judgment on the issues. "Vision" and "framework" render in another way what I call moral stance or horizon. This vision or framework (stance) that he sought to articulate was comprehensive in scope,[4] consistent in application,[5]

An earlier version of this chapter was published as "Horizon Analysis and Moral Stance: An Interpretation of Cardinal Bernardin's 'Consistent Ethic of Life,'" in James J. Walter and Thomas A. Shannon, *Contemporary Issues in Bioethics: A Catholic Perspective* (Lanham, MD: Sheed and Ward, 2005).

analogical in character,[6] and dialogical in its culture and social policy.[7] Each of these descriptions of his vision is important in itself to understand and appreciate, and I return to each of them shortly. However, before moving directly to an analysis of the descriptions, I need to develop more thoroughly what horizon analysis is and how one might use it in general theological and ethical discourse. In other words, by articulating what horizon analysis can contribute to theological and ethical analyses, I am able to articulate better what this analysis can contribute to Bernardin's consistent ethic of life.

Bernard Lonergan has made use of horizon analysis to clarify the nature and importance of both a theological and a moral stance. He used a heuristic metaphor, namely "horizon," to describe the context of all human cognition. For him, horizons can be understood literally as the line where earth meets the sky and where they limit our field of vision. In this ocular model, horizons change when we move from one position to another.[8] So, if I am standing in a valley, the farthest point that I can see is bounded by the hills that block my vision of what might lay beyond them. Though I might be able to ask questions about what may lay beyond the hills, I am not able to answer such a question. The answer simply lies beyond my horizon. If I then move to the top of one of the hills, then my vision is expanded and more of the terrain that lies before me comes into view. What was once hidden from me is now within my horizon or grasp, and consequently I now have an answer to my former question about what might lay beyond the hills. However, just as one's horizon has the possibility to expand, so too does one's horizon have the possibility to recede or diminish so that what was once known and prized is now once again hidden or no longer considered valuable.

If one makes a transition from an ocular to a disclosure model of conceiving horizon, however, we can grasp that, for Lonergan, there are also horizons to our knowledge and desires, and they too can change on the basis of what we care to know and love. In other words, what I am interested in knowing or caring about (values) are likewise bounded. Simply stated, my ability to know certain things or my ability to commit to values has limits. These limits can be exceeded when I am willing to ask different kinds of questions or willing to dedicate myself to new sets of values that have hitherto been beyond my horizon. Similar to the ocular model where I made a change from one location to another, what now comes within my grasp with these new questions and commitments is a different range of data or sets of experiences on which to reflect. When one uses a disclosure model of horizon as a way of understanding stance, then one understands that all stances imply two necessary and interrelated poles: a subject pole and an object pole. Both a theological stance and a moral stance are formed through the interaction between a subject pole, which involves the existential questions of the agent about his or her commitments, attitudes, lived values, actions, and social policies, on the one hand, and an object pole, which involves the range of data (a text, an experience, a collection of statistics, etc.) or "world" that comes into view for the agent to interpret, judge, and act on, on the other.

In essence, the interaction between these two referents fashions how one looks on reality, and it structures one's understandings of and moral judgments about the world, God, and self. To understand how stance can help to interpret theological interpretations, let's turn our attention to the nature of disclosure models and the five models of theological inquiry.

The Nature of Disclosure Models

There are several kinds of models. Scale or picture models copy an object exactly, according to a measure that miniaturizes or enlarges the image, such as the architectural model of a building or the representation of the DNA molecule. On the other hand, disclosure or analog models do not provide exact details, but like the drawing for a sculpture, they evoke the final product. They are a basic sketch, a guiding tool for inquiry, simplifying for the sake of identification. Their imaginative configuration approximates the result and invites understanding. In the investigation below of models of general theological interpretations and ethical interpretations, I use the second notion. In disclosure models, one distinguishes two poles: the subject investigating and the object or world disclosed by the study. In this analysis, I begin with general theological models developed through horizon analysis, and then I turn my attention to ethical models that serve as a moral stance.

Five Models of Theological Inquiry[9]

There have been five basic models of theological inquiry in the history of Christian theology. As we will see, each model places a subject pole (the theologian and his or her questions, interests, values, etc.) in relation to an object pole (the field of data that is consulted or appealed to in the formation of a normative claim to truth or value). No one theologian or author stands completely in one or another of these models. Rather, the models serve as heuristic devices to help the reader understand the subject and object poles of the author and the meaning of his or her writings. We see this more concretely when I turn my attention to Cardinal Bernardin and his speeches on the consistent ethic of life.

Classical Model. In the mode of theology that reigned supreme for some eighteen hundred years, the theologian was a believer within a particular confessional tradition who used various philosophic tools (Platonic, Neoplatonic, Augustinian, Aristotelian, etc.) to investigate the belief within the church. His (during this time, the theologian was almost always male) task was to express a carefully formulated tradition to the world. The world's understanding of itself had no explicit "internal" relevance in theological reflection. As examples, we might think of Thomas Aquinas, Bonaventure, Martin Luther, and John Calvin. Though it can be said quite justly that a theologian such as Aquinas included the intellectual concerns of Muslims and Jews, classical thinkers had as a goal the conversion of others. Their heirs during the later scholastic period (such as the Jesuit Francesco de Suarez [1548-1617] and the Lutheran Johann Gerhard [1582-1637]) exemplified an often logically brilliant organization, together with strict confessional polemics.

Liberal Model. In reaction to the academic form of Christian theologies, the period from 1750 to 1840 experienced an explosion of religious devotion as well as radical cultural departures in painting, poetry, music, and other arts. Romanticism in theology hoped to overcome a dry intellectual assent to doctrines through a resurrection of affective attachment to worship, the Scriptures, and beliefs. Whether in France (with René Chateaubriand [1768-1848]), in England (with Samuel Taylor Coleridge [1772-1834], or later, F. D. Maurice [1805-72]), in Germany (with Friedrich Schleiermacher [1768-1834]), or somewhat later in America (with Horace Bushnell [1802-76] and Walter Rauschenbusch [1861-1918]), the emphasis in theology shifted from the objective contents of faith to the subjective conditions of beliefs. The emerging sciences, developing political idealism, and artistic subjectivity had inner relevance to faith. Thus, the subject in this theological model is committed to modernity as a personal enterprise and sees the object of theology to be the Christian tradition—but as reformulated for the sake of the claims of the modern world.

Neo-Orthodox Model. There were strong responses to the nineteenth century's mode of theological investigation. In the early twentieth century, the Catholic community responded with a broad negative action against what were called modernists (especially Alfred Loisy [1857-1940] and George Tyrell [1861-1909]), condemning any "subjectivization" of Christian doctrines. After the devastating trench warfare of World War I, Karl Barth (1886-1968), especially in his *Commentary on the Epistle to the Romans* (1919) and his *Church Dogmatics* (1932-67), said a resounding no to the optimistic beliefs of liberal theology. Convinced, as the Catholic antimodernists were, that theological study had collapsed the dialectically critical character of the Christian proclamation into the scientific, cultural, and artistic biases of the age, he proposed a return to the prophetic immediacy of the Scriptures with the Reformers as the most authentic interpreters of the message. Because of the Fall, human beings are caught in a realm of sin such that only God's infinite qualitative difference, God's radical otherness, can transform our existence.

Reinhold Niebuhr (1891-1971), in *The Nature and Destiny of Man* (1939-43), mediated the language of dialectical divine presence to the American scene. In a sense, neo-orthodoxy allowed modernity to define the questions of experience, its quest for the infinite, and its sense of sinful personal and social alienation, but maintained that only the unique claims of Christianity could transform the problems into grace. The object pole of theology, therefore, is the wholly other God, a paradoxical mystery whose reality calls into question all our paltry reasoning and religious pretensions. The subject engaging in theology, called into existence by this God, is a human being dedicated to the quest forged by an authentic faith, truth, and love.

Radical Model. This theological endeavor looks at the development of postclassical thought and reminds us that modernity will not disappear. Is not the God who is wholly other busy overturning human expectations? Is not this God constantly competing with human projects? And hence, must not believers in this God conclude that our commitment to moral actions is inconsequential at best, sinful at worst? Can language about such a divinity be in any sense truthful, let alone verified? In this model, the concerns of the modern world are paramount; they define theologians and the world disclosed by their study. The subject is committed to contemporary science, transforming political endeavors and affective honesty; the object remains the Christian message, but this message concerns a person (Jesus), who is the paradigmatic moral person, and doctrines (salvation) without any clearly defined or sharply argued transcendent reference. The theological questions asked use the tools of early linguistic analysis (especially those of Ludwig Wittgenstein [1889-1951] and A. J. Ayer [1910-89]) and cultural commentary to argue that (at least the old classical or neo-orthodox) God is dead. This primarily American phenomenon is associated in the second part of the twentieth century with figures like Paul van Buren, Gabriel Vehanian, Thomas J. J. Altizer, and Joseph Fletcher.

Dialogical Model. A proposal that hopes to integrate the concerns of all these models has been suggested by David Tracy and others. It involves commitments at both poles of the model with a correlative process of interaction. The subject/theologian is committed *both* to an authentic public secularity (note: not secularism) *and* to an authentic Christian quest for truth, justice, and love. The object disclosed by theology is a critical reformulation of secular concerns *and* the motifs of Christian doctrine and value. Because faith *and* the world are taken seriously, they involve a mutually corrective interpretation. Faith must listen to the questions *and* the answers proposed by the world. The truthful character of the investigation is clarified by an examination of the moral claims made for religious as well as worldly "objects." Subject *and* object are correlatively "revised."

These models for theological reflection place the normative dimension, whether of truth or of value, in different places, but the standards at stake are primarily intellectual values. The models then establish a relationship between the conceptualized norms.

In the classical formula, the norm for truth or for value is to be found in the confessional tradition and its doctrines; in the liberal model, the standard is modernity's teachings as they reformulate Christian experience; in the neo-orthodox model, God's otherness is the normative judgment upon humanity's reasoning powers; and in the radical model, modernity shapes both believer and beliefs. In the final model, there is a dialogical norm: beliefs and reason are mutually related, so that if we say that faith is primary, we must recognize that its expressions are always culturally shaped. Since faith and the mystery of the Wholly Other exceed our ability to explicate them, we recognize that the subjective and objective poles of theological investigation, psychologically, socially, and culturally determined as they are, must be willing to "let go" of themselves when more adequate formulations appear.

These five theoretic correlations described above can also be judged according to their engagement in praxis or informed and committed doing.[10] The classical model focuses on the primacy of theory. "Theory regards objective knowledge as the formulation and verification of intelligibilities; it primarily regards possible, probable, or certain constructs of reality."[11] It mediates doctrines and value judgments in a particular cultural context, so that Christian activity implements good theory. One's religious and moral knowing is not intrinsically changed by doing.

In models in which only praxis is important, Christianity gains an internal relation to human activity, religious and secular, but at the cost of losing theoretic criticism of itself. Christian service would always be paramount but without a doctrinal spine or theoretic warrants. Praxis should be understood as what we actually do as involved and committed persons, the intersubjective home in which we establish ourselves as authentic or inauthentic subjects. A theology that stresses this dimension tends to think of doctrine as secondary, teaching as second-rate, and noncommitment to sociopolitical transformation as sinful. Many of the forms of liberal or radical theology fall within this category.

There is also a type of praxis theology that stresses the primacy of faith and love. Christianity stands in judgment on the theoretic formulation and the commitments of human praxis. The primary focus is upon the wholly other God. The prototype remains Karl Barth, for whom theology was always dialectically related to human activity. His Catholic friend Hans Urs von Balthasar (1905-88) can also be understood within this framework.

In the final two models for theology, there is an attempt to include both theory and praxis within religious discourse while maintaining the specific values Christianity has to offer to both. Where theory remains primary, the correlations between life, thought, and Christian conversion are mediated primarily through the extraordinarily tough demands of various contemporary sciences and theoretic disciplines. Matthew Lamb believes that Rudolf Bultmann (1884-1976), Paul Tillich (1886-1965), the Niebuhrs, and Karl Rahner (1904-84) belong in this category. Here theoretic issues are mutually and critically correlated, but nonintellectualized praxis becomes largely the application of already constituted theories. Human praxis fails to be the true origin of Christian knowing and loving. However, those who participate in the dialogical model that I have sketched above, e.g., Bernard Lonergan (1904-1984) and John Baptist Metz, opt for the primacy of critical Christian praxis in which theoretic and practical reflection are mutually informing. Christian praxis, by its loyalty to the suffering and poor, by its commitment to the radically unloved, by its recognition of atonement within creation groaning to be completed, better informs thought and action.

Ethical Stance

The search for the "imperative" or normative judgment in human and Christian moral experience is one of the human desires for meaning. In the moral life, the "ought" is part of the very process of self-transcendence through which we seek to conform our decisions and lives to informed judgments of value. Since judgments are not guesses but probable truths, normative judgments of value are concerned with the way the world and human relations probably ought to be. Yet the discernment of particular imperatives is not enough; there is also the need for coherence among all the normative judgments we make as individuals and as a society. Stated more concretely, it is not sufficient for us to arrive at distinct normative decisions on the issues of the value of human life and the economic policies affecting third-world countries. There must be some congruence, coherence, and consistency between these two sorts of normative value judgments—that is, judgments of virtue, judgments of rightness or wrongness of actions, and judgments of obligation. The desires for coherence and congruence result in what is called a stance. Simply defined, an ethical stance is a coherent combination of value judgments about the world, God, and self. Not only is stance the locus for the determination and justification of value judgments about what is right or wrong, good or bad, virtuous or vicious, stance is also the search for consistency between and among a whole range of judgments of value and oughtness. This search and desire for consistency in the moral life is what ties together one's judgments about abortion and one's judgments about the health-care policies that affect the poor.

An ethical stance, like general theological models, is formed through the interaction between a subject pole (existential questions about our commitments, lived values, actions, etc.) and an object pole (the range of data or "world" that comes into view for us to interpret, judge, and act on). The interaction between these two referents fashions the ways in which we look on reality and structures our understandings and judgments about the world. For example, we have seen that the classical theologian's subject pole comprises a commitment to a particular religious-moral tradition, and the furthest range of the object pole—that is, the range of data consulted and acted upon—includes the beliefs of that tradition. The ethical stance of such a theologian, then, represented an almost monolithic way of viewing and structuring the moral life. Specific imperatives, virtues, values, and actions were understood and judged according to the established moral data (doctrines) of the tradition, and alternative ways of understanding and judging were thought erroneous or were beyond the boundaries of the theologian's consciousness.

When we seek to thematize or make explicit in consciousness the contents of a stance—that is, to make explicit both the subject and object poles of the decision maker's stance—we attempt to make explicit the very foundations of the normative judgment itself and its justification. In other words, the normative judgment—that is, judgments about what kinds of virtues we need to live the moral life well, or judgments about the rightness of actions, or judgments about our moral obligations—arises from within the context of a normative stance, and so the stance is actually the ground and justification of the normative judgment itself. For example, for most classical theologians the ethical imperative or normative judgment arose only from within the confines of their particular religious-moral traditions, because these theologians were committed at the subject pole to the religious tradition and its values, and the object pole was the tradition itself with its doctrinal tradition.

If a theologian is committed to Roman Catholicism, then all ethical imperatives find their ground and justification from within that tradition. Thus, until the middle of the twentieth century, almost all Roman Catholic theologians argued that the primary purpose of marital sexual relations was procreation. They were committed to preserving their long-standing understanding of sexuality that can be traced back to Augustine and Thomas Aquinas. This tradition had understood sexual relations between spouses as acts of nature (and not primarily as acts of love) having a moral intentionality or finality (procreation) built into them by God. To act against this moral finality by some form of artificial contraception was tantamount to acting directly against God. We can see, then, that how we discern, argue, and justify the ethical imperative is a function of how we intend and understand the human world.

There have been several normative stances proposed within the Christian traditions.[12] In classical Protestantism—for example, in Martin Luther's writings—faith was considered the stance for the moral life. *Sola fide* (by faith alone) was the fundamental viewpoint from which the ethical imperative was discerned, argued, and justified. Second, in some forms of Protestant liberalism of the twentieth century, love (*agape*) became an alternative stance to faith. For example, Adolf von Harnack (1851-1930) thought that the entire gospel of Jesus could be embraced under the rubric of love without depreciating the gospel message itself.[13] Thus, von Harnack considered the entire moral life to be founded on the single commandment to love in the New Testament.

Some neo-orthodox Protestant theologians proposed a third stance based on Jesus Christ. For example, in reaction to Protestant liberalism, Karl Barth argued that only through Jesus Christ is the Christian enabled to know and do good. Thus, Barth's ethics was a form of Christological monism in that the ethical imperative and all normative judgments must always be founded on Jesus Christ alone and can be authentically discovered and justified only through belief in him.[14]

Against these stances, James Sellers proposed the stance of promise and fulfillment as the normative horizon of the Judeo-Christian moral life. For him, salvation is best understood as "wholeness," but humanity has not yet possessed this wholeness fully and therefore must search for it. Humanity is moving toward the plenitude of salvation (wholeness) that has been promised, and so the best stance from which to discover and justify the ethical imperative is within the horizon of promise and fulfillment.[15]

Finally, Charles E. Curran in the 1970s proposed a stance based on the fivefold Christian mysteries of creation, fall, incarnation, redemption, and resurrection destiny.[16] For him, each one of these doctrinal themes normatively interprets Christian experience within a comprehensive schema. All these mysteries taken together, then, serve as a way not only to shape and inform the Christian's moral reasoning on concrete issues but also as a way to critique other religious and secular stances in society that underlie and justify normative judgments on moral issues like abortion, capital punishment, and so on.

As helpful as all these stances might be, all of them seem to be far too content-oriented and doctrinaire in their intent and far too narrow in their scope. In other words, these stances are interpreted through content categories alone—for example, Jesus Christ or love (*agape*) or the fivefold Christian mysteries—and the content is too indigenous to a specific confessional tradition (doctrinaire). Surely, the content categories of the believer's stance can and should be specifically Christian, particularly when explicit reference is made to Jesus and his teachings of the kingdom, but I argue that the proper category by which one should understand a stance should be formal or structural in nature. In other words, one should understand a stance by reference to the interaction between the subject and the object poles of human knowing. Furthermore, an ethical stance must be as comprehensive as possible to take into view as many elements of moral experience as possible. Nearly all the stances discussed above lack this comprehensive scope. For example, Barth's stance (Jesus Christ) fails to appreciate that in fact nonreligious people do experience an authentic ethical imperative, although they have no reflective experience of God or of Jesus Christ.

Cardinal Bernardin's "Consistent Ethic of Life" Understood as a Moral Stance

I have already defined a moral stance as a coherent and consistent combination of normative value judgments about the world, God, and self. It is precisely in the interaction between the subject and object poles that the claim to a normative moral judgment about virtues, moral actions, and obligations in the moral life is discovered, articulated, and justified. Thus, like all stances, Cardinal Bernardin's consistent ethic of life structures one's fundamental understanding of moral experience, serves as a critique of others' interpretations of moral reality, and becomes a source of ethical criteria to evaluate particular actions and social policies across a wide range of moral issues. Though a stance is always logically prior to systematic reflection on specific issues—for example, abortion—nonetheless it seeks such reflection by its very nature. Because a stance is the foundation of or matrix within which moral imperatives are discovered and ultimately justified, the validity of the imperatives rests on the validity of the stance. Thus, if a stance lacks comprehensiveness, coherence, or authenticity, then so do the moral imperatives or moral judgments of virtue, value, or obligation that have been discerned and formulated from within the stance.

The vision that Bernardin proposes is comprehensive in that it refuses to leave out any life issue that affects the sacredness of persons. At the subject pole where one's attitudes and commitments come into view, he is committed to a full range of issues where human life and dignity are at stake, and these commitments and attitudes are nourished and informed by various theological themes. Though he argues that these themes are specifically grounded in the New Testament, he believes that neither the themes nor the content generated from the themes are specific or unique only to the Christian stance.[17] By arguing in principle that the themes and content are not necessarily specific to Christians, Bernardin is able, at the level of his vision (stance), to dialogue with others in society who are not Christian. At the object pole where the range of data or "world" comes into view, Bernardin's consistent ethic of life is comprehensive in that the vision encompasses all the particular issues from womb to tomb. Put negatively, his moral stance refuses to exclude any issue that threatens the dignity or sacredness of the human person, and he employs this vision to criticize other groups whose stance is narrowed by commitment to one specific issue—for example, abortion.

On almost every page of his speeches, Cardinal Bernardin calls for a consistency in attitude and in the use and application of certain moral principles. Though I assess here neither the adequacy nor the validity of these moral principles, what is important for my purposes is to indicate how the consistency he calls for is part of his moral vision or stance. Of course, any particular moral stance can be inconsistent, and to that extent it is incoherent, and possibly even inauthentic. People can hold to one thing, yet incoherently do something else that is inconsistent with their basic attitudes and commitments. Likewise, individuals and whole communities can commit themselves to certain moral principles to inform and direct their behavior, but then they can be highly selective and serendipitous in the application of these principles. One of the hallmarks of an *adequate* vision of moral experience is its ability to tie together attitude and doing, commitment and application. It seems to me that in his emphasis on consistency Bernardin seeks to achieve this adequacy. He uses consistency not only to assess the adequacy of others' stances but also the adequacy of various social attitudes and policies.

The moral stance of Cardinal Bernardin is also analogical[18] in character because it seeks to view issues that are not identical but which have some common characteristics.[19] Though he insists that each issue along the spectrum of life must be considered on its own merits, he believes this should not dull our vision to the possible connections among these distinct concerns. A stance that is analogical, then, approaches the interpretation of moral experience with an eye to possible similarities; it refuses to look on our moral lives as disparate and unconnected. The radical existentialist's or situationist's vision is inspired by the novelty of the individual and the particular. As such, their vision is committed to seeing only the disconnections within moral experience and the uniqueness of each moral issue. Bernardin's stance is quite different from this situationist's view, and it is quite different from other stances. His stance is not as radical as their claim to particularity, and his is not narrowed by a desire to concentrate on the importance of a single issue at the expense of seeing connections to other issues. By paying attention to and focusing on the links that exist among a variety of issues, Cardinal Bernardin's stance can allow him to dialogue and form coalitions with others along a whole spectrum of concerns in order to transform people's hearts and actions and society's policies.

I indicated above that a moral stance is logically prior to systematic reflection but that it ultimately seeks that kind of reflection. When the contents of a stance are thematized and made explicit, the attitudes and commitments embodied in that vision make their way into and influence systematic reflection on moral experience. Bernardin is certainly correct in describing his consistent ethic as a way (I would say "heuristic device") of defining the problems that confront human dignity.[20] This is precisely what a stance is and does. But he also claims that the consistent ethic is systematic.[21] He links this term to the nature of Catholic theology, which is the systematic reflection on religious-moral experience. As a reflective discipline, theology has the task of drawing out the meaning of each moral principle and the relationships among them,[22] and it refuses to look at and treat moral issues in an ad hoc fashion.[23] I would argue, though, that not all theologies can accomplish what Bernardin seeks. Some types of theology that have a narrow stance that lies behind them will not in fact look at and treat moral issues in any other way than ad hoc. Because a moral stance is not only the foundation of systematic reflection but also of the moral imperative and normative judgment discoverable by that reflection, the adequacy of a theology will depend upon the comprehensiveness and authenticity of the stance which gives rise to that discipline.

When we turn our attention to placing Bernardin and his writings into one or more of the general models of theological discourse, what we find with him, like with most other authors, is that he does not neatly fit into any one of the models. Rather, he seems to move between two of the general models: the neo-orthodox and dialogical. Though we find Bernardin in each of these models, I would argue that his consistent ethic of life was in fact an attempt on his part to initiate a change from the neo-orthodox to the dialogical model. At first glance, this attempted shift was somewhat unusual or even revolutionary given the standard paradigm of the "teaching church" that was accepted among most of the hierarchy in the church. Whether Bernardin was truly successful in this shift to a dialogical horizon, however, occupies the attention of several of the other authors in this volume, especially chapter 5 by Patricia Beattie Jung.

In some of his earlier speeches, especially those dealing specifically with the moral issue of abortion, Cardinal Bernardin appears to fit more squarely into the neo-orthodox model that I described above. It seems that what he is committed to and the kinds of questions that he asks are determined principally, if not entirely, by the moral tradition of the Roman Catholic Church and its doctrinal tradition. Thus, the range of data that comes into view for him tends to be the doctrinal content of this tradition, though some opening is made to other considerations. On the other hand, Bernardin also adopts the dialogical model in which he regularly reformulates his commitments and questions to include those concerns, values, and normative claims of secular society and other religious traditions. Consequently, I find that the range of data that he consults and is interested in investigating begins to change in that his data now comprise the experiences of people, including the experience of women, and the values and data of secular society. For example, when Bernardin held open sessions for his "Common Ground" initiative or interviews prior to the writing of the pastoral letter *The Challenge of Peace*, he sought input from various secular sources, some of whom for the latter sessions were either military strategists or others who had an expertise in matters of warfare.[24] He did not limit his data at the object pole solely to the contents of the doctrinal tradition of the Roman Catholic Church on issues of peace and warfare. In these instances, Bernardin is committed to dialogue. As he states in the Gannon lecture:

> As we seek to shape and share the vision of a consistent ethic of life, I suggest a style governed by the following rule: We should maintain and clearly articulate our religious convictions but also maintain our civil courtesy. We should be vigorous in stating a case and attentive in hearing another's case; we should test everyone's logic but not question his or her motives. (SG, 14)

What one finds here is Bernardin's commitment not only to the values and normative claims of the Catholic tradition but also a commitment to a dialogue with others and their values and normative judgments. When one is invested in true dialogue, one must suspend for the moment one's own taken-for-granted assumptions and normative judgments and allow the conversation with the other and his or her values and judgments to be included as new data for further reflection. Bernardin's questions about and commitments to including the experiences and judgments of others in society beyond his own ecclesial community and religious tradition were the conditions of the possibility for him to formulate the consistent ethic of life. Had he remained, as head of the Committee for Pro-Life Activities of the United States Conference of Catholic Bishops, only within the neo-orthodox model of theological discourse—with its commitments to the established tradition and its content only—he quite possibly would never have articulated the need for the consistent ethic of life—with its commitments to dialogue with others outside the tradition. As he changed his commitments and questions about a wide range of issues that confront the sacredness of life, the data (people's experiences, scholarly documents, etc.) that came into view for him to consult and reflect upon also changed. As we recall, when the subject pole changes, there is a corresponding change at the object pole. Such an important change signaled and marked his movement from the neo-orthodox model of normative judgment making to the dialogical model. In moving from one model to another, Bernardin was able to challenge two different groups. The first group was the pro-life movement within his own Catholic tradition that had a tendency to focus on only a single issue—namely, abortion—and thus not see how a normative judgment on this issue must be consistent with other normative judgments on a wide range of other moral issues that affect the sacredness of human life—for example, capital punishment, delivery of health care to the poor, and warfare. On the other hand, his consistent ethic was also a challenge to secular society to change its attitudes, practices, and social policies on these same issues related to the sacredness of life.

Conclusion

In the end, Cardinal Bernardin has left us with a great challenge. Understanding the nature or inner intentionality of that challenge as the systematic development of an authentic, comprehensive, analogical, and dialogical stance is the first task in taking up the charge that Bernardin has placed before us. His commitment to placing into dialogue the legitimate secularity of society with its values *and* the authenticity of the Christian tradition and its values is the nexus and challenge of his consistent ethic of life.[25]

2.
THE CONSISTENT ETHIC OF LIFE

A Corrective Moral Vision for Health Care

RONALD P. HAMEL

"Because of its central importance to human dignity, to the quality of our community life, I have felt a special responsibility to devote a considerable amount of attention to healthcare at both the local and national levels."[1] Joseph Cardinal Bernardin spoke these words to the Harvard Business School Club of Chicago in 1995. Indeed, he did have a keen appreciation of the importance of health care, and he did direct considerable energy and attention to it. During his tenure as archbishop of Chicago, Bernardin devoted close to two dozen addresses to topics related to health care, ranging from abortion and euthanasia to managed care, the physician's covenant with patients and society, and health-care reform. In almost every one of these presentations, Bernardin made at least some mention of the consistent ethic of life, and, in most, the consistent ethic of life shaped his approach to and development of the topic.

Given the critical role that Cardinal Bernardin's consistent ethic of life served in his treatment of health-care issues, it seems only fitting to ask how it functioned, what it contributed to those discussions, and what, if anything, it might contribute to ongoing efforts to grapple with old and new challenges in this domain today. Does the consistent ethic of life contribute to health care in any significant way, some twenty-five years after it was first articulated? Or, is its relevance limited, either because of the nature of the consistent ethic of life itself or because of the particular context in which it was developed and proposed?

This essay attempts to address these questions by first considering key features of Cardinal Bernardin's consistent ethic of life and then examining how the consistent ethic of life functioned in Bernardin's own approach to health-care issues while suggesting along the way what it may have to offer health care. The essay concludes with an assessment of the contribution of the consistent ethic of life to health care and proposes that its principal contribution is to provide a "corrective moral vision."[2] "Moral vision" refers to a way of seeing the world that is characterized by a particular set of beliefs and values.[3] Moral vision, essentially an interpretive lens, affects what is seen, how it is seen, and how one interprets what is seen. The vision is "corrective" in the sense that it challenges social and cultural assumptions informed by a different set of beliefs and values and provides either an alternative or complementary (i.e., adding missing elements) way of viewing and interpreting reality. In turn, seeing differently should lead to doing differently. Bernardin's consistent ethic of life offers such a corrective moral vision for health care.

Bernardin's Consistent Ethic of Life

In three addresses over the course of three years (1983-86),[4] Cardinal Bernardin articulated the core elements of his consistent ethic, though he continued to refine and elaborate upon it for the remainder of his career. Given the task of this essay, a brief delineation of those essential features seems to be in order. First, Bernardin's consistent ethic is founded on the conviction that human life is sacred, a sacredness grounded in the belief that human beings are made in the *imago Dei*. While Bernardin most often speaks in terms of the sacredness of human life, he also, at times, uses the language of human dignity—the inviolable dignity of human persons and the need to respect persons. For example, he points out in one of his lectures that theologically the consistent ethic "is grounded in the respect we owe the human person. To defend human life is to protect the human person . . . the core reality in Catholic moral thought" (SG, 103).[5] In addition, he considers human life to be social; as such, we have a personal as well as a social responsibility to protect and preserve human life at all stages of development and across the whole continuum of life. In part, this requires the creation of a social environment that protects and fosters the development of life, that respects the dignity of human persons.

Second, Bernardin's consistent ethic seems to have been born of the insight and the conviction that the Catholic moral tradition can bring a comprehensiveness and a consistency to the treatment of a broad spectrum of individual threats to human life and dignity. As he says in one of his earliest addresses on the topic: "I am convinced that the Catholic moral vision has the scope, the strength and the subtlety to address this wide range of issues in an effective fashion" (SG, 17). That vision "joins the humanity of the unborn infant and the humanity of the hungry; it calls for positive legal action to prevent the killing of the unborn or the aged and positive societal action to provide shelter for the homeless and education for the illiterate" (SG, 17). While distinct, these issues have a common foundation. Each has to do with the dignity of the human person and the sacredness of human life. At the same time, however, Bernardin also recognizes that these threats to human life, both to the preservation of life itself (the right to life) and to the quality of life (promoting those rights that enhance life), are very distinct and require individual treatment.

In a later address, Bernardin employs other terms to describe these features of his consistent ethic. He refers to it as being both "systematic" in its argument and "analogical" in its perspective, both aspects, he believes, arising out of Catholic moral theology.

The systematic nature of Catholic theology means it is grounded in a set of basic principles and then articulated in a fashion which draws out the meaning of each principle and the relationships among them. Precisely because of its systematic quality, Catholic theology refuses to treat moral issues in an *ad hoc* fashion. There is a continual process of testing the use of a principle in one case by its use in very different circumstances. The consistent ethic seeks only to illustrate how this testing goes on when dealing with issues involving the taking of life or the enhancement of life through social policy. (SG, 103)

When he describes his consistent ethic as "analogical," Bernardin intends to emphasize the similarities and the unifying elements among the multiple and varied threats to human life, while not collapsing the differences. "The *differences* among these cases are universally acknowledged; a consistent ethic seeks to highlight the fact the differences do not destroy the elements of a *common moral challenge*" (SG, 103). These two features give rise to the possibility of developing a moral vision that can address the multiple threats to human life and human dignity in a coherent and comprehensive manner. Third, though Bernardin does not develop this characteristic at any great length, he does maintain that "attitude"—a public attitude or societal environment of respect for all of life—is the place to ground and the precondition for sustaining a consistent ethic. Unless there is a transformation of societal attitudes, respect for human life and dignity will not take hold. With such a transformation, there can also be a transformation of public and institutional policies and practices. For Bernardin, a transformation of individual and societal attitudes toward human life is critical.

Fourth, Bernardin maintains that a consistent ethic of life will need to be "finely honed and carefully structured on the basis of values, principles, rules and applications to specific cases" (SG, 11). Ultimately, Bernardin observes, ethics is about principles that help guide the actions of individuals and institutions. The core principle in his consistent ethic of life is the prohibition of directly taking innocent human life. This single principle has diverse applications—abortion, war, capital punishment, and euthanasia among them—and, thereby, links these discrete issues. At the same time, however, Bernardin recognizes that this sole principle is not sufficient, and that there is need for additional moral principles that have more specific applicability to the diverse issues.

Fifth, Bernardin believes that a consistent ethic of life has direct implications for public policy and that it should impact political choices, namely, assessment of party platforms, public policies, and political candidates. In doing this, however, it is also important to recognize that not all issues have the same moral import (for example, abortion is qualitatively more morally grave than lack of health-care coverage).

And, finally, while the church must establish credibility across a wide range of life issues, individuals must establish priorities regarding their own public witness to life, while not denying the interdependence of the issues. The latter is critical. It would be inconsistent for individuals to witness to life at one end of the spectrum of life issues while being insensitive or even hostile to life issues at the other end.

These then are the core elements of Cardinal Bernardin's consistent ethic of life. How do they shape his treatment of health-care issues? It was not until May 1985, in a lecture at Loyola University of Chicago (SG, 77-84), that Bernardin offered his first major articulation of the consistent ethic of life in relation to health care. Several other addresses that deal with health care precede this one (beginning in 1983)[6] and contain hints of the consistent ethic, but neither the ethic nor its application to health care was yet explicit. In the Loyola lecture, after reviewing the major themes of his consistent ethic, Bernardin proceeds to structure his discussion under two major headings— "classical" medical ethics questions and "contemporary" social justice issues. Following Bernardin, I employ these two headings in order to organize and explore Bernardin's discussion of health-care issues from the perspective of the consistent ethic of life. Under each heading, I examine what Bernardin addresses relating to the heading and what the contributions of the consistent ethic might be.[7]

The Consistent Ethic of Life and "Classical" Medical Ethics Questions

Under this heading in his Loyola lecture, Bernardin makes mention of a broad range of technological developments dealing with the entire spectrum of life from artificial insemination to genetics to various means of prolonging life. For him, the basic question vis-à-vis these issues is: how do we decide morally what we should *not* do in an age when we can do most anything technologically? Although he poses this question, he does not answer it, either in general or with regard to one or more specific issues, except to say that "technology must not be allowed to hold the health of human beings as hostage" (SG, 80). The only hint of an answer comes when he briefly describes advances in genetics and some of the benefits of these advances, ending with a comment on their dark side, the challenges they pose. Bernardin notes in particular sex selection and terminating the lives of those who are "undesirable" genetically. Similarly, he mentions the enormous technological possibilities of preserving and prolonging the lives of infants, children, and adults usually for the good, but also mentions the pursuit by some of legalized euthanasia.

Bernardin concludes this section of his lecture by making three claims for his consistent ethic of life. First, the consistent ethic provides "additional insight" into the new challenges that arise in classical medical ethics. How? By "taking into consideration the impact of technology on the full spectrum of life issues" (SG, 81). Second, the consistent ethic "enables us to define the problems in terms of their impact on human life" (SG, 81). And, third, the consistent ethic enables us to "clarify what it means to address them [the new challenges] from a Catholic perspective" (SG, 81). Bernardin offers no further elaboration on these claims. Given the core features of his consistent ethic of life, however, one might infer that Bernardin regards his consistent ethic as providing a particular perspective toward issues that fall under the category of classical medical ethics questions—that is, those of a more clinical nature. That perspective would likely be comprehensive and analogical in that it would consider the full range of technologies that might have an impact on human life recognizing both the commonalities and the differences. It would also place the person and human life (both preserving human life against harm or destruction and enhancing human life by promoting those rights that contribute to human enhancement) and the impact of these technologies upon them, at the very center of those considerations. In addition, any technology that involves the direct taking of innocent human life would be judged morally unacceptable.

Another way to say this is that Cardinal Bernardin's consistent ethic seems to provide something more than tools for a moral analysis of specific biomedical technologies or even judgments of these technologies. While this and other of his addresses are not devoid of such, these elements do not appear to be his primary concern or emphasis. Instead, Bernardin offers a *moral vision*, a way of seeing the full range of developments in science and medicine as well as in health-care delivery. The most telling comment in his Loyola lecture is that the consistent ethic offers "additional insight" (or, in the words of William F. May, a "vision"). It offers another way to "see into" and interpret the issues, a way that underscores the centrality of human life and human dignity and that views all the disparate issues as related to human life and dignity. In doing so, this "additional insight" or "vision" is also "corrective" in that it lifts human life and dignity to the status of primary concern and attempts to demonstrate relationships among issues that would otherwise be considered in an isolated or fragmented manner.

A year following the Loyola address, Bernardin delivered a lecture at the Catholic Medical Center in Jamaica, New York (SG, 109-16), where he again returns to "classical" medical ethics questions. In this lecture, however, he turns to the issue of ordinary-extraordinary means. He begins by iterating two fundamental principles. The first is that innocent human life can never be directly attacked. Hence, euthanasia is always morally wrong. The second principle he appeals to is the nonabsoluteness of earthly life. "Life on this earth is not an end in itself; its purpose is to prepare us for a life of eternal union with God" (SG, 112). Flowing from this principle, he states, is the distinction between ordinary and extraordinary means, concluding that "a

Catholic is not bound to initiate, and is free to suspend, any medical treatment that is extraordinary in nature" (SG, 112). After a brief explanation of the ethical meaning of ordinary and extraordinary, appealing to Pius XII and the 1980 Vatican "Declaration on Euthanasia," Bernardin comments on the usefulness of the consistent ethic of life to end-of-life matters. He makes two observations. The first is that in the face of a societal disregard for the sanctity and dignity of life, "We must develop social attitudes, policies, and practices that guarantee the right of the elderly and the chronically and terminally ill to the spiritual and human care they need. The process of dying . . . should not be allowed to be dominated by . . . purely utilitarian considerations or cost-benefit analyses" (SG, 113). The second observation is that the Catholic Christian community's care of the terminally ill must be shaped by the conviction that dying and death are fundamentally good in that they are a transition into eternal life (SG, 113-14).

While Bernardin appeals to two principles in his discussion, principles that help determine the morality of particular actions, he identifies the usefulness of the consistent ethic primarily as calling for and contributing to the transformation of personal and societal attitudes (toward greater respect for human life and human dignity), which in turn will lead to different social and institutional policies and practices. Though Bernardin does not specify what he has in mind with regard to policies and practices, one might surmise (given the subject of his lecture) that he intends those having to do with euthanasia, physician-assisted suicide, forgoing life-sustaining treatment, advance directives, futile treatment, how we care for the dying, and the like. Bernardin also notes in this lecture that the consistent ethic "enables us to define the problems in a broader, more credible context" (SG, 114). This comment hearkens back to a constitutive element of his approach, namely, comprehensiveness. In other words, our approach to end-of-life issues should see them all as having to do with respecting human dignity and both respecting life and enhancing life. In this context, that would mean opposing euthanasia and physician-assisted suicide, but also enhancing care for the dying or the way that people live while dying.

Bernardin's comment about the transformation of attitudes above is, perhaps, the more important. It, too, points to moral vision. A moral vision that focuses on the sacredness of human life and inherent human dignity can both challenge prevailing cultural visions and help transform them by providing an alternative, one that does not approach human life in a utilitarian manner and human dignity as conferred.[8] Here we see Bernardin's moral vision as being *corrective*. Such a corrective moral vision is most important because, as Bernardin suggests, it ultimately influences society's policies and practices. Seeing rightly will affect acting rightly.

In 1988, Bernardin devoted an entire lecture to the topic of euthanasia (SG, 154-63). Much of the lecture has to do with euthanasia as a public policy issue, but in it, Bernardin also addresses the ethics of euthanasia and, in doing so, appeals explicitly to the consistent ethic of life. "The founda-

tion of my position on euthanasia is to be found in what I have described as
a consistent ethic of life" (SG, 159). He goes on to identify the "grounding
principle" of this ethic, namely, the fact that human life is sacred because God
is its origin and destiny. Because of the "distinctive dignity and meaning or
purpose" of human life, "innocent human life must not be directly attacked,
threatened, or diminished" (SG, 159). The "second principle" that informs
the consistent ethic of life is the belief that human life is also social. "To be
human is to be social, and those relationships, structures, and institutions
which support us as individuals and as a community are an essential aspect
of human life" (SG, 159). From these two principles, Bernardin draws two
obligations for both individuals and society: a *positive* obligation to protect
life, and a *negative* obligation not to directly destroy or injure human life,
especially that of the innocent and the vulnerable.

    One gleans from this lecture additional dimensions of Bernardin's cor-
rective moral vision. It rejects the notion that some individuals or categories
of individuals no longer have a dignity that must be protected. Bernardin
reaffirms his conviction that the dignity of innocent human life is absolute
and never ought to be violated, regardless of the condition of that life. Equally
important, Bernardin rejects the notion that euthanasia is a private matter
based on individual choice. His vision challenges the individualism and the
privatization of moral choices so entrenched in American society, especially
as related to abortion, assisted suicide, and euthanasia. Against those who
maintain that the decision about how to end life is essentially a private decision beyond the interests of the state, Bernardin argues:

> Human beings are meant to live in community. Social order is
> not an enemy but a necessary good that protects personal and
> social life. Kept in proper balance, the tension between personal
> rights and social goods can be healthy. And nowhere is this more
> evident than in matters pertaining to the defense and enhance-
> ment of life itself. Neither individuals nor society can long survive
> when respect for the inviolability of life is diminished. It is for this
> reason that the protection of innocent life must be understood
> as part of the public order of society. As such, it legitimately fits
> within the scope of civil law.
>   . . . We may never agree to this privatization of life because,
> if we were to do so, we would undermine our ability to live in
> community. Life is both a private and a public good, and, therefore,
> social legislation to defend and protect it is both appropriate and
> necessary. (SG, 160-61)

Over against individualism and an emphasis on individual rights and autonomy, Bernardin underscores our social nature, our social obligations, and the
necessity of individuals and the State to work for the common good of all.
    Further insight is gained into the consistent ethic of life itself and into

its contributions to health care in Bernardin's 1990 address to the Wood-stock Theological Center on "The Consistent Ethic of Life after Webster" (SG, 188-99). Here he makes the observation that "the consistent ethic . . . is helpful in that it illustrates the consequences on a range of issues when we fail as a society to protect the sacredness of every human life. A moral vision which does not have room in the circle of the human community for unborn children will inevitably draw the circle of life too narrowly in other decisions of social and economic policy" (SG, 191). Bernardin then points out that while we failed to protect unborn life in the 1970s, we subsequently failed to care adequately for children in the 1980s as evidenced in high infant mortality and lack of sufficient health care, nutrition, and housing. He observes, "There must be a connection . . . between our lack of moral vision in protecting unborn children and our lack of social vision in the provision of basic necessities for women and children" (SG, 191). The consistent ethic, he argues, must refocus attention from the question of "Who decides?" to the real question of "What is being decided?" In other words, *Roe* protects freedom of choice, but ignores what is being chosen about. The central question for Bernardin is the moral status of fetal life and what kind of legal protection it should be given. Bernardin's corrective moral vision focuses attention where he believes it needs to be focused—on the protection of fetal life and dignity—and helps define issues in light of that focus.[9]

But Bernardin does not stop here. The consistent ethic leads him to broaden his considerations. He expresses sensitivity to the difficult circumstances surrounding some pregnancies and the plight of women in these situations. He argues that practical alternatives and support must be offered to these women.

> We should be second to none in our sensitivity to the problems pregnant women face. But we should offer a different moral response to individuals and society at large. . . . We must combine moral wisdom with specific social policies of health care, housing, nutrition, and counseling programs in our own institutions. We must also support public programs which provide an alternative to the hard and narrow choices pregnant women often face. (SG, 194)

Protecting life is clearly joined here to enhancing life, illustrating well the comprehensiveness of Bernardin's moral vision, a vision that encourages both breadth and depth. It fosters breadth of perspective in that it encourages consideration of a full range of threats to human life and dignity. It also, however, fosters depth, namely, the "protecting life dimensions" as well as the "enhancing life dimensions" associated with any particular issue. Those who care about human life and dignity must concern themselves not only with the morality of abortion or euthanasia or embryonic stem cell research in themselves, but also with what gives rise to these practices, what surrounds them, and what does or can result from them in terms of protecting and enhancing human life and dignity.

An example of this depth dimension of Bernardin's moral vision is his consideration of the impact of a permissive abortion policy upon society itself. Bernardin refers to a double moral failure in the social practice of abortion: destruction of human life, and society's permitting this. "The basic question is the kind of society we want to be—one that destroys its unborn children, or one that commits itself to a decent life for the most vulnerable in our midst, especially women and children" (SG, 192). Damage is done to a society that permits, sustains, or encourages abortion. Among other things, it weakens that society's commitment to human rights.

> A consistent ethic will ask, What happens to other rights in a society when protection of the right to life is selective? What happens to our moral imagination and social vision if the right to life is not protected for those who do not look fully human at the beginning or end of life? What happens to the vulnerable along the full spectrum of life, if the right to life is denied to inherently vulnerable and dependent unborn life? (SG, 193)

For these and other reasons, Bernardin maintains that civil law must somehow reflect the judgment that abortion is morally wrong.

What, then, does Bernardin's consistent ethic of life contribute to "classical" medical ethics? Put simply, not what one would expect. What might be expected is a moral analysis of technologies that threaten human life or human well-being, perhaps, or an extended discussion of the various moral principles and norms that are relevant to the analysis of life issues, or an attempt to develop a consistent methodology for both the life and the enhancement issues. But this is not the case. Bernardin does not engage a wide range of difficult cases beyond abortion and euthanasia—for example, induction after viability of fetuses with anencephaly or other conditions incompatible with life, the use of methotrexate for tubal pregnancies, the withdrawal of medically administered nutrition and hydration in patients in a persistent vegetative state. Nor does he discuss or analyze all the moral principles that are pertinent to life issues in order to determine their adequacy or their applicability to particular types of issues or to a variety of issues. Nor does he attempt to move beyond the dual methodologies that are present in Catholic moral theology—one for sexual/medical issues and another for social issues.

Instead, what the consistent ethic of life offers to "classical" medical ethics questions is a perspective, a corrective moral vision. And what does this corrective moral vision actually contribute? It offers a way of seeing and interpreting, a way of considering issues in classical medical ethics that:

1. Focuses attention on the sacredness of human life and inherent human dignity as the primary moral consideration and the fundamental value for guiding moral deliberation and judgment.

2. Encompasses the whole range of issues that pose threats to the protection of human life itself while pointing to those issues as well that enhance life, thereby fostering breadth and depth in moral analyses. In other words, it is not sufficient to only oppose abortion. We must also be concerned about and address those factors that contribute to the procurement of abortions. We must not only oppose euthanasia, but also be concerned about and address those factors that give rise to euthanasia and find ever better ways to care for the dying and ensure the dying the opportunity to forgo treatment and to live their lives fully while dying.

3. Raises awareness of basic social attitudes such as individualism, utilitarianism, the privatization of moral choice, and the supremacy of autonomy, which can threaten human well-being and the common good. In their place, Bernardin offers a view of the individual as possessing inherent dignity and as inherently social with responsibilities to other individuals and to society.

4. Calls for the transformation of personal and societal attitudes and, in turn, the transformation of individual behavior and social policies and practices. Bernardin's moral vision is corrective not only with regard to attitudes, but also with regard to social and institutional policy and practice. In other words, do our social policies (e.g., with regard to euthanasia) and practices (e.g., care for the dying) both protect human life and dignity as well as enhance it?

The Consistent Ethic of Life and "Contemporary" Social Justice Issues

Under this heading, Cardinal Bernardin shifts his emphasis to the second pole of his consistent ethic, namely, life-enhancing issues. In his 1985 Loyola of Chicago lecture, he takes up a concern that he returned to often during the course of his career—health care for the poor and vulnerable. At the outset of his discussion, Bernardin raises what he sees as the defining question in this area: How does the evangelical option for the poor shape health care today? Bernardin is appalled over the state of the health-care system that results in so many people not receiving the basic health care required for nurturing life. Delineating some of the factors contributing to the situation—government regulations and restrictions, cutbacks in health programs, maldistribution of health-care personnel to provide services, lack of access, cost, and the like— Bernardin states that what is required by a consistent ethic of life in response to this situation is a change in societal attitudes, and social and institutional policies and programs.

At this point, Bernardin challenges Catholic hospitals by posing several questions about their practices with regard to the poor and vulnerable (e.g.,

transferring indigent patients to another institution, requiring large cash
deposits from nursing home applicants, and giving staff privileges to physicians who do not accept Medicaid or uninsured patients) and offers concrete
proposals for action that he believes follow from a consistent ethic of life
(SG, 83). In short, Bernardin believes that Catholic hospitals must change
some of their practices and take the lead in changing social policy so that the
poor receive the care they need. This is required by a consistent ethic of life
because, ultimately, "the fundamental human right to life . . . is the source
of all other rights, including the right to healthcare" (SG, 83).

Given the state of health care in the country generally, Bernardin believes that Catholic health care faces issues of survival and purpose. How
shall it survive? And for what purpose? He responds, "The consistent ethic
of life enables us to answer these questions by its comprehensiveness and the
credibility which derives from its consistent application to the full spectrum
of life issues" (SG, 84). While this statement does not seem to answer the
first question about survival, it does suggest something about the purpose of
Catholic health care. It must be about a profound respect for human life *and*
human dignity across the full continuum. It must be about protecting life *and*
enhancing life; about avoiding abortion, assisted suicide, and euthanasia; but
also providing excellent care for the elderly, the dying, and the poor.

What role does the consistent ethic play in this first lecture devoted to the
consistent ethic and social justice issues? First, Bernardin's moral vision and
its various elements seem to be operative here. It is because of his profound
regard for human dignity that Bernardin is able to recognize how the health-
care system as a whole and how particular practices within Catholic hospitals
harm human dignity. And it is precisely because of his profound regard for the
sacredness of human life that this matters. Hence, his vision sensitizes him to
threats to human well-being, brings these threats to the foreground, inspires
alternative approaches and practices, and motivates for change. Second, Bernardin suggests that the consistent ethic and, hence, his moral vision, offers
to Catholic health care a way of thinking about its purpose in a time of great
turmoil in health care generally. His moral vision serves as a laser beam to bring
into focus what is most important. While this is not new to Catholic health
care, it does serve as an important reminder at a time when Catholic health
care is buffeted by economic concerns, strong competition, and other forces.

Although the injustice of the health-care system was clearly an early
concern of Bernardin's, it was only in 1993 and 1994 that he began to give
it sustained attention explicitly in the context of the consistent ethic of life.
Perhaps the most important address on the topic was his 1994 address to the
National Press Club, "The Consistent Ethic of Life and Healthcare Reform"
(SG, 238-48). In this address, Bernardin observes that health-care reform
brings together both social justice and pro-life values because it requires
people to defend both the unserved and the unborn, to work *for* universal
coverage and *against* abortion coverage. Hence, for advocates of a consistent
ethic of life, the debate about reform is an opportunity and a test. "It is an

opportunity to address issues and policies that are often matters of life and death, such as, who is covered and who is not; which services are included and which are not; will reform protect human life and enhance dignity, or will it threaten or undermine life and dignity? It is a *test* in the sense that we will be measured by the comprehensiveness of our concerns and the consistency of our principles in this area" (SG, 239).

As would be expected, Bernardin identifies the sacredness of human life as the foundation for debates about health-care reform. "The foundation for all of these discussions is a deep conviction about the nature of human life, namely, that human life is sacred, which means that all human life has an inalienable dignity that must be protected and respected from conception to natural death" (SG, 238-39). In addition to this foundation, Bernardin articulates several other convictions that he considers to be "bedrock" for the consistent ethic; there are certain goods and values that all humans share because we share the gift of human life (in turn these goods and values can serve as common ground for a public morality); inalienable human dignity gives rise to certain rights and duties; a true community protects human rights; individuals and institutions have an obligation to pursue the common good so that individuals can realize their human dignity (SG, 241).

In light of these convictions, Bernardin argues that health care is "an essential safeguard of human life and dignity and that there is an obligation for society to ensure that a person be able to realize this right" (SG, 243). For this reason, Bernardin believes that universal access to health care is not sufficient. Rather, justice and the common good demand that health-care reform include universal coverage.[10] This must become a social reality. Such a program of universal coverage must be person-centered and community-based. It is a program that must be supported by all sectors of society. All must be willing to help meet this demand of justice and be willing to share in the sacrifices it might require. Furthermore, a consistent ethic of life requires that there not be mandated abortion coverage in a program of health-care reform.[11] Bernardin considers that "it would be a grave moral tragedy, a serious policy mistake, and a major political error to link healthcare reform to abortion" (SG, 247). Health-care reform for Bernardin is not primarily a political challenge, as it is for so many. It is fundamentally a *"moral* challenge—finding the values and vision to reshape a major part of national life to protect better the life and dignity of all" (SG, 247).

There are several things to be noted about the role of the consistent ethic of life in this particular presentation. First, Bernardin's moral vision again serves a very important corrective function. It enables him to define the issue of health-care reform as primarily a moral issue, whereas most others would define it as primarily a political or economic issue. Second, his vision enables him to view health care as a basic human right because it is essential to human dignity. Third, it allows him to link life-protection and life-enhancement concerns, thus underscoring "consistency" and "comprehensiveness." And, finally, it enables Bernardin to articulate the social dimension of human reality in terms of the common good and the obligation of all to contribute to the common good, in contrast to American society's preoccupation with the pursuit of individual interests and rights.

It is precisely Bernardin's view of health care as a basic human good, necessary for the protection and enhancement of human life, that leads him to argue in a 1995 address to the Harvard Business School Club of Chicago that health care is best delivered by the not-for-profit sector.[12] Bernardin is troubled by the growing commercialization of health care and the progressive abandonment of values that should be at its core. He sees as one of the consequences of this trend the increasing possibility that not-for-profit hospitals become for-profit enterprises. Among the causes that Bernardin cites is a body of opinion that believes health care is a commodity, exchanged for profit, just like anything else. Like food, clothing, and shelter, it should be subject to unbridled market competition.[13]

While Bernardin does not explicitly appeal to his consistent ethic of life in this address, its influence is apparent and affirmed by his appeal to human dignity. Early on, he notes that there are some "institutions" (family, education, social services) whose essential purpose is a noneconomic goal, namely, the advancement of human dignity. Quoting Pope John Paul II, Bernardin maintains that health care is one of those goods " 'which by their nature are not and cannot be mere commodities.' "[14] Health care, he maintains, is special, like family, education, and social services. "It is fundamentally different from most other goods because it is essential to human dignity and the character of our communities."[15] Bernardin believes this "because healthcare involves one of the most intimate aspects of our lives—our bodies and, in many ways, our minds and spirits as well. The quality of our life, our capacity to participate in social and economic activities, and very often life itself are at stake in each serious encounter with the medical system."[16] Furthermore, health care, Bernardin argues, is critical to the well-being of our communities.

> We would not think well of ourselves if we permitted healthcare institutions to let the uninsured sick and injured go untreated. We endeavor to take care of the poor and the sick as much for our benefit as for theirs. . . . There is a practical aspect to this aspiration as well because, like education, healthcare entails community-wide needs which it impacts in various ways: We all benefit from a healthy community; and we all suffer from a lack of health, especially with respect to communicable disease."[17]

Given this, "The primary end or essential purpose of medical care delivery should be a cured patient, a comforted patient, and a healthier community, *not* to earn a profit or a return on capital for shareholders."[18] For these reasons, Bernardin concludes that the not-for-profit structure is the preferred model for delivering health-care services because it is uniquely designed to provide essential human services.[19] Here is a very concrete example of how a shift in attitude (i.e., health care as a basic human good) can affect a practice (i.e., how health care is organized).

Bernardin's moral vision is clearly operative here in its "corrective" dimension. Its focus on human dignity and the social nature of the person shape his understanding of the very nature of health care and the best overall means of delivering it, both of which are at odds with strong social currents. It serves as a type of compass, redirecting people to what Bernardin would consider to be the "right" course.

One of Bernardin's last addresses relating to health care was titled "Managing Managed Care" (SG, 275-86). Here he explicitly takes up the topic in the context of the consistent ethic of life. The influence is evident. Early on in his lecture, Bernardin enunciates the criteria for assessing managed care. He says:

> What are the healthcare principles and values against which managed care should be measured? The goal of healthcare is healing. To heal is to restore wholeness, "to make whole that which is impaired or less than whole." Achieving wholeness requires attention not only to the physical condition of the patient, but also to his or her spiritual and social well-being. Further, healthcare is focused not only on curing illness, but also on preventing it and building "wellness." Healthcare focuses not only on the patient, but also on the overall health of the community. No person can be completely well if his or her community is unhealthy, and a community's health is dependent on that of its members (SG, 277).

In order to achieve these purposes, a health-care system must, according to Bernardin, embody the following values, values influenced by his consistent ethic: regard health care as an essential social good; preserve the human dignity of all; consider health care as a basic human right; serve the common good; give special priority to the needs of the poor; exercise prudent stewardship of resources; be provided at appropriate levels of organization (SG, 277-78). In light of these values, Bernardin examines the promise and the peril of managed care especially with regard to its relationship to the common good, its impact on quality of care, and how it addresses stewardship and rationing (SG, 282-86). He concludes by saying, "By evaluating and responding to those changes [in the health care system] in terms of our consistent life ethic and our healthcare values, we have the opportunity and the obligation to manage managed care so that it advances the goals of human dignity and the common good" (SG, 286). Once again, Bernardin's moral vision provides his discussion with a certain orientation, helps him to frame it in a particular way, leads him to highlight certain values, and, in the end, offers a corrective vision that implies the need for social transformation.

In sum, what does Bernardin's consistent ethic of life contribute to "contemporary" social justice issues relating to health care? Interestingly, in this domain, unlike the previous one, Bernardin does tackle a few specific issues, in particular, health-care reform, the organization of health care (i.e., for-profit or not-for-profit), and managed care. His treatment of these issues, however, while important, is not where the contribution of his consistent ethic of life lies. Nor does it lie in providing tools for the moral analysis of social justice issues relating to health care. As with "classical" medical ethics questions, the value of the consistent ethic seems to lie in offering a moral vision, a way of seeing, that:

1. Sensitizes one to aspects of the health care system that fail to respect or do not adequately respect human dignity and do not sufficiently enhance human life. The consistent ethic provides insight into aspects of the health-care system that need strengthening or need reform.
2. Places human life and human dignity at the center of these issues, so that they do not get lost in political and economic consider-ations. This in turn leads to a special concern for the poor—the vulnerable, the underinsured, and the uninsured.
3. Proposes alternative attitudes to those that tend to dominate in American society. For example, in the health-care domain, Ber-nardin's consistent ethic leads him to see health care as a basic human and social good rather than as a commodity; health care as a basic right; health-care reform as primarily a moral issue rather than a political and/or economic one; community and common good as essential considerations in social life and public policy.
4. In turn, these attitudes or this moral vision, shaped by the consistent ethic of life, require doing things differently at the personal and social levels in practices and in policies. They challenge the way things are and call for transformation toward how they should be.

Conclusion

This essay began by asking about the contribution of Joseph Cardinal Bernardin's consistent ethic of life to health care, both then and now. After examining his treatment of a variety of topics in health care in light of the consistent ethic, it seems possible to make the general observation that the greatest contribution of Bernardin's consistent ethic of life to health care is that it provides health care with a moral vision—a way of seeing and a way of thinking about particular challenges to human life and dignity, and a motivation for action. More needs to be said about each.

First, the consistent ethic offers a way of seeing, interpreting, and think-ing. It offers a way of seeing by focusing attention on the sacredness of human life and on human dignity. Reality is seen through this lens. The lens or vision determines what is seen and what is not seen, what comes to the foreground and what recedes to the background, what is most valued and what is less valued. It offers a way of interpreting many aspects of health-care reality, of making sense out of them, and even of giving them meaning. This moral vision is possible only because of Bernardin's insistence on comprehensiveness and consistency.

In the most general way, the consistent ethic offers a way of thinking, a "framework for analysis" to use Bernardin's expression, by highlighting certain values and fundamental convictions—the sacredness of human life, inherent human dignity, human rights as constituting fundamental human goods, the person in relationship with others, the common good, the role of the state, and so on. These do provide critical points of reference and evaluation when considering various medical technologies and dimensions of the health-care system.

The consistent ethic also provides some assistance in the moral analysis of specific issues by affirming a few well-known principles. But the principles and rules are few, despite Bernardin's early observation that the consistent ethic will be structured on the basis of values, principles, and rules and that ethics is about principles. And the few principles he mentions are generally limited to the "protecting life" issues. When dealing with the social justice issues, Bernardin speaks more in terms of values and fundamental convictions. Bernardin's consistent ethic is in need of greater development in this area. What moral principles flow from and support his moral vision? How is the principle prohibiting the direct taking of innocent human life to be understood?[20] How are conflicting goods and conflicting obligations to be resolved? Do any of the principles that relate directly to "life enhancement" issues have a bearing on "life protection" issues? In the end, despite claiming a consistent ethic, Bernardin cannot claim a consistent methodology across the two types of issues. Had Cardinal Bernardin more fully developed his consistent ethic along these lines, it might have been far more helpful and significant, though almost certainly controversial.

Second, the consistent ethic, the moral vision, offers a motivation for action. It does so in two ways. It is, first of all, a corrective vision. Richard McCormick describes a corrective vision in this way: "I borrow the phrase to state in shorthand what I take to be the major contribution of moral-theological reflection: opening peoples' eyes to dimensions of reality they may have missed."[21] The consistent ethic of life, by focusing on the sacredness of human life and on human dignity, brings to light problematic social attitudes—individualism, a utilitarian assessment of persons, privatization of moral choices, excess autonomy, the commodification and commercialization of health care, the technological imperative, and the like. These attitudes are threats to human life and dignity and are, therefore, unacceptable. Hence, Bernardin's moral vision offers a critique of attitudes associated with particular medical technologies and aspects of the health care system as well as personal and social attitudes and behaviors. Implicit, and very often explicit, in Bernardin's analyses is a call for change. And this is the second way in which his moral vision constitutes a motivation for change.

The consistent ethic is not only a corrective vision, it is a transforma-
tional vision. It is inherently oriented toward change: change in personal
attitudes and behaviors; change in social and institutional attitudes, policies,
and practices; as well as change of and within the health-care system itself
and the use of particular procedures and technologies. As applied to health
care, Bernardin's moral vision does not allow for the status quo unless and
until all of health-care delivery is respectful of human life and promotes
human dignity. As such, it serves as both a foundation and an incentive for
advocacy efforts.[22]

We have been speaking about the contribution of Bernardin's consistent
ethic to health care in general. But what about its contribution to Catholic
health care in particular? Several observations can be made here. First, the
moral vision offered by the consistent ethic is one that is shared by Catholic
health care. Respect for human dignity and human life are at the core of
Catholic health care's identity (as are the values that flow from them) and
are expressed in most of its policies and practices (though, unfortunately,
sometimes falteringly in its practices). Second, Catholic health care's regard for
human life and dignity tends to be both life-protecting (it opposes abortion,
euthanasia, etc.) and life-enhancing (it is involved in healing the sick; caring
and advocating for the poor, the elderly, and the dying; fostering healthy
communities; promoting universal access, etc.). It tends to be marked by the
comprehensiveness for which Bernardin calls. Third, Catholic health care's
commitments do lead it to take action toward self-transformation as well
as the transformation of social policies and practices. Advocacy is inherent
to its mission.

Like all human realities, however, Catholic health care is marked by
the effects of sin. It often falls short of the ideal and sometimes loses its way,
buffeted as it is by numerous social forces, market pressures, and technological developments. In this context, Bernardin's corrective moral vision
can assist Catholic health care to keep focused, to be shaped by the right
beliefs and values, and urge it toward continuous self-transformation and
increased efforts at transforming social polices and practices as they relate
to human health.

Toward the end of 1987, Cardinal Bernardin wrote this about his consistent ethic: "Such an ethic provides both the vision and the norms needed
to guide and direct individual and communal behavior in a great variety of
contexts" (SG, 138). This is likely claiming too much for his consistent ethic.
Even nine years later at the conclusion of his life, there was still much else
that had to be worked out, as so many of his critics have pointed out over
the years.[23] But even if the consistent ethic of life is not complete and is not
without its many rough edges, there is a richness and a power in the fundamental vision it offers that is capable of guiding and motivating and even
transforming during very challenging times in medicine and health care.

PART 2
ENGAGING MORAL REASONING

3.
THE CONSISTENT ETHIC OF LIFE AS MORAL ANALOGY

Thomas A. Nairn, O.F.M.

On December 6, 1983, when Joseph Cardinal Bernardin delivered the Gannon Lecture at Fordham University, the "consistent ethic of life" was born. He had been asked to address some aspect of the Catholic bishops' pastoral letter, *The Challenge of Peace*, which had been approved by the then National Conference of Catholic Bishops earlier that year. (The NCCB changed its name in 2001 to the United States Conference of Catholic Bishops, or USCCB). Bernardin, who had also recently been named chair of the NCCB's Committee for Pro-Life Activities, used this lecture as a forum to launch a moral analysis based on the "linkage" among a variety of ethical issues, some usually characterized as "life" issues and others usually characterized as "justice" issues. The understanding of linkage among these issues has come to be known as the "seamless garment," or more precisely as the consistent ethic of life.

As early as October 1984, the cardinal described the consistent ethic as analogical, explaining that a "key concept in the formulation of a consistent ethic is an analogical understanding of issues which recognizes certain thematic ideas among them and is still capable of identifying the specific character of each problem along the spectrum of life" (SG, 52-53). Two years later, he would describe this understanding of similarity in difference used in analogical reasoning as part of the "very character of Catholic moral thought" (SG, 103).

At first, this conclusion might seem somewhat unusual in light of the fact that if one were to investigate the books of moral theology written prior to the Second Vatican Council, one would have difficulty finding references to "analogy" in general, and, I believe, one would find no references at all to "moral analogy." It was not a term typically used in the moral theology in the time immediately prior to the council. Nevertheless, I do believe that Cardinal Bernardin was correct when he said that analogy has been part of the very character of Catholic moral thought.

To defend this insight, I investigate what the cardinal might have meant when he spoke of Catholic moral thought as analogical, and then ask how the analogical nature of Catholic morality, however it is construed, can help shape a consistent ethic of life. As soon as one embarks on such a defense, however, one runs into an apparent obstacle. As important as this question is, there is a difficulty in answering it because there does not seem to be one meaning of analogy at work in the cardinal's lectures. On the contrary, I believe that there are at least three distinct uses of the term in the consistent ethic of life. Each of these three uses can be a point of departure from which to criticize both the cardinal's theological analysis and his ethical conclusions.

One of the most traditional understandings of analogy suggests that there is some general resemblance among a group of notions usually thought of as different. This understanding is the broadest and probably most ancient understanding of analogy in the tradition. A second understanding of moral analogy is a rather technical one that can best be understood by recourse to an ordering (or taxonomy) of notions by similarity and difference from a particular paradigm "the truth of which no one doubts."[1] This understanding of analogy is at the heart of the tradition of casuistry. A third understanding of analogy is also the most intriguing. Authors such as David Burrell have explained it as part of the "dramatic dimension" of language usage in which we "break out of accustomed usage to describe the unfamiliar or reveal forgotten facets of the too familiar."[2]

This chapter first analyzes each of these understandings of moral analogy in general. It then looks to Cardinal Bernardin's consistent ethic of life and analyzes how each of these understandings helps shape the ethic. The chapter then uses these three understandings to raise some questions regarding the consistent ethic of life itself. To acknowledge these three senses of moral analogy is not the same as stating that only three senses of moral analogy exist. The history of theological and philosophical interpretation has articulated a wide variety of notions and types of analogy. The Thomistic philosopher George Klubertanz, for example, has described over a dozen understandings of analogy, broadly categorized under what he calls predicational analysis, formal analysis, and material analysis.[3] I have limited my own analysis to the three senses of analogy mentioned above because I believe that they are the understandings of moral analogy that are evident in the lectures of Cardinal Bernardin.

Analogy in General

Analogy as Family Resemblance

The first question that arises when one analyzes the consistent ethic of life is the most obvious: what in fact links the variety of (at first glance disparate) moral issues analyzed in the consistent ethic? Each of the three uses of analogy mentioned above gives a slightly different answer to this question. Bernardin himself typically simply asserts that there exists a certain commonality or family resemblance among the issues he tries to link. In doing so, he makes use of one of the broadest and most ancient elements of analogical reasoning: the simple statement that similarities and differences exist among the terms under discussion. To understand this use more fully, one can look to the way in which analogy has functioned in the Catholic theological tradition. Ralph McInerny, for example, adopts the terminology used by sixteenth-century theologians such as Thomas de Vio and Cajetan, suggesting that to understand what I have called family resemblance is to understand the relationship between the *ratio communis* of a term and its *ratio propria*.[4] According to Cajetan, a *ratio* is a single account or mental construct.[5] The *ratio communis* then refers to the account or mental construct common to all terms in question, while the *ratio propria* refers to that which is particular to a specific term. The relation between the *ratio propria* and the *ratio communis* therefore accounts for the distinctions one makes between univocal language, equivocal language, and analogical language. Univocal terms, for example, would have a single account common to all the things named by the term. With analogical terms, however, the "*ratio communis* and *ratio propria* involve the same name, with the latter suggesting a shrinking or appropriation of the common meaning of the term."[6] Note, however, that to state that there is a family resemblance, in the above analysis, is merely to say that a relationship exists among the terms of the analogy. It does not explain the basis for the relationship.

Similarly, George Klubertanz has divided the various Thomistic understandings of analogy into three general categories: the predicational approach, the formal approach, and the material approach. The understanding of analogy as family resemblance is closest to what he called the formal approach to analogy, which he described as considering "the analogous community in the most abstract possible fashion," considering the "bare formal notion: 'an analogous community of the many.'"[7] In employing this formal approach, one is simply articulating the intelligible structure of the analogous community, "without any consideration of the things that enter into this structure."[8] One acknowledges that the elements are related, but does not analyze the nature of this relatedness.

This first use of analogy thus simply recognizes that the analogates under consideration are related. It states, for example, the fact that we are able to understand that there are both the similarities and differences in language when we describe a "good musician" or a "good ballplayer" or a "good moral theologian." What this first sense of analogy does not do is explain *why* or *how* the analogates are related. Klubertanz suggests that this formal analysis leads to a material analysis in which one analyzes the "concrete nature of the relations which constitute the various unities."[9] This first sense of analogy, in which a relationship is simply posited, thus seems to demand that one move to an analysis of the nature of the analogy. In doing so, one moves from the first sense of analogy mentioned above to either the second or third sense I mentioned above.

Analogy as a Language of Ordered Relationships

Much of the work on moral analogy that has occurred within the past twenty years has been focused on the second sense of analogy mentioned above, that of an ordering by similarity and difference from a clear paradigm case to more ambiguous or difficult cases. This has also probably been the most prevalent usage of moral analogy in the Catholic tradition. Albert Jonsen and Stephen Toulmin quote the seventeenth-century Jesuit Gabriel Daniel, who commented that "the resolution of a difficult case—for example, whether one can kill another in anticipation of deadly danger—'is a consequence drawn by analogy with the earlier decision on self-defense under attack, the truth of which no one doubts.' "[10]

In a contemporary retrieval of this tradition, David Tracy states that "analogy is a language of ordered relationships articulating similarity-in-difference. The order among the relationships is constituted by the distinct but similar relationships of each analogue with some primary focal meaning, some prime analogue."[11] He continues to describe such analogy in theological language: "Order is developed by explicating the analogous relations among various realities (self, others, world, God), by clarifying the relationship of each to a primary analogue, the meaning chosen as the primary focus for interpreting reality."[12] William Spohn further develops this analysis on the level of ethics: "Analogies exercise a normative function by implying actions and ways of living that are congruent with the prototype."[13]

Jonsen and Toulmin explain the specific shape of a morality using analogy as a return to the method of casuistry.[14] While, for many, this latter term conjures up all sorts of pejorative connotations, these authors portray it as the task of choosing appropriate moral paradigms and ordering the relation between these paradigms and more ambiguous or complicated cases by developing appropriate taxonomies. The casuist looks to paradigms because "in unambiguous ('paradigmatic') cases we can recognize an action as, say, an act of cruelty or loyalty, as directly as we can recognize that a figure is triangular or square."[15] One then moves from these clear paradigms to circumstances of greater complexity and likely more conflict. Jonsen and Toulmin describe this movement as practiced by the casuists of the sixteenth and seventeenth centuries:

> The paradigm cases enjoyed both "intrinsic and extrinsic certitude." . . . Then, in succession, cases were proposed that moved away from the paradigm by introducing various combinations of circumstances and motives that made the offense in question less apparent. . . . This gradual movement from clear and simple cases to the more complex and obscure ones was standard procedure for the casuist; indeed, it might be said to be the essence of the casuistic mode of thinking.[16]

In this movement, however, "there is little resemblance to those forms of moral reasoning that seek to 'deduce' a particular conclusion from a moral premise that serves as a universal premise."[17] Principles may apply but only "so long as their applicability to new cases is clear, meaningful and unambiguous."[18]

In this understanding of morality, a principle such as that proscribing the direct killing of the innocent can be meaningful, and in straightforward situations it may be seen as an absolute. It cannot, however, govern all applications, especially as one moves away from the rather clear-cut paradigms. Questions arise regarding the very meaning of the principle in its applicability to particular circumstances. The further one moves from the paradigm, the more questions there are that may arise. Supporters of casuistry claim that this is not a flaw in this method of reasoning but rather is an aspect of practical morality itself. It was Aristotle who maintained that morality ought not be considered a science but rather practical wisdom. He reminded his readers that "matters concerned with conduct and questions of what is good for us have no fixity, any more than matters of health. The general account being of this nature, the account of particular cases are yet more lacking in exactness."[19] Similarly, Thomas Aquinas spoke of the difficulties inherent in moving from the first principles of natural law to concrete practical conclusions.[20] The movement from principle to practice, or from paradigm to application, is never mechanical. Nevertheless it continues to maintain distinctive features: the moralist begins the process with clear and relatively unambiguous cases in which the determination of the rightness or wrongness of an action is rather straightforward and then moves from these clear cases to those of greater complexity and therefore of possibly greater moral conflict.

Analogy as Breaking from Accustomed Language Usage

Related to the understanding of moral analogy used in casuistry is a third understanding of analogy. This third use, however, contains a critique of both of the other two senses of analogy under discussion. On the one hand, this understanding would agree with Klubertanz that a formal approach to analogy must move to some material account. On the other hand, this third understanding also criticizes the "excessive demand for clarity" that might be associated with the second understanding discussed above.[21] David Burrell has noted that the various attempts to account for analogy display a shared presupposition, "that something is recognized to be the same; that there must be some 'ground' for the predication."[22] Demonstrating his mistrust of this presupposition, he articulates his own assumption, namely that "the 'ground' for deliberate and opposite ambiguous usage is neither a common referent nor a common formula (or meaning) but rather . . . the demands germane to reason itself."[23] He articulates two characteristics of analogous expressions: "(1) a resistance to definition and to an account that will not vary from one context to another; yet (2) a propensity to employment in diverse contexts in spite of the acknowledged differences in meaning."[24] Burrell thus suggests that rather than attempting to see in analogy a sort of "super-logic" that attempts to discover common qualities among elements first thought of as different, one rather sees analogy as "concerned with facts about life and language that reach beyond logic to reveal something more of the shape and texture of our language."[25]

But what is this "something more"? Burrell suggests that analogous language is part of the "dramatic dimension" of language usage. We use analogies, he proposes, because "we clearly need to break out of accustomed usage to describe the unfamiliar or reveal forgotten facets of the too familiar."[26] Analogies, therefore, are "neither susceptible of a rigorous account nor in need of logical justification."[27] Nevertheless, this language is not simply arbitrary. Burrell discusses the use of models and metaphors to explain why such language is not arbitrary, suggesting that "this capacity is shared by poets, scientists, some philosophers, and nearly all ordinary [people]."[28]

Within this context he speaks explicitly about the fact that the language of morality is itself analogical and suggests that one can only understand moral principles by "molding their meaning to fit relevant features of different situations." He continues:

> Hence we teach a moral principle not simply by enunciating it, but we also feel it necessary to show what it means by illustrating how it might give shape to our activity in typical situations. That process of shaping, however, involves making a decision; and a decision of this sort helps us understand the principle-in-use. So teaching a principle is understanding what it is to be a principle. Part of understanding a principle is understanding how to apply it. So the locution "applying principles" proves to be misleading.[29]

Such a process, however, is never straightforward and without ambiguity:

> We are invited to look for, to formulate the standard, and then to use it as a common measure. But standards resist unambiguous formation and take refuge in analogous expression. This frustrates the initial leads of grammar, for we expect a standard to function like an ordinary rule and to be a straightforward measure easily applied to the thing to be measured.[30]

Analogous expressions are necessarily vague, and their very ambiguity forces their users continuously to refine, modify, or alter their conventional understandings of the terms themselves.[31] Thus, Burrell suggests that analogous terms help their users to become more aware of what is happening in the process of assessing itself, employing this language with ever more finesse and discernment.

The Consistent Ethic of Life and the Three Understandings of Analogy

There is evidence in Cardinal Bernardin's series of lectures on the consistent ethic of life for his use of each of the three senses of analogy described above. He preferred, however, the first sense, that which Klubertanz called the formal approach to analogy. Nevertheless, at least early in his developing thought he had recourse to the other two senses. I will therefore begin my analysis of his use of the three understandings with these early articulations of the second and third senses of analogy discussed above.

Analogy as Series of Ordered Relationships

The larger discussion of the understanding of analogy as a series of ordered relationships has shown the major thrust of the casuistic tradition— that is, that the resolution of a difficult case often takes place by analogy from simpler, clearer cases called paradigms. Although Cardinal Bernardin's use of moral analogy has several points of intersection with this second sense of moral analogy articulated above, two areas distinguish him from typical casuists: (1) his strong defense of moral principles absolutely understood and (2) his choice of abortion as his paradigm case.

Regarding the first point, in high casuistry, analogy seems to have been used as an *alternative* to what were perceived to be antiquated moral principles. James Keenan, for example, has shown that "in the face of antiquated principles, 16th-century ethicists, attentive to the newness of contemporary projects, turned for guidance to cases, circumstances, new distinctions, and analogous logic."[32] Albert Jonsen has taken this insight even further by contrasting theory, with its emphasis on principles, with practice. He explains that theory "likes to be a whole, uniform, original construction, laying its foundations on fresh soil and building its own conceptual rooms in Palladian symmetry." In practice, however, "reasoning moves by analogy from case to case, sorting out what is similar and what different and how those differences demand different resolution." Rejecting the notion that moral theology is properly understood as "the application of theory to practical judgment," he adds that "it is analogy that makes practical judgment move."[33]

Bernardin, however, consistently defended the centrality of moral principles in moral theology in general and his consistent ethic of life in particular, especially the principle that absolutely proscribes the direct taking of innocent life. In his very first lecture, he stated, "Attitude is the place to root an ethic of life, but ultimately ethics is about principles to guide the actions of individuals and institutions" (SG, 12), insisting that the consistent ethic "will have to be finely honed and carefully structured on the basis of values, principles, rules and applications to specific cases" (SG, 11).

Later, in his Seattle University address, responding to Richard McCormick's critique[34] of the place of absolute principles in his consistent ethic of life, Bernardin countered:

> I think the reduction of the prohibition against the intentional killing of the innocent to a status less than an absolute is not correct. . . . The justification of the use of force and the taking of human life is based on a presumption against taking life which then allows for a series of exceptions where the presumption is overridden. But within this general structure of reasoning . . . the direct killing of the innocent has not been regarded as a legitimate exception. (SG, 105)

Still later, the cardinal articulated that he based his consistent ethic on two principles, deriving from the sacred and social character of human life. For example, at an address at the University of Chicago in 1988, he stated:

> If one accepts these two principles about human life, then one may argue that two precepts or obligations necessarily flow from these principles. The first is that, as individuals and as a society, we have the *positive* obligation to protect life. The second precept is that we have the *negative* obligation not to destroy or injure human life directly, especially the life of the innocent and vulnerable. (SG, 159)

Bernardin never reconciles his use of analogy with the principlism displayed in these quotes.

The second issue deals with Bernardin's choice of abortion as the paradigm case for moral analogy. As he asserted in his 1985 Georgetown lecture, "Abortion anchors a consistent ethic because the unborn child symbolizes the fundamental challenge innocent life poses for individuals and society at every stage of human development" (SG, 53). He thus sees abortion as the prime example of the prohibition against the direct killing of the innocent. On one level, this choice of abortion as the paradigm case can be seen as a response to those critics who claimed that the consistent ethic of life tended to destroy important differences among the issues of life and justice addressed by the cardinal and tended to diminish the pro-life stance of the Catholic Church in the United States. Those critics claimed that linking abortion to issues such as capital punishment or nuclear deterrence would only serve to reduce the importance of the abortion issue. By making abortion merely one of several "life causes," they claimed, one weakens its urgency and visibility.[35]

Nevertheless, this choice of abortion as his paradigm case raises further questions about his understanding of moral analogy. In the first place, if the description of this second sense of analogy is apt, difficult cases simply should not be used as paradigms. The logic of moral analogy demands that one begin with straightforward cases around which there is basic agreement and move to more complex ones by citing similarities and differences between those cases and those more generally agreed upon. Because it is the focus of so much public (and private) debate, abortion fails as a paradigm case. The current task of the consistent ethic of life in fact may be to find that paradigm which may enable us better to understand the issue of abortion today.

Such a task would involve asking difficult questions. It would look to the similarities and differences between, for example, abortion and infanticide. It would ask on the one hand regarding the similarities and differences between abortion and murder and on the other may make a similar comparison between abortion and self-defense. Those who engage in this task cannot claim a priori where sameness or difference lies among the cases.

Second, Bernardin himself notes in a different context that "abortion is not a 'single issue,' because it is not even a single kind of issue" (SG, 25). He then goes on to discuss abortion as an issue of equality, of the nature of the family, and of societal responsibilities. There is another way, however, to interpret Bernardin's statement. The term "abortion" itself comprises a spectrum of concrete issues (or cases), each with similarities to and differences from one another. Understanding analogy, one must acknowledge that circumstances do not merely add some further information to the already understood issue of abortion but (as Burrell has suggested) in fact *constitute* the cases as different, though related.[36]

If one accepts moral analogy as an appropriate moral method, one must ask whether and how the similarities and differences among these circumstances change the morality of the act of abortion itself. Some questions have been forced upon us by science and technology. Early detection of anencephaly or gross genetic anomalies creates questions that were not the object of earlier moral analyses. New paradigms are also being developed which place the question of abortion in new interpretative matrices involving complex personal and societal analyses. For example, Christine Gudorf has suggested that society's moral callousness has so victimized women that "many of those victims are now sacrificing another group of victims in their attempts at self-assertion and self-defense."[37] Such an analysis forces us to ask troubling questions not present in the more traditional analysis of abortion based solely upon the absolute moral principle proscribing the taking of innocent human life. To ask such questions and to probe new answers should not be seen as a sign of bad faith. Rather, it is the very task and responsibility of the moralist. There are indeed dangers of misuse; and moral analogy, as any moral method, can be used as rationalization by those in bad faith. Nevertheless, in the face of this danger, it is wise to recall the words of Stephen Toulmin: "Casuists may occasionally have been lax; but they grasped the essential Aristotelian point about applied ethics: it cannot get along on a diet of general principles alone. It requires a detailed taxonomy of particular, detailed types of cases and situations."[38]

Bernardin does seem to understand the difficulties in relating his enterprise to this second understanding of analogy. In fact, in his Georgetown address discussed above, he attempted a justification for his use of abortion as a paradigm, but in doing so changed the understanding of paradigm itself. As we have seen, paradigms are chosen because of their "intrinsic and extrinsic certitude."[39] Bernardin, however, articulates a variety of different reasons that abortion should function as paradigm: (1) the antiquity of the church's tradition regarding abortion, (2) the symbolic nature of abortion as an attack against "innocent human life," (3) the vulnerability of the unborn, and (4) the relation between attacks against the unborn and the moral and social order (SG, 53). It is interesting that the cardinal's very attempt to articulate a variety of other reasons for choosing abortion as paradigm for the consistent ethic of life seems to underscore the traditional demand that paradigms be clear, enjoying both intrinsic and extrinsic certitude.

Analogy as Breaking from Accustomed Language Usage

As we have seen, Burrell suggested that the strategy one uses in articulating this third understanding of analogy is "to expose the attitudes and convictions embedded in our ordinary usage, including the uncanny sense for similarity-in-dissimilarity we display in our frequent recourse to metaphor."[40] Returning to the lectures of Cardinal Bernardin, one sees that from the earliest of his talks he not only spoke of a linkage among a variety of issues, but he also tried to investigate the relationship between moral attitude and moral principle. In this chapter, I have frequently quoted his first lecture, in which he stated, "Attitude is the place to root an ethic of life, but ultimately ethics is about principles to guide the actions of individuals and institutions" (SG, 12). He thus seems to resolve the tension between attitude and principle in favor of principle. His articulation of the absolute nature of moral principles, his straightforward movement from principle to application, and his willingness to accept consequences stemming from this movement all seem to be attempts to limit wide-sweeping change in moral theology. He sees principles as providing consistency and stability to the moral enterprise.

Nevertheless, the very fact that Bernardin needed to articulate the need for moral attitudes in addition to principles seems to illustrate the point that Burrell is trying to make. As we have seen, Burrell himself speaks of the need for attitudes and convictions to articulate "those aspects of our linguistic comportment which are neither susceptible of a rigorous account nor in need of logical justification."[41] It seems that for Cardinal Bernardin moral attitudes give voice to the complexities inherent in morality, pushing one to the differences to which moral analogy must attend. Attitudes lead to development in morality. This can be seen as utilizing the third sense of analogy I have described.

Quoting the Jesuit theologian John Courtney Murray, Bernardin spoke about a "growing edge of tradition," which he explained as follows: "The Catholic style admits of change—indeed requires change, but it is change rooted in continuity" (SG, 92). Within a similar context, Bernardin spoke of Murray's understanding of the "fallacy of archaism." In his Georgetown address, for example, he stated, "Father Murray would be the first to warn theologians against the fallacy of 'archaism'—his characteristically elegant way of describing how people keep repeating the formulas of the past when the need is to reverence the tradition by renewing it" (SG, 49). Bernardin's broad understanding of tradition allowed him to move beyond some of the limits that his adherence to absolute principles might impose. Cardinal Bernardin's early lectures thus exhibit an understanding that moral attitudes help one break out of accustomed usage, of those formulas that merely repeat the older formulation of a tradition rather than renew it.

Examples of this third sense of moral analogy, however, disappear from lectures on the consistent ethic of life almost as soon as they appear. The two examples I have given in this section come from 1984 and 1985. There do not seem to be any more examples of this third understanding until the very end of the cardinal's life. In a February 1995 lecture in Melbourne, Australia, Bernardin again made several allusions that can be construed as endorsing this third sense of analogy, in which he challenged that the consistent ethic of life "requires us to broaden, substantively and creatively, our ways of thinking, our attitudes, our pastoral response" (SG, 260).[42] He ended this lecture with reference to a "Spirit-filled, living Church" and challenged his listeners to move beyond "petty criticisms and jealousy, cynicism, sound-bite theology, inaccurate, unhistorical assertions, flippant dismissals," calling for the "realization that there is room for considerable diversity among us" (SG, 266). Granted a possible return to this third understanding toward the end of his life, Cardinal Bernardin did not in the end seem comfortable with the direction this most radical use of moral analogy might take him. Furthermore, he had already been strongly criticized for his use of Murray in this context. It must be acknowledged therefore that the cardinal's most frequent use of analogy remained that of formal analogy, in which he acknowledged the fact that a family resemblance existed among the issues he was treating, without necessarily explaining how or why this was the case.

Analogy as Family Resemblance

Cardinal Bernardin used this broad understanding of analogy understood as family resemblance as his entry into a range of moral issues, in some respects similar and in other respects different, acknowledging that it is analogical reasoning itself that "identifies the unifying elements which link two or more issues, while at the same time recognizes why similar issues cannot be reduced to a single problem" (SG, 103). Nevertheless, throughout his three dozen lectures on the consistent ethic, he spent more time speaking of similarity rather than articulating differences.

One of the cardinal's tasks in his early lectures was that of identifying the unifying element in the consistent ethic. In his first lecture, he simply suggested that what links the issues discussed was a profound respect for all human life (SG, 12). The following year he would expand this notion, suggesting that respect stems from the fact that human life is both sacred and social: "Because we esteem human life as sacred, we have the duty to protect and foster it at all stages of development, from conception to death, and in all circumstances. Because we acknowledge that human life is also social, we must develop the kind of social environment that protects and fosters its development" (SG, 42). Later in the same lecture, he added, "Human life has always been sacred, and there have always been threats to it. However, we live in a period of history when we have produced, sometimes with the best of intentions, a technology and a capacity to threaten and diminish life which previous generations could not even imagine" (SG, 42).

On several occasions, Bernardin suggested that the linkage among the issues under consideration was connected to the understanding of the challenges that technology, peace, and justice pose for society (SG, 149-50, 166-67, 202, 213). In a 1986 lecture, during his visit to Chile, the cardinal again suggested that the issues under consideration are linked "because of the impact they have upon the human person" (SG, 126). Still later, the cardinal tried to articulate his understanding of linkage in terms of "micro-questions" such as medical ethics and "macro-questions" such as war and peace or justice, suggesting that the linkage among these is "the technological revolution which has unlocked the genetic code and unleashed the power of the atom within the space of a lifetime" (SG, 148). He added, "Technology provides the material link between the 'micro' and the 'macro' threats to life in our time. The moral link is the unique value of human life" (SG, 148). Still later, he spoke of the linkage between "life-threatening" issues and "life-diminishing" issues, maintaining that "wherever human life is considered 'cheap' and easily exploited or wasted, respect for life dwindles and, eventually, every human life is in jeopardy" (SG, 235).[43]

These several attempts to articulate the unifying element or elements that establish the linkage in the consistent ethic of life point to that which is both positive and problematic in Cardinal Bernardin's moral enterprise. On the one hand, his search for linkage is itself a reaction against the perception of single-issue voting on the part of Catholics. He explicitly states, "Properly used, the consistent ethic will refute decisively claims that we are a 'one-issue' constituency. The essence of the consistent ethic argument is that no one issue can exhaust the moral significance of our public policy concerns" (SG, 152). On the other hand, the cardinal is reacting to the opposition between pro-life groups and justice groups that he had experienced. He claims, "The consequence of a consistent ethic is to bring under review the position of every group in the Church which sees the moral meaning in one place but not the other. The ethic cuts *two* ways not one" (SG, 152).

This drive to understand the linkage, the family resemblance among the issues under discussion, therefore is understandable. Nevertheless it obscures the fact at the basis of analogy that one is dealing with similarity *in difference*. Although Bernardin mentions the fact that these issues remain different, his desire to understand the linkage keeps him from developing in any meaningful way how the differences, as well as similarities, may be morally significant. He has at hand the tool for this more nuanced analysis. The very difficulty he seems to have had articulating the unifying element that is at the basis of the family resemblance would seem to show the importance of both sides of the dialectic, both the similarity and the difference. The considerations that the cardinal articulated—that life is both sacred and social; that there are both "micro" and "macro" threats to life; that the issues addressed are both life-threatening and life-diminishing; that technology, peace, and justice all constitute challenges to a consistent ethic—might be developed into a sort of matrix out of which both ethically significant similarities and ethically significant differences are explored. This would result in more nuanced understanding of his consistent ethic of life.

Conclusion

Even though Cardinal Bernardin characterized analogical reasoning as part of the "very character of Catholic moral thought" (SG, 103), he actually never used the term "analogy" again after his 1986 Address to the Consistent Ethic of Life Conference,[44] preferring rather to speak simply of "linkage." There may be good reason for this. David Burrell describes analogical language as dangerous but useful.[45] It may very well be that Bernardin saw a danger in his use of analogy, that it would take him where he did not want to go—or to where he felt that he, as spokesperson for the Catholic Church, could not go. Nevertheless, the analogic of the consistent ethic of life does raise necessarily troubling questions. In answering these questions, the three senses of analogy I have tried to analyze above will all be at work. They will call adherents of the consistent ethic of life (1) to complete the moral analysis begun by Cardinal Bernardin—but, in doing so, to acknowledge morally significant differences as well as linkage among the issues addressed; (2) to question whether or not abortion is able to function as paradigm in the consistent ethic; and (3) to understand that analogy itself breaks open language and thereby forces its users continuously to refine, modify, or alter their conventional understandings of moral terms themselves. Moving to this third sense of analogy, the consistent ethic may finally contribute substantially to the development of moral theology itself.

4.
VIRTUES, PRINCIPLES, AND A CONSISTENT ETHIC OF LIFE

JAMES F. KEENAN, S.J.

"Virtues without principles are blind; principles without virtues are impotent."[1] So said William Frankena more than thirty years ago, just as the field of virtue ethics was at the dawn of its renaissance.

Frankena was trying to acknowledge a place for the virtues. He understood ethics to be predominantly about norms, principles, or rules—that is, specific guidelines for or against certain forms of action. Ethics according to Frankena was predominantly about determining what actions ought or ought not to be performed.

Frankena had his pulse on the way most people thought and still think about ethics: ethics is about whether we can do research on stem cells, prohibit gay marriage, attack potentially belligerent countries, use condoms for HIV prevention, ban abortions, and so on. But Frankena wanted to provide space for virtues, because virtues tell us not what to do but rather how to be. Rather than giving us principles that tell us "do this," "don't do that," virtues tell us how to be: "be just," "be faithful," "be loving." Virtues tell us to adopt certain kinds of character traits or dispositions.

At first glance, then, Frankena's little adage makes a lot of sense: if I tell soldiers to be just and send them into war without a principle like "never directly attack the innocent," then I am offering them an upright disposition but no real direction about how to express in action that disposition to justice. They would be "blind," Frankena remarks, as to how to proceed.

Frankena's adage seems even more plausible when we consider the second half of it: if I inform soldiers to heed the principle "never directly kill the innocent" and send them into war without helping them to acquire the virtue of justice, then I cannot expect that they will have the strength to withstand the enemy and still follow the principles. If they are not disposed to justice, what will happen when all they know is that there is a principle of justice to heed? For this reason, Frankena says knowing a just principle without having the virtue of justice to heed the principle leaves a person impotent.

This seems fairly simple, until we push the adage one step further: which comes first, the virtue or the principle?

For the most part, philosophers and theologians usually say that ethics is predominantly about principles. Usually they think of ethics as mostly about these guidelines for certain forms of actions and then expect that we should develop complementary virtues so that we can execute those guidelines.

At first glance, this seems reasonable. The church teaches us the principle, "No sex outside of marriage," and then exhorts us to be chaste. The church teaches us, "Fast during Lent," and then helps us to develop the ascetical disposition that helps us to do that. The Bible commands our children, "Honor your parents," and expects them to develop the virtue of obedience so as to follow parents' orders.

In fact, when we think for a moment on the commandments, we can think of Moses coming down from Mount Sinai with the Decalogue. Were Moses's commands about virtues or principles? Did they say, "Be just," "Be obedient," "Be chaste"? No, they were about principles for actions: "Do not bear false witness," "Do not kill," "Do not commit adultery." If the commandments were about specific forms of action, then it seems reasonable to recognize that principles come first.

Thus, the German moral theologian Bruno Schüller dismisses the virtues as completely exhortative, that is, virtue informs us of nothing. Once the norm is given, virtue simply urges us to follow the norm. For Schüller virtue ethicists are at best auxiliary, ancillary handmaidens waiting on the bridal principlists.[2]

James Gaffney, however, wisely reminds us that virtues are instructive. They are never without content and information.[3] If, for instance, I were giving a lecture and midway pause and say to an audience member, "Be respectful," you would all comment to one another, "Somebody must have been talking or somehow offended Fr. Keenan." But imagine, if I were to pause and say, instead, "Sir, be chaste." Here I would be communicating something very different. Gaffney then proves Schüller wrong: any exhortation has content and therefore gives direction itself.

People who write about the virtues do not like being treated like second-class citizens, waiting for those in normative ethics to generate new principles, norms, and rules, and then in subservience having to articulate a virtue or two that can make their principles work. People in the field of virtue are not that passive. Here I think of Alasdair MacIntyre,[4] William Bennett,[5] Stanley Hauerwas,[6] Elizabeth Anscombe and her husband Peter Geach,[7] and Gilbert Meilaender.[8] Of course there are others like Jean Porter,[9] Diana Fritz Cates,[10] Joseph Kotva,[11] Anne Patrick,[12] and the late William Spohn.[13]

We do not think that virtues are attendant to principles. In fact, quite a number of people have argued that giving predominance to principles really misses a great deal of what the moral traditions have said in sustaining our communities for centuries. For instance, Courtney Campbell and Marcio Fabri dos Anjos both ask whether the whole prophetic nature of ethics is demolished by simply vesting the normative with predominance without understanding the relevance of virtue.[14]

To pacify virtue ethicists, Tom Beauchamp offers us a certain compromise. He sees normative ethics and virtue ethics as two independent systems each making comparatively similar claims on one another, broadening both our understanding of ethics and our ideas about how we should proceed morally.[15] But that leaves us with either two systems of thought for ethics or a bipolar one.

We also have no need for a principlist system like Frankena's that depends on virtues solely for motivation or willingness. Rather, for any virtue ethics to be worthy of being called ethics it has to, in itself, offer us guidelines for action. In fact, I would argue, as David Solomon has, that a virtue-based ethics that generates its own norms and principles is more capable of guiding us in action than a simple normative ethics.[16]

I argue, moreover, that inevitably any normative ethics finds it origins in a virtue ethics. Virtue ethics actually generates its own principles, norms, and rules on a regular basis, and all principles eventually emerge from some community that has certain anthropological expectations, expressed in the form of virtues, which it needs to protect and develop.

Every community has a constellation of virtues that are offered as normative character traits for the community's own members. In order to promote these goals, these communities generate rules, norms, and principles which prompt members toward actions and practices that keep these virtues as realizable. For this reason, every community has principles, norms, and rules of justice that actually embody the very specific virtue of justice which they want to see embodied in their culture. Likewise, every community promotes its own notion of the virtue of fidelity or loyalty in a variety of specific forms and subsequently articulates particular rules, norms, and principles in order to direct their members toward the actions and practices that secure the specific trait of loyalty.

In this essay I contend that the late Cardinal Bernardin's consistent ethic of life thrives predominantly in the context of virtues and from there promotes its relevant norms.[17] To make this case, I proceed in three stages. First, I demonstrate how virtues generate norms; second, I ask the question whence norms and argue for the historical rootedness and development of principles and norms in cultures promoting virtues; and third, I explore the ramifications of this for Bernardin's consistent life ethic.[18]

Virtue Ethics as a Comprehensive System

From the outset, we must appreciate that virtues are not simply subjective dispositions.[19] We have known since Plato and Aristotle that virtues exist not primarily for private purpose, but to form and improve our communities. They are, as James Drane wisely points out, social. We can see easily how even virtues that form us at the depths of our being are social—for example, love, faith, charity, justice, and fidelity. A simple virtue like self-care is, then, hardly a subjective virtue; rather, it has enormous social ramifications, without which we would be parenting one another our entire lifetimes.[20] In fact, d argue, as I have elsewhere, that virtues actually perfect us in the forms of social relationships that distinguish us.[21]

ues, therefore, offer us guidelines. Joseph Kotva remarks that virt us to become a person with certain character traits, and therefore ist teach us not only who we ought to become but also how we ome that type of person. Therefore, virtues must provide us with or directives for acquiring the virtues we aim to have.[22]

general claims of Solomon and Kotva are illustrated by Lawrence Solum when he writes specifically about the virtue of jurisprudence, calling it "a normative and explanatory theory of law that utilizes the resources of virtue ethics to answer the central questions of legal theory." Later he explained, "A virtue-centered theory must claim that judicial virtues are a necessary part of the best theory of judging and that judicial virtue plays a central explanatory and normative role. A theory does not lose its status as virtue centered simply because it does not limit its explanatory resources to the virtues alone." Solum derives normative standards for right judging from moral judges themselves and demonstrates how norms are the directives for the right appropriation of the virtues themselves.[23] Here again norms are articulated so as to help us grow in virtue and are therefore derived from the very understanding of the virtues we are pursuing. This is, of course, the basic thesis of Alasdair MacIntyre in his work *After Virtue*: virtues have to tell us, not only who we are, but also who we ought to become and how we ought to become that person with those character traits.

Still, it is important for us to realize that when virtues direct they often do not have specific instructions, but are rather heuristic. If I say, "Pick up this eraser," I am giving a very specific action command. Most action commands are in their nature specific. But imagine that this essay is a lecture that I am reading before an audience. If I turn to one in the audience and suddenly say, "Sir, be respectful," I am giving that person a direction: I am aiming him to attend to a type of disposition by which he considers others, and even though the command lacks a lot of specificity, still it prompts the listener to attend to the way he treats me in this instance.

He may respond, "I think I am respectful. I think this argument about virtue is nonsense, but I'm still sitting here. I haven't quit your lecture and said what I think." If I were to respond, "Sir, I think respectful is more than simply being passively resigned," I am beginning to give my statement "Be respectful" some further determination.

As a heuristic, then, a virtue gives a general sense of direction though it is still waiting further definition. We want our audience member to show evidence that he is *aiming* at promoting a disposition of respect; how he is to actually promote it and in what way still awaits manifestation and definition.

Imagine, however, that my comment is made in front of a very diverse audience. For instance, a couple from Thailand notice that my interlocutor's feet are specifically pointing in my direction, a very disrespectful gesture in some Buddhist cultures. They might well turn to one another and say, "Keenan has a legitimate complaint. That man's feet tell the whole tale." But then Americans turn to the Thais and say, "Excuse me, but in our culture if you want to show respect you don't use last names like that." Then someone from Latin America or Africa turns to the Americans and says, "On our continents calling a person by the last name is completely respectful."

If we understand that heuristic means pointing us in a certain direction without complete finality and specificity, then we can see how "being respectful"—a virtue for so many cultures (if not all)—requires a further explication and more specific practices, rules, norms, and principles that help us to grow in our own specific communities in the virtue of being respectful, a very social virtue.[24]

Here let me develop my argument further by considering parenting. The work of parents in teaching their children to become fine human beings is a long one, and parents are constantly generating rules so as to guide their children not only nor primarily to right conduct but rather to becoming responsible, virtuous people. That is, every parent gives a rule to the child precisely as a way of helping the child to grow in virtue.[25]

Think here of the basic rule of all families, setting the time for a child to return home. We can easily imagine a parent saying this to a ten-year-old: "Tommy, be back from Johnny's by 5:30 p.m. I don't want you out past dark." Here the parent is teaching the child to socialize on his own, to develop new bonds of friendship beyond the family household, and at the same time to realize the responsibility to participate in family life while being vigilant of the fact that growth toward greater maturity means assuming forms of self-governance one step at a time. This particular rule, then, is training Tommy to engage a variety of virtues like friendship, responsibility, self-care, and prudence.

Imagine, however, we were to meet Tommy ten years later, at twenty years of age, and we hear his father say, "Tommy, be back from Johnny's by 5:30 p.m. I don't want you out past dark." This would be a startling rule. We would wonder why Tommy has not become more social, more autonomous, more self-caring, more prudent, and we would probably wonder the same about Tommy's father.

Family rules are the paradigm for moral rules.[26] Families engage in practices that help children keep their room in order; develop and maintain relationships; come to degrees of self-understanding and self-guidance; study and learn; articulate goals and agendas for the realization of self, relationships, and dreams; and appreciate the world, the neighbor, the needy, and the Lord. All these practices come with rules, and the engagement of these practices help children to grow into a more virtuous way of living. Of course, these family rules come within very specific cultures and the command, "Tommy, be back from Johnny's by 5:30 p.m. I don't want you out past dark," would probably be very rarely uttered in a little place like Tarime, Tanzania, where a family member would never go to another family household individually and unaccompanied and where without electricity it would be unthinkable for most people to imagine one another walking around in the dark.

Still, in Tommy's household, like those in Tarime, parents are not always able to so easily or clearly monitor their children. Here, for instance, I think back at my late father's constant (and desperate) complaint to his brood of five children, "Please try to get along with one another." This simple command (yes, command) was not simply a rule he wanted followed. Rather he wanted us to develop dispositions and to change our hearts. He would say, "You know, my parents only had two children, and I wanted you to have more siblings than I did." He wanted us to love one another. The rule was not only to stop us from engaging our vices; it was articulated out of his perception of the virtue he wanted us to develop with one another. That is, the rule grew out of a need for virtue, and he wanted us to engage a practice, the practice of getting along with one another. If we continued with this least of all expectations of exasperated parents, I am sure he would have taught us other practices.

Of course, he did. When we were older and my brother Bobby died at the age of twenty-six, my father and mother wondered whether we told one another enough that we loved one another. They also wondered whether they had said that to my brother before he died suddenly from a drowning. So they developed the practice of concluding a phone call with the words, "I love you." Now all of us do it. My dad died years ago, but my mom continues the practice, as do my siblings and my cousin, and now their children do it, not only with their family members but with their aunts and uncles, nephews and nieces, cousins and now close friends. The practice is about promoting the virtue of love, of course, and the practice is also an indication that my father's earlier rule for us (to get along with one another) was a successful admonition in getting us to where we are today.

Now, what bearing does this have on the topic of a consistent life ethic?

When we think of a consistent life ethic, generally we think of particular rules and principles such as, no direct killing of the innocent. We think too that our opposition to abortion and to euthanasia, for instance, should extend to our opposition to the death penalty and to assisted suicide and possibly to many, if not all, forms of war. We might even think that we should form policies for opposing cruelty to animals and environmentally damaging forms of conduct.

In all these instances, our imaginations take us to certain rules and principles about a consistent life ethic and the subsequent policy positions we should maintain. But as a matter of fact, you and I only move toward those positions if we are already disposed, and if we are not disposed, we will not move. This is the most stirring problem with a consistent life ethic: it only makes sense to those disposed to it. Most others who do not heed a consistent life ethic simply do not see the claim to oppose abortion as even analogous to the claim to oppose euthanasia.[27]

People who heed the consistent ethic of life share not only the deriva-
tive principles, but more importantly they share the original dispositions that
predetermine them for the consistent life ethic's claim.[28] Strangely, instead
of first asking whether we have the predisposition or not, many adherents
turn right to the policy issues. One reason for turning in this direction is that
often when we think of the consistent ethic of life we turn toward an ethics
of action rather than first to an ethics of being or virtue. That is, we go to
the end of the process rather than to the beginning.

Until we appreciate that the direction of our discourse is going in the
wrong direction, we find ourselves often stymied, wondering why those who
support abortion and oppose capital punishment or vice versa do not see
their inconsistency. Shouting "inconsistency" might be a ploy to awaken our
conversation partner, but to date it has not been terribly effective.

Aristotle told us that we see things as they appear to us, and therefore
he decided we should ask questions about whether we had, in the first place,
the right dispositions to see things clearly.[29]

The more important discussion for a consistent life ethic is not "Do we
have consistent action policies?" but rather "Do we understand the virtues
and attendant practices that could help us as a community of faith and as a
civic entity to promote a vigilant regard for the sanctity of life?" Rather than
promoting policies and consistencies, I think we need first to articulate and
promote virtues and their practices that could make us disposed to articulating
and promoting subsequently the policies that would be consistent.

Whence Principles?

We should be able to see that virtues promote not only the virtues
themselves but also the rules that we need and the practices that they govern
which furthers our ability to be and live virtuously. In other words, virtue
ethics is a complete system. In this light we need to ask, in such a complete
system, whence principles?

There are two types of principles: methodological and material. The
first are so called because they are principles like double effect, cooperation,
toleration, and *minus malum*, which are formal principles that provide us
with a method for adjudicating particular claims. The latter are not formal
but have a specific content: they are articulated as "no direct killing of the
innocent," "no separation of the unitive and the procreative," and so on. In
both instances any principle, whether it is methodological or material, has had
some history, and that history means there is a beginning, that is, that there
was some point in human history that the principle was not yet articulated.
This claim contends obviously against those who presume that principles are
eternal or that principles always existed as such.

Thus, the question, whence principles, assumes that they came from
somewhere and were not always with us. That principles have histories means

that new principles need to be articulated and others fall into disuse.

The historical development of methodological principles like double effect is worthy of note. Though Joseph Mangan once argued that Thomas Aquinas first expressed the principle of double effect,[30] Josef Ghoos proved otherwise.[31] Ghoos showed that the moral solutions from the thirteenth through the sixteenth century were of isolated concrete cases. These cases dealt, for instance, with whether a pregnant woman could flee from life-threatening danger even if the flight were to prompt a premature delivery and whether one could attack places where noncombatants were. Casuists began to note the similarities in these cases, and in the sixteenth century Bartolomeo Medina (1528-80) and Gabriel Vasquez (1551-1604) traced the common factors among these cases, which earlier casuists had already determined. As Ghoos proves, eventually, John of St. Thomas (1589-1644) articulated the factors into the conditions of the principle as such. At that point in time, and not earlier, the formal principle of double effect became a methodological tool for determining the moral validity of an action that produces two very different results.

Though we will momentarily look at a material principle, we should see from the above case that, over a period of time, moral teachers recognize an interrelatedness of particular cases and begin articulating their points of connection. Thus, the philosopher John Kekes in *The Examined Life* comments on the way that we constantly interact with principles. First, he claims that principles are simply shorthand endorsements of already accepted conduct; they are "extracted from conventional conduct prevailing in the society." Second, principles are revised or rejected to the extent that they continue to conform with our "prevailing practice." Their developments are conditioned by the social practices that originally validated them. Third, the degree that the practice is commonly accepted, to that degree the principle has force, and vice versa. In sum, principles are derived from conventional conduct: "Practice is primary and principles are secondary."[32]

Martha Nussbaum makes a similar point and writes with an Aristotelian assumption that "principles are perspicuous descriptive summaries of good judgments, valid only to the extent to which they correctly describe such judgments."[33] Elsewhere she writes, "A good rule is a good summary of wise particular choices and not a court of last resort."[34]

In their study of the history of moral reasoning, Albert Jonsen and Stephen Toulmin agree with Kekes and Nussbaum. They write of a variety of historical instances where rules and principles evolved from the particular judgments of wise leaders, whether pontiffs or rabbis. Dependence on these leaders evolved into a dependence on formulated methods and rules. On those occasions, a shortage of prudential leaders led to the formulation of such rules to guide the judgments of the less skilled and the less experienced.

For instance, the authors describe the transition in classical Roman society from an arbitrating society to a more rule-based one, from pontiffs to statutes. First, as Rome expanded so did the caseload, and less experienced judges had to settle disputes. Since their judgments were not always trusted, rules were articulated to measure the correctness of their decisions. Second, since rules were needed, law schools were established that found the teaching of rules more expeditious than the formation of prudential character. Third, the entrance of non-Romans into Roman society required a concordance between the laws of the new peoples and Roman law itself. Fourth, as the empire grew, so did its bureaucracy, and its operating procedures made further appeal to rules a form of life.[35] The pontiffs articulated into common denominators the points of congruency among successfully resolved cases. These points of agreement became the foundations and then validating insights for the rules.

In sum, principles are summaries of summary judgments. They are late-stage articulations of the basic considerations of relevant judgments that further a community's attempt to determine its future. Their relevance to us depends on our need for them as we continue to develop a society whose members conform with the type of people we are to become. The entire heuristic that we find in Aristotle's discussion on virtue is played out, then, throughout history and across geography. Principles, like rules and norms, are then key factors in guiding us expeditiously toward the goals we are seeking. They briefly encapsulate enormous insights that have taken years, decades and sometimes even centuries to achieve. Moreover, like telling Tommy when he is to return home, they not only presume an enormous number of concerns about where we are going but they also embody a marker of sorts regarding where we have been and where we hope we are now.

Behind these principles are shared dispositions about what it means to be human. A people who develop a principle of double effect evidences a community that seeks to be prudent and not promote harm intentionally, but yet determines courses of action that navigate adeptly through seemingly dangerous distinctions. They believe that the right answer is more important than a simply clarified one, and they therefore seek clarity, resist simple solutions, and insist that the moral action is as complex as the world. Religious fundamentalists would never have formulated double effect, or toleration, or worse, cooperation.

Let us then turn to the history of another principle, this time the material principle of the sanctity of life, a principle that rolls out of Catholic mouths with such frequency and familiarity today that we probably all think of it as having been a part of our language for centuries.

We may be surprised to learn that were we to investigate its history we would find no entry for the sanctity of life in the fifteen-volume collection of the *New Catholic Encyclopedia*. There also is no entry in *The New Dictionary of Theology*, *The Oxford Dictionary of the Christian Church*, *The Theological Dictionary*, or the German *Concise Dictionary of Christian Ethics*. In Palazzini's Italian *Dictionary of Moral Theology* there was only "Life, Respect for: see Murder, Suicide."

Certainly, the term has its roots in modern Christian writings, and it is linked with earlier concerns that we previously referred to as "the inviolability of life." Before that concept, we spoke about God having both dominion over us and Lordship over life. But today the term "sanctity of life" has become the quintessential expression for explaining why we need to promote among one another practices that express a deep respect for human life. It serves as a marker of the development of our community of faith. Let me explain.[36]

If we go back a hundred years we could see how the Jesuit moralist Thomas Slater discussed suicide: "The reason why suicide is unlawful is because we have not the free disposal of our own lives. God is the author of life and death, and He has reserved the ownership of human life to Himself."[37] We see here, then, that at its roots sanctity of life is about God's ownership: we do not own our lives; God does. Therefore we are not free to dispose of them.

Later Pope Pius XI declared in *Casti connubi*, "The life of each is equally sacred and no one has the power, not even public authority, to destroy it."[38] In a manner of speaking, then, in these and other writings, our life was construed as an object; human life was something God owned and therefore only God could dispose of it; we, on the other hand, only had use but not dominion over this object.[39]

The phrase "sanctity of life" first explicitly appeared in papal writings in the encyclical *Mater and Magistra*.[40] In its original form, sanctity of life functioned as a euphemism for God's dominion.[41] Thus, in *Humanae vitae*, life is sacred because its owner, God, willed it so; like other objects that God owned and sanctified, for instance, the marriage bond and the temple, life can not be violated.[42] The sacredness rests not in anything intrinsic to the marriage bond, the temple, or human life; rather it rests on the claim of God who made and owns the sacral quality of the marital bonds, temples, and human lives.[43]

During his papacy, Pope John Paul II significantly developed the term. In 1987, in his apostolic exhortation, *Christifideles laici* (38), he spoke at length about the inviolable right to life: "The inviolability of the person, which is a reflection of the absolute inviolability of God, finds its primary and fundamental expression in the inviolability of human life."[44] Nowhere did he refer to God's dominion or prerogatives. Rather the argument is simply that we are in God's image; as God's person is inviolable, so is God's image.

In the same year, in *Donum vitae*, we read:

> From the moment of conception, the life of every human being is to be respected in an absolute way because man is the only creature on earth that God has "wished for himself" and the spiritual soul of each man is "immediately created by God"; his whole image bears the image of the Creator. Human life is sacred because from its beginning it involves the "creative action of God" and it remains forever in a special relationship with the Creator, who is its sole end. God alone is Lord of life from its beginning until its

end: no one can in any circumstance, claim for himself the right
directly to destroy an innocent human being.[45]

This latter section is repeated later in *Evangelium vitae* (53) and becomes the
singular text in the *Catechism of the Catholic Church* (2258) to interpret the
fifth commandment. The entire paragraph is the most extensive statement on
both the sanctity of life and God as Lord of life prior to his lengthy encyclical
dedicated to the sanctity of life, *Evangelium vitae*.[46] In it we see some of the
key elements that later appear in the encyclical: that human life is singular;
in God's image; uniquely created by God for a special relationship with God
that is, in turn, the human's destiny; and, finally as source and end of human
life, God is Lord of life. While not at all abandoning the "God's ownership
or dominion" argument, the pope gives it newer meaning by highlighting the
uniqueness of the human subject.[47]

The act of creation is where God invests each human life with its inviolable character that now lies *within* the human, the image of God.[48] The
human is not to be killed therefore because of who the human is. Human
life is not an object that God owns: human life is a subject who bears the
inviolable image of God. This image of God is hardly extrinsic. Speaking of
the Yahwist account of creation, the pope writes in *Evangelium vitae* that we
have within us that divine breath which draws us naturally to God.[49]

Elsewhere in the encyclical we read: "At this point we come to the
decisive question, Why is life a good? Why is it always a good? The answer
is simple and clear: because it is a gift from the Creator, who breathed into
man the divine breath, thus making the human person the image of God."[50]
In John Paul II's personalist writings all people are invited to see within human life an indelible mark of its sacredness. The pope breathes life into the
concept of sanctity of life. Sanctity of life now means that the human life as
created in the image of God is no longer primarily an object that belongs to
God but a subject whose inviolability is indisputable.[51]

Clearly this principle reflects then enormous shifts in self-understanding
within the Catholic community. Having already shifted their attention from
objects to persons, the Catholic community began asking itself, who are we
as humans? Understanding themselves as made in God's image they began to
see a need to promote a respect not only for God's dominion but also for humanity itself. This newfound and newly developed disposition of self-respect
eventually needed to be expressed in the form of a new principle.

Conclusion

What, then, do we need to do in order to develop the consistent ethic
of life? We could go in the direction of principles. We could simply do what
many people do, argue logically from one way of human life being under
attack to another and look to extend the claims of a consistent life ethic. We

could expect that people agree with us and then when they do not we can shout at them, "Where's your consistency?"[52]

A more successful way of proceeding I think is what is at stake here. Rather than looking to the principle itself we need to look at how we develop the dispositions to appreciate the sanctity of life and how we name the practices appropriate for developing those dispositions.

We need to advance the principle by advancing the constellation of virtues and practices that originally gave it life. We need to promote, for instance, the virtue of mercy so that people in their respect for life are not so parsimonious with it to only restrict their understanding of respect for life for those in the womb or on death row. Through the virtue of mercy we can help others to see the extent of such great suffering in the world, whether from hunger, thirst, disease or infection, that they will want to be disposed to a very broad consistent ethic of life.

What then do we need to do to promote mercy? What practices would help people to open their eyes to the human condition, not just here in the States, but throughout the world? How do we help people to overcome their fear of other cultures and other forms of human life? What practices do we need to promote to develop dispositions of human sensitivity to those without? And how then do we break down the deep-seated judgmentalism with which so many persons from the industrialized world blame those from the developing world for their context? How do we help people to become aware of the biases that prompt us to categorize people as more or less worthy of our concern? What do we do when people entrench their biases in religious language? All these questions are simply issues for raising up possible strategies to help people expand the quality of mercy in their lives. But mercy is hardly enough.

How can persons develop the virtuous disposition of a vigilance that allows them to see how so many different forms of human life are under threat every day? I remember, when I lived in Europe, that I saw much more suffering in the world on Italian news than I did on American news. There is something about American media that wants to shelter us from seeing too much suffering, that filters out news about the way human beings live here and elsewhere. How do we promote a culture of vigilance that willingly finds out how the other half lives?

I remember the importance of teaching high school students and getting them to participate in Christian Service programs and how that practice of exposure helped to introduce students to the "other half," but how do we continually develop that sensitivity for the infirmed, the disabled, the imprisoned, and the homeless in populations that never attended our schools? If the entire American culture is based on advancement, how do we promote a willingness to look back, to look at the sidelines?

Similarly, how do we promote a sense that as people become more merciful and vigilant, they do not begin to look condescendingly at their neighbor? How instead of condescension do we promote solidarity, a very new virtue, which calls people to see themselves as related to one another? What practices can we encourage to develop solidarity for people they do not know, cannot see, have never heard? How can we invite others to see the real import of the Good Samaritan parable? How can we help them to hear in their newfound vigilance the call to solidarity?[53]

The companion virtue to solidarity is humility. I remember when I first worked on migrant camps in upstate New York I thought I knew how everyone should live until one day I asked a woman migrant laborer why her child was not in school, and she answered, shamefully, "Because I have no decent clothes for him." I began to learn how little I knew and how much I needed to do to find out why people were in their situations. I realized I was not the Good Samaritan but a clod and that I needed a humility to see my neighbor as one who could teach me more than I could teach her.

How, then, can we promote mercy, which I define as the willingness to enter into the chaos of another, when so many simply believe that people get the chaos they deserve?[54] How do we encourage others to realize that the circumstances people are in are more historically complicated than they presume them to be? How do we invite people into what Margaret Farley calls the grace of self-doubt, this epistemic humility that helps people to want to learn about their neighbors rather than to judge them?[55]

These are just a few questions. I think, however, when we realize with Aristotle that we can only see if we are rightly disposed, then we need to promote the principle of a consistent life ethic not by simply making logical connections with other instances of the principle but rather by promoting the virtues and practices that could make us a people more sensitive to promoting the principle itself. And, of course, we articulated the principle in the first place, precisely for that reason.[56]

5.
CONSTRUCTING A CONSISTENT ETHIC OF LIFE

Feminist Contributions to Its Foundation

PATRICIA BEATTIE JUNG

Introduction

Cardinal Joseph Bernardin claimed that deep within the Catholic moral tradition there was a consistent ethic of life (hereafter CEL). This essay evaluates that claim by critically assessing the tradition in this regard and constructively suggesting foundations upon which the church might establish a more consistent ethic.

The response made to Bernardin's claim by Christian feminists has been ambivalent. Noting that there is much to applaud in a call for consistency, moral theologians such as Christine E. Gudorf, Daniel C. Maguire, and Charles E. Curran maintain that the Catholic ethical tradition has been profoundly inconsistent, especially when traditional approaches to social and sexual issues are compared. Upon close analysis, it is clear that this pattern of differential treatment is methodological and ultimately theological in origin.

If we are to build a genuine CEL, the reasons for this methodological inconsistency need to be identified and analyzed, and if found to be without justification, this pattern of differential treatment needs to be uprooted. I will argue that, in Catholic moral theology, two mutually reinforcing misunderstandings of the approach to ethical reasoning espoused by Thomas Aquinas, along with an inadequate theological account of the moral ambiguity of human life, are among the primary sources of this ethical discrepancy. If genuine consistency is ever to characterize Catholic moral theology, then a foundation for it must be (re)constructed which avoids these errors. This essay aims not so much to delineate that foundation as to establish what must be part of its agenda.

Feminist Ambivalence about the Consistent Ethic of Life

The response of Christian feminists to Bernardin's CEL was and remains divided. On the one hand, there is much to applaud in the proposal. There is great affinity between the CEL and many feminist insights and concerns.

On the other hand, the assertion that such consistency has already informed the tradition still does not ring true. There are key points of tension, if not disagreement, about central theological claims regarding the moral ambiguity of much of life and the existential nature of evil. The feminist response to the CEL was and is profoundly ambivalent.

Affinities between Feminist and CEL Concerns

As noted, Christian feminists find much to appreciate in the commendation of a CEL. Much that is foundational to Bernardin's CEL coheres with and reinforces tenets commonplace to Christian feminist ethics. Three closely intertwined base points of the CEL are of particular import to Christian feminists.

First, there was the appeal Bernardin made to the ethical centrality of the sacredness of all human life as affirmed in *The Challenge of Peace*. Because human dignity is intrinsic to us as beloved sons and daughters of God, men and women can do absolutely nothing to lose or establish our worth as persons. From this point of view, a person's value can be neither socially nor individually (de)constructed, because it is God-given. The root of human dignity is not a matter of social attribution or personal merit. It is God's love for all that is the basis for both the general obligation to respect (that is, to promote and protect the sanctity of) all of creation in general and the moral presumption in particular against the taking of personal life. This—the sacred value of human life—is the axiological basis for the critical analysis of all those domestic, socioeconomic, and political contexts in which some people are not treated as worthy of such respect. These people are often women, but also people of color; gay, lesbian, bisexual, and transgendered persons; and the poor. These are precisely the ones whom feminists are committed to uplifting with respect.

Second, such respect for the value of all human life is reinforced by another moral stance foundational to both Christian feminism and Bernardin's proposal for a CEL. I am here referring to the appeal within the CEL to a sense of fairness that rejects unjustifiable forms of discrimination, like the double standard that still prevails in our culture regarding gender and other caste systems. There is an abiding and deeply rooted moral consensus among people that similar cases ought to be treated alike (and dissimilar cases differently). One can trace this notion back through its expression in Kant's principle of universalizability to Aristotle's conception of justice. Indeed, part of Sidney Callahan's case for pro-life feminism hinged on the claim that it alone was genuinely consistent with feminism's demand for justice.[1]

Bernardin appealed to this sense of fairness when he compared official church teachings on abortion and just conduct in war. Bernardin noted that if it is always wrong to intend directly the taking of innocent human life—as the Catholic Church teaches is the case in abortion—then justice required a consistent approach to the analysis of military strategies. The church also ought to teach that "directly intended attacks on civilian centers are always wrong" (SG, 12). Such an appeal to evenhandedness in the promotion of what Bernardin recognized to be a heroic ethic promotes both personal integrity and social justice. "The principle which structures both cases, war and abortion, needs to be upheld in both places." Indeed, Bernardin concluded "the viability of the principle depends upon the consistency of its application" (SG, 12). Precisely this same sense of (in)justice informs much feminist analysis as well and underlies the import of consistency.

Finally, building upon the argument sketched in *The Challenge of Peace* Bernardin emphasized the new context in which Christians find themselves, particularly the powerful way technologies can threaten life today. As reflected in this pastoral letter's teaching on deterrence, the modern development of nuclear weaponry has resulted in significant developments in church teachings about what might justify strategies to avoid war, recourse to war, and particular forms of conduct in war. In regard to war, this "new context shapes the *content* of our ethic of life" (SG, 11), noted Bernardin.

Such differences in context are not completely unique to the military arena. For example, analogous changes have taken place in many modern penal systems. Our increased ability to "incapacitate" murderers through imprisonment has triggered related changes, at least at the level of application, in church teachings on capital punishment.[2] Such attention to context and its significance, not only to pastoral considerations and applied and/or practical ethics, but also to the normative content of Christian ethics, is a mainstay for many, if not all, Christian feminists.

In sum, like advocates for a CEL, Christian feminists affirm the sacred value of human life, share the sense of fairness that demands such consistency, and recognize the substantive moral significance of the context in which decisions are made. Yet many Christians remain suspicious of those who advocate a CEL. In the next section I identify the roots of that suspicion.

Tensions between Feminist and CEL Concerns

Fifteen years ago Susan L. Secker identified the disagreement between advocates of CEL and many feminists. She noted that close attention to what we experience as the context for our decision making can shape the content of ethical reflection in two distinct ways. It can increase (1) the descriptive accuracy of our understanding of the situation and (2) the normative adequacy of the criteria we bring to our decision making.[3] The former, I would argue, has generally been recognized by the most thoughtful proponents of the CEL, while the latter has not. Let us consider this distinction in more detail.

Increasingly careful attention to the concrete particularities of many women's lives has recast the abortion debate in official Roman Catholic Church teachings in recent years. As early as 1988, John Paul II noted that often a woman is "abandoned with her pregnancy, when the man, the child's father is unwilling to accept responsibility for it."[4] In his 1989 address on the consistent ethic of life and the *Webster* Supreme Court decision, Bernardin also took note of the problems some pregnant women face (SG, 180-87). The recognition that pregnancy can be problematic, and other related insights into the realities of many women's lives, is developed further in the 1995 encyclical letter *The Gospel of Life*. Here, John Paul II noted that however widespread it is, a "contraceptive mentality" may not accurately characterize the thought process of every woman who chooses to abort. His analysis of the situation faced by many women is worth quoting at length.

> It is true that the decision to have an abortion is often tragic and painful for the mother, insofar as the decision to rid herself of the fruit of conception is not made for purely selfish reasons or out of convenience, but out of a desire to protect certain important values such as her own health or a decent standard of living for the other members of the family. . . . The father of the child may be to blame, not only when he directly pressures the woman to have an abortion but also when he indirectly encourages such a decision on her part by leaving her alone to face the problems of pregnancy. . . . Nor can we overlook the pressures which sometimes come from the wider family circle and from friends.[5]

While attention to the concrete particularities of women's lives may correct our description of the problem, John Paul II is adamant that it does not have a normative impact. "Nevertheless, these reasons and others like them, however serious and tragic, *can never justify the deliberate killing of an innocent human being*."[6] In contrast, Secker notes, Catholic feminists such as Margaret A. Farley have argued that close attention to the "features of women's experience, if taken seriously, would alter the very moral norms that are being brought to bear in particular judgments."[7] Consciousness of the distinctive features of women's experience constitutes for feminists not only a "new" context for decision making, but can and should impact the assessment of the normative adequacy of traditional approaches to these decisions.

So, while there was much about it to be appreciated, Bernardin's claim that a "seamless" attitude toward life ought to inform the tradition was also met with suspicion by Christian feminists. Christine E. Gudorf gave sharp voice to the sentiments of many when she replied to Bernardin's claim by declaring that the tradition has in fact not been consistent. "Abortion stands alone along our spectrum of moral issues."[8] The principle that one ought to never directly intend to kill innocent life has indeed found regular expression in traditional rules prohibiting abortion and promoting noncombatant immunity. But these rules have not been applied evenhandedly to concrete historical realities. Despite Bernardin's claim of consistency, Gudorf easily demonstrated that "in Catholic teaching on abortion and war we have two significantly different methods of moral decision making."[9] In one approach, circumstances impact normative arguments; in the other, they do not.

Bernardin was clear that his call for a systematic vision of life issues had to "honor the complexity" of the problems people face (SG, 18). The church has a long and time-honored tradition of recognizing the complexity of human decision making in time of war. Thomas Nairn wrestles with the question of whether abortion provides the sort of straightforward, paradigmatic case that can fruitfully illumine a CEL.[10] I am suggesting in this essay that in the just war tradition one might find cases better able to illumine what remains obscured and forgotten in the multifaceted practice of abortion.

While there is a strong presumption against taking life, exceptions have been made. One such exceptional situation may occur during a war. Direct attacks upon civilians are absolutely prohibited, even when the resort to war is just. And yet, some civilian deaths can be permitted morally, if they are the result of an attack directed elsewhere. (Thomas A. Shannon notes that one finds in *The Challenge of Peace* a justification, albeit reluctant, of nuclear deterrence, which must intend the "indirect" death of millions of innocent civilians.[11]) The church has respectfully recognized the need for prudential judgments "in the field" by soldiers and commanders alike, especially regarding what might count as a direct attack upon civilians. Pilots often know that children live near their intended targets and that even "smart" bombs miss their targets with a measure of predictable certainty. Only military officers are perceived as capable of discerning the level of innocent civilian death that could be judged morally tolerable as "collateral damage," whether under the standard justification (principle of double effect) or newer ideas like group liability.[12] The point here is that this was not considered by the bishops to be a matter appropriately regulated in detail even by international or military courts of law, except in retrospect in the case of its extreme violation. In *The Challenge of Peace*, noted Gudorf, "even the instruction of Catholic military personnel offers moral principle rather than specific commands."[13]

This pattern continues. Though not totally silent on such matters, the bishops tread and judge comparatively "lightly" when addressing issues like U.S. detention policies and its torturous interrogation techniques of "enemy combatants" (as young as eight years old) in Guantánamo Bay, Cuba, and of prisoners in Abu Ghraib, Iraq, and Afghanistan by military and intelligence personnel under the "guidance" of psychologists. I am unaware of any public criticism of the horrendous impact of phosphorous shells, allegedly used only for illumination purposes, on civilians sleeping in Fallujah when the U.S. attack on that city began. While objections might have been raised, they were certainly done *sotto voce*, presumably with the hope of engaging officers and politicians in dialogue about alternative strategies.

In contrast, there has been little recognition—except perhaps on the pastoral level noted earlier—of the moral complexity of the situation faced by women who experience pregnancy as problematic. Even though, as Nairn notes in chapter 3, Bernardin recognized that abortion entails the consideration of several moral issues, I do not think he wrestled with their potential for conflict. Despite Bernardin's call to "honor the complexity" of these problems and his concomitant invitation to "expand the moral imagination" (SG, 19) of our society regarding these issues, many women and men find that his vision of a "seamless garment" simply short-circuits their efforts to reflect afresh about the complexities and distinct conflicts associated with abortion.

For example, Gudorf pointed out that the value of women's bodily integrity, while hypothetically "recognized by the church as a basic human right in other contexts,"[14] is not seen as objectively relevant to the abortion debate. The point I want to make here is not that respect for a woman's right to bodily integrity and to bodily self-determination in this context would automatically trump concern for the sanctity of fetal life. The point I want to underscore is that these are values of great moral significance. It may well be that upon close inspection, the church as a community of moral discernment might decide that there are significant differences between involuntary child-bearing and other instances of the violation of bodily integrity (like slavery, forced labor, and torture). A claim to analogy between these situations—or more positively, a claim to an analogy between childbearing and a practice like organ donation—may not ultimately prove illuminative of the many values at stake in abortion.[15] Feminists are themselves divided on whether this and other ways of reconceiving pregnancy in light of the concrete particularities of women's experience are fruitful.[16]

This essay is not basically about abortion per se, but rather about how the traditional Catholic approach to it differs from its approach to conduct within war, the death penalty, and other life issues. The question at stake here is not under what conditions, if any, might the values of the mother's bodily integrity and well-being and her responsibilities to other dependents override the sanctity of fetal life. Rather, I am concerned with a more foundational question: why have the values of a woman's freedom regarding parenthood and her moral obligations to others and herself not been recognized as relevant *in any respect* to her responsible decision making regarding childbearing?[17] In arguments about family planning it is falsely presumed that in virtually all marriages, wives freely consent to coitus with their husbands. The fact is that often women and girls have no real choice about when or whether to have sex; the fact is that many wives have no real choice in the matter either. Some have been schooled to "render the debt," whether they think having children would be responsible or not. Many experience sexual activity in marriage as simply coerced, if not violent. Yet, whether consensual or not, the Vatican teaches that all sexual activity must be open to the possibility of procreativity.[18]

If a woman decides it is in the best interest of her other children, her spouse, her marriage, and/or herself not to conceive, Rome teaches that her only choice is to practice sexual abstinence. The fact is, however, that this is not a real option for many women around the world. Although this aspect of the context within which women make decisions about abortion is not new, the feminist consciousness of the moral implications of this concrete particularity of women's experience certainly is. Traditionally, female bodily self-determination has not been recognized as relevant to the moral analysis of contraception and sterilization either. Thus, it is not surprising that it carries no weight in traditional arguments about abortion.

Furthermore, unlike military personnel, women—who alone bear and who for the most part still take primary responsibility for the rearing of children, who live in the "reproductive trenches," so to speak—have not been viewed as capable of or trustworthy in regard to making prudential judgments about the resolution of the potential value conflicts that may arise in concrete, specific cases of pregnancy. The bishops continue to press to outlaw all instances of abortion. This is part of a larger pattern associated with sexual issues.

Until the second half of the twentieth century the U.S. bishops pressed to outlaw all forms of contraception as well.[19] By the 1960s, however, there was widespread noncompliance and no enforcement of those few remaining statutes in states like Connecticut and Massachusetts that imposed fines and potential sentences of imprisonment on those "caught" practicing contraception. Despite church teaching to the contrary, few in North America could then (or do now) see that allowing individuals to make concrete decisions about "artificial" contraception would seriously undermine the foundations of society or gravely damage the moral life of the community. In addition, many non-Catholic religious leaders approved as "responsible" this approach to parenthood. The claim that this practice eroded obvious and minimal standards of public morality or "generally accepted standards" was no longer credible. The point here is not to obscure important differences between the debate about contraception and the debate about abortion, but to suggest that in regard to sexual issues the church has not always been clear or convincing about when and why some issues should be properly matters of public policy and others matters of private conscience.

The U.S. bishops employed a listening process in the development of their pastorals on war and the economy that acknowledged the complexity of those moral issues and the moral significance of the contemporary context.[20] Many perceived this approach as endorsed by the Second Vatican Council in its "Dogmatic Constitution on the Church" (*Lumen gentium*). Here a bishop is advised "not to refuse to listen to his subjects whose welfare he promotes as of his very own children and whom he urges to collaborate readily with him" (§ 27). In reference to the laity, bishops are later told "they should willingly use their prudent advice and confidently assign duties to them in the service of the Church, leaving them freedom and scope in acting" (§ 37). To my knowledge, the Vatican has never fully employed this process. In the formation of his teaching on contraception and abortion in *Humanae vitae*, Paul VI chose not to adopt the Majority Report of the Birth Control Commission which had listened carefully to the expert testimony of the married couples and reproductive health practitioners who had addressed the morally complex realities of sexual activity, pregnancy, and child rearing in the modern world. Why? What accounts for this difference?

A Methodological Inconsistency

Gudorf correctly argued that these inconsistencies are foundational in origin. Overall, "the Catholic Church uses proportional consequentialism in public-realm issues and a deontological natural law approach in private-realm issues." She argued that the reason for this discrepancy was "the separation of reality into two spheres, the public and the private."[21] So, while abortion may "stand alone" among issues regarding life, this "deontological natural law" approach is not peculiar to abortion. It is the method most typically adopted by the church when it tackles virtually all issues in sexual ethics.[22]

The current debate over what has become known as "proportionalism" was for all practical purposes sparked by an "untidy" (to use Richard A. McCormick's apt descriptors) yet "seminal essay on the principle of double effect" written by Peter Knauer, S.J., in 1965.[23] In the early 1970s Louis Janssens sought to show how the consideration in tandem of intention and proportion could illumine the distinction between justifiable and immoral evil.[24] These essays probably enabled Daniel C. Maguire in 1976—some eight years before Gudorf drafted her response to Bernardin—to identify as problematic on a methodological level the Vatican's increasingly deontological approach to sexual issues. In an essay he wrote in response to the 1975 "Declaration on Certain Questions Concerning Sexual Ethics" (*Persona humana*), Maguire declared that the Congregation for the Doctrine of the Faith (hereafter the CDF) had not done justice to the tradition.[25] In his commentary on responses to this declaration in 1977, McCormick summarized Maguire's specific criticisms as including "methodological shortcomings (e.g., the separation of the idea of moral disorder from the notion of moral harm; abstractionism; aloofness from the empirical basis of ethics)."[26]

In 1982, as part of this exploding debate over the nature of moral norms, McCormick argued that the notion of intrinsic moral evil should not be based on the object of an act "in a narrow sense,"[27] "apart from all morally relevant circumstances, side effects, consequences, and intentions."[28] Such considerations were precisely what enabled "proportionate reason" to reform (when warranted) assessments of activities like surgery that might have traditionally been seen as instances of "mutilation." Indeed, "Proportionate reason enters into the very definition of what one is doing."[29] Obviously a morally wrong action could never be justified, but an evil like mutilation could be morally justified as proportionate, if it was life-saving (as an amputation might be), just as a homicidal assault could be morally justified, if it was a proportionate act of self-defense.

Of course, the term *ex objecto* has become ambiguous precisely because in the manualist tradition it was used inconsistently. In his essay McCormick conceded that in the manualist tradition the term sometimes "includes morally relevant circumstances," as when theft was defined as "taking another's property against his reasonable will." Other times, however, it did not, as in the treatment of masturbation.[30] Then he asked the sixty-four-thousand-dollar question:

> Why, if we are to be consistent, does not such utterly traditional moral reasoning apply to all areas where moral norms attempt to state the rightness and wrongness of human action? Specifically, there are two areas where this *Denkform* has been excluded. They are: (1) actions considered wrong because *contra naturam* (e.g., contraception, masturbation); (2) actions considered wrong *ex defectu juris* (e.g., direct killing of an innocent person). These actions were said to be intrinsically evil in the manualist tradition.[31]

The practice in the manualist tradition of employing thick descriptions for sociopolitical and economic practices and thin descriptions for sexual practices found expression in official church teachings of the twentieth century.

While noting that there is "great merit" in the call of the episcopacy for a CEL, Charles E. Curran began to develop further these insights of Maguire, McCormick, and Gudorf. In 1985, he argued that "a lack of consistency exists between the positions taken by the American Catholic bishops and the universal hierarchical teaching office in the sexual and medical areas and the approaches taken in social ethics."[32] In a carefully documented comparison of modern official Catholic social and sexual teachings, Curran identified in 1988 three important methodological differences between these strands in the tradition: "Whereas the official social teaching has evolved so that it now employs historical consciousness, personalism and a relationality-responsibility ethical model, the sexual teaching still emphasizes classicism, human nature and faculties, and a law model of ethics."[33] What are the reasons for such a methodological inconsistency? How deeply is the tradition shaped by these differences? Only when the rationale for such inconsistency is exposed and analyzed can we determine whether it can be justified. If not, then it must be uprooted and the foundation for a genuinely CEL rebuilt. It is to these tasks that the rest of this essay is devoted.

The Depth of This Methodological Inconsistency

While proportionate reasoning about what will contribute to human flourishing has deep roots in the Catholic tradition, it is not the only approach to moral norms within that tradition. Much of the church's official teaching in the area of sexual ethics is currently grounded on what has been labeled a "basic goods theory" rather than proportionate reasoning. In his insightful, comparative study of the differences between these two foundations, Todd Salzman makes it clear that they can be distinguished on several fronts.[34] My focus here is on the differences in their approach to moral norms.

In my opinion, the basic goods theory, and hence the methodological inconsistency within the tradition, rests on two mutually reinforcing misunderstandings of the methodological approach to the ethics of Thomas Aquinas. One problem is the misunderstanding of the role in moral discernment of Aquinas's threefold criteria for the evaluation of moral acts. The second is a misunderstanding of Aquinas's view of what makes certain acts unnatural. The roots for the methodological inconsistency within moral theology are established when these two misunderstandings are coupled together.

As is well known, in the *Summa Theologiae* Aquinas analyzes in great detail the structure of human acts. But as Selling notes in his review of Janssens's interpretation of Aquinas "when Thomas shifts from speaking of the structure of human action (qq.6-17) to speaking about its evaluation (whether it is good or evil) he appears to shift emphasis on what is important about human action."[35] Aquinas appears to shift his focus from the object of the act to its end, which is always "presented" by human reason. This is the locus of considerable controversy.

Jean Porter's analysis of the problem is helpful. Everyone concurs that Aquinas identified three criteria for the moral judgment of an act: (1) its object or the act-in-itself, (2) the circumstances, and (3) its aim or intention. However, according to Porter, these concepts are commonly misappropriated. Contrary to popular opinion, "Aquinas does not in fact hold that the criteria for moral judgment set forth in I-II 18 jointly provide a methodology for the moral evaluation of specific actions."[36] Aquinas is not suggesting that we can reach a moral judgment by inquiring *sequentially* first into the object of the act, then into the agent's aim, then its circumstances, and finally by applying his dictum regarding what causes defective choices and what is required to produce good ones. Such a process—which suggests that one might be able to describe an act apart from its circumstances and the agent's aim—is not what Aquinas has in mind.

Aquinas recognized that the object of an action could not be described prior to its moral evaluation.[37] The act-in-itself cannot be evaluated apart from considering the agent's intention (I-II 20.3.1). For Aquinas it is clear that different intentions can constitute different acts. Furthermore, whether a means is proportionate to or congruent with an end is determined by its circumstances (I-II 18.3). Indeed, Porter argues that within a genuinely Thomistic framework, no one can morally describe an action as, say, murder or theft, without employing some sort of generic moral notion as an interpretative lens: "[These are] prior evaluative judgments, in terms of which we determine what is morally relevant and what is not, and how the different components of the action should be interrelated to one another. . . . To describe an action from the moral point of view is to form a moral evaluation of the action."[38] Aquinas refused to evaluate the parts of an act apart from the assessment of it as a whole. A genuine CEL must refuse to do so as well.

Porter's analysis goes on to make it clear that for Aquinas the object of an act is not always perspicacious. Generic notions of murder, theft, just execution, and so on deployed by Aquinas in II-II of the *Summa*, function as key reference points in the process of moral discernment. Once it is decided that a particular action can be truthfully described as an instantiation of one or more of these basic moral concepts, then the objective evaluation of the act is complete.[39] Because such analyses focus on the truthful description of particular cases rather than the more generic notions themselves, absolute moral certainty in regard to all the synthetic moral prohibitions and prescriptions that might flow from such deliberations was inevitably out of reach.

In the majority of cases for Aquinas, it was clear that such moral descriptions could not be made by crudely equating a particular physical behavior with one of these generic moral concepts. For example, while many homicides might be murderous, Aquinas recognized some as just punishments, just acts in war, or proportionate acts of self-defense. The description of an act as a justifiable or murderous homicide entailed its objective moral evaluation.

In a few cases, however, Aquinas appears to many interpreters to identify generic moral notions with particular forms of physical behavior. For example, certain sexual sins (II-II, 154, 11) seem to many to have been identified this way. Indeed, Aquinas does argue that while lust is in every instance a disproportionate experience of desire, all noncoital sexual activities also fall short of the form proper to sexuality. They are thereby *deformitas* or unnatural. Aquinas saw such sexual activities as in conflict with God's design for human sexuality.

In my opinion, this description was not based on a source of wisdom—an order of nature—distinct from reason and revelation, as many modern commentators argue. A reasonable case can be made that Aquinas reached this conclusion on the basis of the best scientific and exegetical understandings of human sexuality available to him. Both the biology of his day and the prevailing biblical interpretations (especially of the story of the creation of woman) reinforced as reasonable his perception of the sheer "naturalness" of coital activity. In the end, I think there is really only one source of moral wisdom for Aquinas, and that is reason, but it is not a source of insight properly understood (by the scholastics) to be independent of the authority of revelation.[40]

Clearly, Aquinas commended both the "scientific" observation of physical structures and reflection on human experience more broadly than is often conceived today. In this sense he is rightly interpreted as taking up and integrating both strains of the natural law that he inherited from the classical traditions of antiquity. Yet, I think for Aquinas this so-called order of nature is a subset of the order of reason illumined by revelation. The breakdown of the synthesis of these strains achieved by Aquinas is at the root of the difference in the methodological approach that has deformed Catholic moral theology in recent centuries.

Rebuilding the Foundation

In order to develop a genuinely consistent ethic of life, a solid methodological foundation for it must be (re)constructed. While this project is undoubtedly complex, let me identify two elements that I wager will prove central to its success. (1) One such agenda item is the normative (re)consideration of human embodiment. How might further reflection on the body contribute to our conclusions about what will prove requisite to human flourishing? Certainly it enhances our identification of the full range of goods basic to it. (2) Another element key to the reconstruction of an ethical methodology that could support a genuine CEL is the recognition of the ambiguity of the moral life. Experience(s) of irreconcilable conflict(s) among basic goods are real throughout all of life. It is simply illusory to think they are not part of interpersonal relationships and domestic life. The ethical, as well as theological, implications of this ambiguity need delineation.

Human Embodiment and the Identification of Basic Goods

Many Catholic feminists believe that the church has not approached abortion in a manner consistent with other life issues. One reason is that abortion was identified by the church as a sexual as well as a life issue. Long ago, in her analysis of Bernardin's initial proposal regarding the CEL, Christine Gudorf pointed out that the Catholic Church teaches that abortion not only unjustly violates the sanctity of life but also "thwarts God's will, as expressed in human biology, that intercourse be open to procreation."[41] For this reason, the church teaches that the practice of abortion, not its prohibition, poses the real threat to the true "bodily integrity" of women.

Such an account of God's design does not square with women's experience of the relationship between human sexuality and reproduction. It rests on accounts of human physiology and biology that long ago were proven inaccurate, among other reasons, because they were androcentric.[42] Therefore, central to the development of a genuine CEL is the development of an adequate account of the relationship between procreativity and sexuality.

On the one hand, fear of a revival of physicalism—and of the false forms of gender "essentialism" that frequently accompany such arguments—has led many feminists to avoid reflecting on what embodiment contributes to our normative understanding of human flourishing. On the other hand, tempting as such a strategy of avoidance may be, it will short-circuit efforts to develop a strong foundation for moral arguments. Persons simply cannot be "adequately considered" apart from attention to the body.[43] Intellectual cowardice must not be confused with authentic humility before the real difficulties that accompany such an endeavor. In the end, a refusal to face this challenge will serve the status quo and put at further risk all those not presently well served by these systems.

Following the lead of Lisa Sowle Cahill, many Catholic feminists believe that "forceful moral critique, especially in an intercultural context"[44] requires a foundation greater than can be minimally established by Kant's universalism. Judgments about and resistance to injustices of all kinds suffered throughout the world will prove broadly unintelligible and ineffective if they rest solely on subjective, communitarian/sectarian or procedural foundations. As Cahill concludes, it is politically "crucial to bring postmodern social critique into connection with some understanding of reason which can surmount moral agnosticism even while appreciating cultural difference."[45] Without some sense of our commonality and shared humanity, feminists recognize that the global struggle for the recognition of women's full humanity and equality will be futile.

Of course, Catholic feminists are divided over the specificity and strength appropriate to such global claims, but even Porter, who argued in 2001 that "it is difficult to arrive at a statement of principles that would be universally acceptable,"[46] concluded in 2003 that there are realities or "pre-conventional aspects of human life (that) give rise to and place constraints upon our moral practices."[47] Building upon the feminist Aristotelianism of social philosopher Martha Nussbaum, Cahill argues that through inductive and dialogical reflection on particular experiences—especially of bodily experiences like aging, mortality, hunger, sexual desire, and reproductivity—feminists can produce modest, reformable generalizations about basic goods.

Though socially constructed in a variety of ways, Cahill argues that these goods are recognizable across the globe: "The essential point to emphasize for an ethics which begins with, and remains respectful of, differences in experience, while not giving up the possibility of normative ethics, is that the shared is not achieved beyond or over against particularity, but rather in and through it.[48] While the pursuit of them is not in all cases necessarily moral, the identification of such basic shared goods provides reasons (premoral values and the norms and rules that express them) for various courses of action, practices, and public policies. These have engendered, Cahill argues, normative commitments to the environment and human rights evidenced across the globe.

One methodological prerequisite for the development of a genuinely consistent ethic of life is the proper identification of such objective, shared premoral values, especially in regard to sexuality. However, the recognition of these basic goods does not automatically entail their classification as absolute. In the abstract, these premoral values may appear incommensurable, but in the concrete lives of pregnant women they are not.

Christian Realism about Evil and Morally Tragic Choices

Obviously, not every imaginable way basic goods might be socially institutionalized and/or culturally scripted within the human community contributes equally well to human flourishing. While procreativity is recognized as a basic good by many Catholic feminists, they are usually among the first to judge as immoral political and religious constructions of gender and sexuality that make openness to pregnancy "compulsory" for all sexually active women.

What makes such a judgment even possible? The entire process of discernment hinges on the feminist commitment to pay attention to and reflect upon the concrete lived experiences of women as well as men. Only then will the absence of bodily integrity in general, and of sexual and reproductive integrity in particular, be recognized as a *real* privation. This reconceptualization of pregnancy—in light of women's concrete experiences of sexuality, childbearing, and child rearing—illumines as partial and inadequate those assessments that would describe situations that involve the denial of bodily self-determination to women as merely entailing the absence of a good. The absence of "bodily integrity" is sensed, experienced, and felt as a *real* loss, indeed as a violation, as a "compulsion," just as the termination of pregnancy or bodily life support is sensed, experienced, and felt as the *real* letting die of fetal life.

This is in part what is at stake in the distinction between ontic and moral evil introduced by Janssens. Whether a problematic pregnancy is aborted or carried to term, it is unrealistic to describe the evil that inevitably accompanies either choice as nothing more than the mere absence of a good. Evil may be primarily a privation, but it is also always experienced as real. In this sense it is important to recognize as real, not merely apparent, the inescapable experience of irreconcilable conflicts among basic goods. In her book, *Out of the Depths: Women's Experience of Evil and Salvation*, Ivone Gebara gives an articulate voice to women's "muddy" experience of suffering as concrete, domestic, and often mixed with salvific experiences of solidarity and understanding.[49]

Over thirty years ago, Janssens theorized that there are four sources of ontic evil: temporality, spaciality, sociality, and sin.[50] Selling summarizes his proposal as follows.

> Because every choice entails the letting go of other possibilities, because we can never completely control the material world in which we live, because the very accomplishment of being a moral person entails a maturity that is inescapable from being involved in many social roles and tasks that cannot all be satisfied at once, and because sin and immorality will always be a part of our earthly environment, ontic evil will always be part of whatever choices (*electio*) we make of our external, material actions or omissions. It is inescapable.[51]

Close attention to the concrete judgments women make about particular experiences of pregnancy likewise reveals that the scope of the impact of finitude and sin is in this sense ontological, not merely anthropomorphic. Realism about human finitude and sin comes easily to those who give considerable weight to the moral reasoning of ordinary people who wrestle what good they can from such conflicts.

In her book, *Escape from Paradise: Evil and Tragedy in Feminist Theology*, Kathleen Sands argues that much of Christian theology lives under a delusion, that is, lives in denial of the real losses and conflicts inescapable in life. She argues that both of the traditional interpretations of evil within Christianity are inadequate. For her, neither Platonic rationalism, with its account of evil as mere privation, nor dualism, with its account of evil as the demonic enemy, does justice to the tragic way good and evil are interwoven in the lives of people.

While basic goods are incommensurable in the abstract, they can and must be prioritized when they are considered in the concrete. Such decisions do *not* rest on the basis of a predetermined hierarchy of values (in which, for example, fetal life is always ranked over bodily integrity or in which bodily integrity is always ranked over fetal life). Nor does such commensuration rest on the illusion that "clean hands" in such situations are possible. Like most soldiers in the field, most women who opt to abort do not want innocent life destroyed. Like soldiers in the field, most women who opt to carry a problematic pregnancy to term may suffer serious consequences for that choice and may perhaps see those for whom they feel responsible suffer as well. Yet certainly in both cases, it is the height of moral self-deception to conclude that what in either case can be so clearly foreseen is not also in some sense willed, even if it is unwanted.

The magisterium has long recognized that on the battlefield what matters is whether one has a proportionate reason for harming innocent life. The church has also recognized the significance of proportionality in some of its other teachings about life, such as in its arguments about the permissibility of a private citizen killing in self-defense and the licity of "electing" to amputate a limb for "therapeutic" reasons. In their article, "Assisted Nutrition and Hydration and the Catholic Tradition," Thomas A. Shannon and James J. Walter establish that "historically, the method for making a determination about the use of a medical intervention was the proportion between the benefits of the intervention and its harms or burdens to the individual, family, and community."[52]

I believe the legitimacy of the moral significance of such proportion finds oblique recognition in the church's teachings about the moral acceptability of both (1) removing a Fallopian tube in the case of an ectopic pregnancy and (2) the removal of a pregnant woman's cancerous uterus. This remains obscure, because in such cases the church refuses to recognize such practices as abortive in any moral sense. Ask any woman who has lost a child this way and she will tell you the truth about her decision.

The church has not generally recognized the role of proportionalism in relation to either contraception or abortion, because it "sees" a necessary connection between these acts and an intention or a motive that is "contralife." In what strikes me as among the most bitter of ironies, some bishops continue to argue that one may not use condoms to prevent the transmission of HIV to one's spouse. Incredibly, they interpret the use of a condom in this circumstance as necessarily "contralife"! Careful attention to the life experience and wisdom of laypeople in general, and women in particular, suggests that this may not be so. It is certainly not self-evidently true. Many faithful Catholics would concur that not every imaginable instance of either contraception or abortion may be necessarily or intentionally "contralife."

It is important to affirm the value of innocent (fetal) life especially under difficult circumstances. Many Catholic feminists agree: just as there can be no just targeting of population centers, there can be no just targeting of fetal life. And yet, on the battlefield soldiers recognize that even when the target is properly military, often some civilians die in the conduct of war. This loss of innocent life may be justified if there is proportionate reason for that loss. Likewise, in an effort to balance responsibly the many basic goods that may conflict when a pregnancy is problematic, some choose to terminate the pregnancy. Consider cases of medically therapeutic abortion. Admittedly rare, it is clearest in such cases that there is no necessary connection between the decision to terminate a pregnancy and an intention that is "contralife." It is crucial that there not be, as Shannon and Walter put it in their discussion of assisted nutrition and hydration, an eliding of the axiological affirmation of the sanctity of life with the distinct but related normative determination of what obligations a person may have in the concrete to maintain this particular valued life. Their point is worth quoting: "Failure to make this important and traditional ethical distinction between axiology and normativity leads one to affirm wrongly that the affirmation of the value or sanctity of life of the patient in and of itself imposes normative obligations with respect to medical interventions."[53]

My point here is that in at least some imaginable cases, the loss of innocent valued fetal life may be justified. Though properly valued as sacred, there may sometimes be proportionate reason for aborting fetal life. However, from what I can determine on the basis of admittedly anecdotal conversations with my students (who are largely privileged women from North Atlantic countries) about why they may have chosen to have abortions, in many instances there was not what I would recognize as proportionate reason. Indeed, it is important to recognize that electing to abort a pregnancy may often not be justifiable.

There are undoubtedly many reasons that women may opt to abort without proportionate reason. But I am firmly convinced that such unethical decisions stem in part from our failure as church to lead serious public conversations about the merits of alternative strategies for solving the problems faced by some pregnant women and about what might, and what might not, constitute proportionate reason for an abortion when those alternative solutions are not available or fitting. Instead, like some elements within the feminist community, the church is contributing to the ongoing polarization of our public conversation about abortion, supporting only those who cry that abortion ought never to be permitted and reacting against those who cry it is always justified. Frankly, this polarity strikes many of the wise women and men who live in the "reproductive trenches" as absurd. And equally, it leaves many of us without the thoughtful guidance we both desire and deserve.

At the very least, such dualistic moral views distort reality by forcing everything onto one side or the other of a battle with the "forces of darkness." Whatever else might be helpfully illumined by dividing people along a "culture of life"/"culture of death" axis, much is obscured by such dualistic thinking. In her editorial, "Either/Or? Catholicism Is More Complex," Cathleen Kaveny notes that polarized thinking about the film *Million Dollar Baby* "occludes our awareness of our own sin and shortcomings" and "corrodes the charity" that prompts us to understand the other person's perspective and to "ask ourselves hard questions about whether and how persons acting in good faith might reach the position they have reached."[54]

Conclusion

My goal in this essay was to identify some of the methodological work that must surround our response to the late Cardinal Bernardin's call for the development of a truly consistent ethic of life. This call for a CEL elicited both positive and negative reactions among feminists: advocates for a CEL and Christian feminists both affirm the sacredness of human life, uphold a sense of fairness as necessary for such consistency, and recognize the significance of the context in which decisions are made. However, Catholic feminists have also pointed out methodological inconsistencies along a "public-realm" vs. "private-realm" divide. Specifically, these theologians have argued that in the area of social ethics, Catholic teachings employ models of historical consciousness, personalism, and proportionate reasoning, whereas in the realm of sexual and medical issues—areas that interface with women's experiences of pregnancy significantly—a more classicist, deontological natural law approach is prevalent.

Much of the church's official teaching in the area of sexual ethics is not currently grounded in proportionate reasoning. In this essay I have argued that two mutually reinforcing understandings of Aquinas's methodological approach to ethics reinforce this reluctance to employ proportionate reason. Put positively, a more faithful understanding of Aquinas's refusal, when evaluating a particular act, to divorce parts of the act from the assessment of it as a whole, as well as his reliance upon the order of reason (of which the order of nature must be considered a subset), will have important implications in building a true CEL.

A (re)construction of its methodological foundation is necessary in order to develop a genuine CEL. Two elements central to this task include, first, a reconsideration of human embodiment—particularly in light of women's bodily experiences, with special attention to sexuality and reproductive issues—and second, a recognition of the ambiguity of the moral life, which entails engaging in open, honest dialogue about important ethical issues rather than encouraging dualistic moral views.

I have argued that when women's and men's bodily experience is taken seriously, the moral landscape changes. Traditional Roman Catholic conceptions of the relationship between human sexual and reproductive potential are problematized. Conflicts among values are shown to be existentially real, and "dirty hands" are proven to be sometimes unavoidable. These conflicts cannot be "dissolved"; they must be faced. I have argued, and the tradition (at least in regard to problems like war) has long taught, that conflicts among premoral values involving life are best—most consistently—addressed, when these basic goods are prioritized through the concrete prudential guidance of proportionate reason.

Richard M. Gula provides a fair summary of the conversation to date about how a truly proportionate reason may be recognized. In 1973 Richard McCormick proposed three specific criteria whereby proportionate reason might be identified. Gula summarizes them as follows: "(1) The means used will not cause more harm than necessary to achieve the value. . . . (2) No less harmful way exists to protect the value. . . . (3) The means used to achieve the value will not undermine it."[55]

According to Gula, McCormick argued that we will know whether in a particular case there was proportionate reason for violating one of the moral life's basic goods either through experience, through an affective intuition (such as moral outrage), or through trial and error.[56] James J. Walter has argued that there are additional ways to come to know whether and when a reason might be proportionate. He suggests that the rational analysis of evidence and of the logic of arguments, consideration of (especially the long-term) consequences of a decision or practice, and personal feelings of disunity or unity (despite the fact that it is notoriously difficult to discern whether a particular experience of guilt is legitimate or not) can each illumine proportionality.

I have tried to demonstrate in this essay that a genuine CEL will only be developed under two conditions. First, the social as well as the personal dimensions of evil must be recognized. Second, the role proportionate reason has in enabling people to negotiate life's existential moral ambiguities—including those related to sexuality—must be recognized. I have argued that Roman Catholic Church teaching about abortion—if it is to promote a genuinely consistent and realistic ethic of life—must be reformed. The church must continue to illumine the sanctity of fetal life. But attention must also be given to the realities of women's lives and to the normative implications of the ambiguities therein. Sustained attention must be given to the specific criteria whereby proportionality might be discerned. Their relevance as guides to moral decision making in the face of problematic pregnancies must be tested. Only then will the church bear witness to a true CEL and hopefully thereby successfully reduce the number of abortions chosen without proportionate reason.

PART 3
FORMING THE ECCLESIAL VOICE

6.
RHETORIC AND THE CONSISTENT ETHIC OF LIFE

Some Ethical Considerations

ELISABETH BRINKMANN, R.S.C.J.

From his first lecture at Fordham University, throughout his various major addresses on the topic, Bernardin repeatedly stated that one of his key concerns in proposing a consistent ethic of life was to build on the success of the pastoral letter, *The Challenge of Peace*, in influencing public policy debates. Just as the peace pastoral made space for public discussion of the "moral factor" in considerations of nuclear armaments, Bernardin wanted to create space for the public discussion of the "moral factor" in issues such as abortion and the death penalty (SG, 9). Creating the space for public discussion of moral issues, Bernardin suggested, has the potential to shape public policies in line with Roman Catholic moral teachings as much as any particular moral doctrine upon which the Catholic Church may insist. As he stated, "The principle conclusion [to be drawn from the policy impact of the peace pastoral] is that the Church's social policy role is at least as important in defining key questions in the public debate as in deciding such questions" (SG, 9). If we raise the right questions, then people may eventually come to the right conclusions. I argue in this essay that viewed as a vehicle for influencing public policy debates, Bernardin's proposal for a consistent ethic of life can be understood not simply as a pro-life ethic in and of itself, but as a rhetorical device for promoting a genuinely consistent ethic of this kind.

Rhetoric Defined

To claim that a consistent ethic of life is a rhetorical device may be surprising, given popular notions of "rhetoric" as a pejorative term implying style with little or no substance, and connoting audience manipulation. In this view, rhetoric is what we hear politicians doing when they are on the campaign trail. Though I am not using this term here in this manner, the connection to politics is on the right track. In the ancient Athenian *polis* of Plato and Aristotle, where rhetoric originated, it was (for free-born males) the essential skill and civic practice of political discourse.[1] Rhetoric as I am using it, in other words, includes the art of speaking well, which requires

81

some years of disciplined study to acquire. As David Fleming explains, "It is rather a rich and rewarding course of study whose end is the development of a certain kind of person: engaged, articulate, resourceful, sympathetic, civil—a person trained in, conditioned by, and devoted to what was once called *eloquence*." The purpose of this training is the development of skills necessary for "effective and responsible participation in public life." [2]

While the study of rhetoric involves the acquisition of particular skills necessary for civic discourse, this still does not fully encompass the meaning of "rhetoric" as I am using it in this paper. More than a set of skills, rhetoric is an *"acquirable virtue,"* according to Fleming.[3] "The goal of rhetorical training," he writes, "is neither a material product, nor a body of knowledge, nor technical proficiency in achieving pre-determined ends; it is rather to become a certain kind of person," one with the characteristics necessary for good citizenship.[4] In the same vein, Richard M. Weaver argues that the "true rhetorician" is "a noble lover of the good, who works through dialectic and through poetic or analogical associations" to move souls toward the good.[5] Understood thus, rhetoric is a civic virtue—one of the dispositions necessary for engaging in civic discourse, especially in a pluralistic democracy such as the United States. It is something like the moral virtue of "civic amity" that John Courtney Murray suggests as "the sentiment proper to the City." Characterized by "reason and intelligence, laboriously cultivated by the discipline of passion, prejudice, and narrow self-interest," civic amity, according to Murray, is the prerequisite for dialogue which turns a "community" into a "political community."[6] As I am using it, then, "rhetoric" is a set of skills and virtues necessary for fruitful public discussion of contentious issues. As such, I suggest that it is among the "virtues and attendant practices"[7] essential for promoting a consistent ethic of life.

The Rhetoric of a Consistent Ethic of Life

That Bernardin himself was conscious of the importance of rhetoric in promoting a consistent ethic of life is clear from his first lecture on the topic. There he said:

> In the public policy exchange substance and style are closely related. The issues of war, abortion, and capital punishment are emotional and often divisive questions. As we seek to shape and share the vision of a consistent ethic of life, I suggest a style governed by the following rule: We should maintain and clearly articulate our religious convictions but also maintain our civil courtesy. We should be vigorous in stating a case and attentive in hearing another's case; we should test everyone's logic but not question his or her motives. (SG, 14)

In other words, not only *what* one says, but *how* one says it is important in shaping and promoting a consistent life ethic.

Promoting a consistent ethic of life requires fostering social respect and concern for all life. This, I suggest, as much as working out the details of such an ethic, is what Bernardin hoped efforts to articulate a consistent ethic of life would help to achieve. Raising the right questions is key: if the church raises the questions, and does so credibly, people can engage with each other over the issues. Presuming the church's insistence that its natural law morality is universally comprehensible and applicable, such engagement can help to "frame a new consensus" around the moral resolution of difficult issues (SG, 9). This rhetorical dimension of a consistent ethic of life, I maintain, is an asset that, if understood and used correctly, can contribute to advancing such an ethic in both the Catholic and civil context.

The rhetorical appeal of a consistent ethic of life is evident in the speed with which it was taken up by the U.S. Conference of Catholic Bishops (USCCB). Just two years after Bernardin first proposed it, a consistent ethic of life was adopted as the official policy of the USCCB in its revised Plan for Pro-Life Activities.[8] Furthermore, prior to every presidential election since 1988, the bishops have asserted their conviction "that a consistent ethic of life should be the moral framework from which to address issues in the political arena."[9] To that end, the statements addressing "the responsibilities of Catholics to society," issued every four years by the Administrative Committee of the USCCB, spell out a whole range of social issues affecting the "life and dignity of the human person." From abortion to poverty alleviation, all these issues must be taken into consideration by the Catholic faithful in deciding how to cast their votes. As the bishops insisted in 2003, "For Catholics, the defense of human life and dignity is not a narrow cause, but a way of life and a framework of action," a claim that they support with the Congregation for the Doctrine of the Faith's assertion that "a political commitment to a single isolated aspect of the Church's social doctrine does not exhaust one's responsibility toward the common good."[10] Given this constant and by now rather well-established commitment of the U.S. bishops to a consistent ethic of life, it is somewhat surprising that the general population seems largely unaware of the Catholic Church's very wide-ranging commitment, flowing from such an ethic, to issues of social justice.

The Failure to Communicate: A Case Study

Ask my students—Catholic and non-Catholic alike—what the Catholic Church stands for, and they will immediately name three things: no birth control, no abortions, and no women priests. (They will also, invariably, bring up the recent sex-abuse scandals.) Press them a little to identify how the church's commitment to life is expressed beyond opposition to abortion,

and some can tell you that the church opposes euthanasia and physician-
assisted suicide (although, especially since the publicity surrounding Terry
Schiavo's death, they are confused about what this actually means). A few
may also know that the Catholic Church opposes stem cell research that
involves the use of embryos. After more than twenty years of insisting on a
"consistent ethic of life" that cuts across issues of social and personal ethics,
most of my students—even those who went to Catholic elementary or high
schools—are surprised when I point out to them that the "pro-life" position
of the church includes support for a whole range of social policies. To name
just a few discussed in the 2007 preelection document, "Forming Consciences
for Faithful Citizenship," these include protection of income security for the
elderly; health-care reform to assure access to decent medical care; creation
and maintenance of "safe and affordable housing" for all; protection of the
rights of immigrants, both documented and undocumented; and so on.[11]
Certainly, my students are not a representative sampling of the U.S. population, but I suspect that their lack of familiarity with the Catholic Church's
stance on social policies is not atypical. Given the population demographic
that my students represent, moreover, their unfamiliarity with the full range
of the Church's "pro-life" stance seems particularly unfortunate.

I teach at a small, Roman Catholic liberal arts college that serves students
who typically have had limited access to a postsecondary education. Many of
my students are first- or second-generation immigrants, predominantly from
Latin America, the Caribbean Islands, and other "developing" nations. They
tend to come from working-class families—that is, from the lower-middle or
lower socioeconomic class. Most rely on financial aid and work one or even
two jobs during the school year to help pay tuition costs. Almost all are the
first generation in their family to attend college. Since the traditional-aged
(i.e., eighteen to twenty-two years old) undergraduate program in which I
teach only admits women, all my students are female. As such, many (because
they come from female-headed, single-parent households) already are, and
all of them are at risk of, suffering from a social phenomenon that Cardinal
Bernardin singled out as being of particular concern for a consistent ethic of
life: the "feminization of poverty." As Bernardin put it in an address given
at the Catholic University of America in January 1985:

> I cite . . . the case of women in poverty not because it is the only
> issue we must face as a Church in the policy debate but because
> it is one we should face with special emphasis. I have argued the
> case for a consistent ethic of life as the specific contribution which
> the Church can and should make in this nation's public debate. . . .
> To stand for life is to stand for the needs of women and children
> who epitomize the sacredness of life. (SG, 68)

Bernardin points out that one of the ways in which the church "stands for
the needs of women and their children" is through its social service agencies

that work to "sustain women seeking to raise families alone and to provide their children with the basic necessities." A second and complementary way is in its role as "advocate and actor in the public life of society." This includes the church's tradition of social teaching and its prophetic task of questioning "how we organize our life as a society," particularly in relationship to those who are most vulnerable. It also must include, Bernardin insists, the church's participation in the public debate to work for "compassionate, just, social policy." As he states, the church must recognize that "it cannot simply address the problem of the feminization of poverty through its own resources. It must also stand in the public debate for such programs as child care, food stamps, and aid to families with children" (SG, 68).

It has been more than twenty years since Bernardin spoke about the feminization of poverty at the Catholic University of America, but the situation for women has not improved significantly since then—if, indeed, it hasn't declined. Based on U.S. Census Bureau data, in 2006 women generally were 41 percent more likely to be poor than men; women over sixty-five years old were 74 percent more likely to be poor than men over sixty-five; and children in single-mother-headed households were 102 percent more likely to be living in poverty than those living in households headed by single fathers.[12] This, no doubt, is why the bishops have voiced support for several programs that directly benefit women and their children, including "efforts to overcome barriers to equal pay and employment for women and those facing unjust discrimination."[13] Furthermore, "Forming Consciences for Faithful Citizenship" expresses concern "about the income security of low- and average-wage workers and their families when they retire, become disabled, or die," and points out that "in many cases, women are particularly disadvantaged." Consequently, it insists that "any proposal to change Social Security must provide adequate, continuing and reliable income for low- and average-wage workers and their families."[14]

Given this professed concern of the U.S. Catholic bishops specifically for women and their children, why is it that so few of my students have any knowledge of the church's stance on these issues that are so directly relevant to their own lives? I suggest it is because, while the bishops may recognize the rhetorical *appeal* of a consistent ethic of life, they seem to misunderstand the importance of rhetoric in *promoting* such an ethic. If anything, frequently their rhetoric actually appears to contradict their stated commitment to a consistent ethic of life. A brief look at the bishops' public participation in the 2004 presidential election is illustrative.

U.S. Catholic Bishops and the Presidential Election of 2004

In May 2004, an *America* magazine editorial lamented the lack of substantive discussion and debate of issues in the presidential campaign then under way. The editorial pointed out that, while promising to be the most expensive election campaign in U.S. history, it also threatened to be one of the least enlightened. The enormous amounts of money being spent by the campaigns was disproportionately going to television advertising, a forum better suited to distilling issues and candidates' stand on them into oversimplified sound bites than to in-depth examination of the choices voters faced. In comparison, the editorial pointed to the ambitious and comprehensive agenda for the "national debate that presumably takes place in an election year" as it was set forth by the U.S. Catholic bishops in "Faithful Citizenship." Yet here, too, according to the editorial:

> The formidable challenge the bishops posed in defining their agenda stands in disappointing contrast to the actual record of Catholic participation in the campaign so far. An inordinate amount of public attention has been paid to a few Catholic bishops who have inserted themselves into the campaign by publicly warning that they would refuse Communion to Senator John F. Kerry, the presumptive Democratic candidate.[15]

The editorial was referring to Archbishop Raymond Burke of St. Louis, Missouri, who, along with a number of other bishops, insisted that Kerry and other Catholic politicians (and even Catholics who cast their votes for these politicians) should refrain from receiving Communion because their voting records on abortion-related policies placed them outside "the state of grace."[16]

Regardless of one's opinion about these bishops' pastoral theology or the appropriateness of their statements in the midst of a national election campaign, it is not surprising that such statements leave the voting public, including the Catholic voting public, with a mistaken impression that the Catholic Church's pro-life agenda is limited to the issue of abortion. This is particularly true when there is not equally strong concern expressed by the bishops about candidates' stances on other life issues, such as the war in Iraq or fiscal policies benefiting the wealthiest citizens at the cost of social programs for the poorest. Rather, their response to Archbishop Burke was to develop "a policy statement on the responsibility of Catholics in public life."[17] Even though Cardinal McCarrick, the head of the committee charged with developing such a statement, expressed reluctance to use "exclusion from participation in the Eucharist as a sanction for Catholic politicians whose legislative decisions seem inconsistent with Catholic teaching,"[18] the debate itself served to once again reinforce the Church's already well-known opposition to legally available procured abortion. In so doing, it undermined the bishops' stated insistence that Catholics must go to the polls having examined "the position of candidates on the full range of issues, as well as on their personal integrity, philosophy, and performance" and that "for Catholics, the defense of human life and dignity is not a narrow cause, but a way of life and a framework of action."[19]

Ironically, the focus on imposing ecclesial sanctions may have served also to undermine the bishops' agenda for ending legal availability of abortions because it suggests, in the words of *America*'s editors, "that the abortion issue is one of denominational discipline, a 'Catholic issue,' rather than an issue of human rights, around which a broad coalition of religious and nonreligious traditions can unite."[20] This certainly seems to have been borne out by the commentary of Robert Grant on the June 18, 2004, meeting of the U.S. Catholic bishops. Writing in the *Humanist*, Grant stated that the bishops "approved a statement on 'Catholics in Political Life' that brands Catholic politicians who *support abortion rights for non-Catholics* as 'cooperating in evil.'"[21] The not-so-subtle implication here clearly is that ending legal access to abortions in the United States would be imposing specifically Roman Catholic religious morality on non-Catholic citizens.

Some might argue that the problem here lies not with the bishops, but with anti-Catholic bias or the media's predilection for emphasizing the most controversial and divisive stories while ignoring other equally important but less dramatic ones. Yet this only serves to underline the importance of rhetoric in effectively promoting the bishops' agenda. Rhetoric, as I argued at the beginning of this essay, involves a set of skills and virtues necessary for fruitful engagement in public discussion. Most fundamental among those skills must be a proper understanding of the context within which one is speaking. This context, at this time in our nation's history, is one in which the public discussion of moral issues has become polarized to the point of fragmentation. Certainly, some news media contribute to this situation by oversimplifying complicated matters into easily digestible stories that play on pre-existing stereotypes and capitalize on controversy. Yet this is hardly a secret and should, therefore, be a factor in shaping the rhetoric of the Catholic bishops who otherwise contribute to the increasing divisiveness of public debates. Not only does this serve to undermine the bishops' own stated agenda, it also squanders what Bernardin identified as the Catholic Church's unique potential for bridging the divide at the heart of America's culture wars.

Bridging the Divide

In an address delivered at Columbia University in November 1993, Bernardin pointed out the tension that had existed from the founding of the United States, between the nation's Enlightenment and its religious heritage. On the one hand, said Bernardin, "Like many of their European confreres, our Founding Fathers were suspicious of the heteronomy and authoritarianism that characterized the religious heritage."[22] This bred "a healthy sense of skepticism" in the American citizenry, which tends "not to be convinced simply by the dictate of authority" but wants "to hear persuasive arguments."[23] Yet on the other hand, Bernardin goes on to say, "Alongside this

Enlightenment influence, there has been, from the beginning of this nation, an enormously powerful religious influence. . . . In the end, one cannot ignore or bracket the influence of religion in the social, political, and cultural life of the United States."[24] Bernardin saw the interplay between these two aspects of the U.S. cultural heritage—the autonomous ideals of the Enlightenment on the one hand and the heteronomy of religious traditions on the other—as "creative and enlivening, indeed the animating force that makes our cultural life distinctive." He cautioned that danger lies in the "one-sided emphasis on one at the expense of the other."[25]

An overemphasis and uncritical acceptance of Enlightenment autonomy, individualism and rationalism, he argued, can be blamed for "much of the poverty, inequality, and lack of economic opportunity in our nation" as well as for "a debilitating loss of purpose and identity" and a resulting "breakdown in moral sensibility [and] falling away from those convictions and principles that give structure and depth to human life." Yet at the same time, he warned, a one-sided emphasis on religious heteronomy is "self-destructive and inimical to society." In fact, he asserted, "The attempt to impose a narrowly conceived Christian political agenda, simply on the basis of biblical authority, is an act of intellectual and cultural aggression that is understandably resisted by a pluralistic society." One might add that the imposition of such an agenda on the basis of *ecclesial* authority alone is equally inimical and destructive.[26]

Yet Bernardin went on to argue that the Catholic Church was particularly suited to bridging the gap between autonomy and heteronomy in U.S. culture. It is worth quoting him at length:

> As the proclaimer of the God who became *human*, the Church can gratefully and enthusiastically celebrate all that is positive in the autonomous culture born of the Enlightenment: freedom of the individual, the dignity of the human person, the right to express oneself and seek one's own destiny. And, as the proclaimer of the *God* who became human, the Church can speak the word of judgment over all demonic distortions of autonomy; it can embody what is best in the heteronomous tradition that has shaped our nation. Standing, as it were, above the split between autonomy and heteronomy, the theonomous Church of Jesus Christ can serve as a uniquely powerful leaven to U.S. society.[27]

While Bernardin went on to illustrate how the church can function in this way by examining the role of the Catholic intellectual in the university, I suggest that an examination of the way Bernardin functioned as pastor and bishop is equally illustrative.

At the heart of Bernardin's ministry was his vision of the church as leaven in society, a vision that informed and shaped not only the projects he took on, but the rhetorical style with which he promoted them. It is to an examination of his style, then, that we now turn. What are the skills and virtues inherent in his rhetoric, and how do these negotiate the tensions built into the culture of the United States? Since this essay is specifically concerned with Bernardin's proposal for a consistent ethic of life, how did his rhetorical style serve to promote the social attitudes and atmosphere necessary for supporting and sustaining a genuinely consistent ethic of life?

Bernardin's Rhetorical Style

Bernardin once told an audience that it was his "trust that, through open and honest dialogue, differences can be resolved and the integrity of the gospel proclaimed" that "prompted [him] to move beyond the family of faith and speak to our society about a consistent ethic of life."[28] The context for these words was an address, given just three weeks before he died, to the first meeting of the Catholic Common Ground Project committee in Chicago. Here we see the essence of Bernardin's style; it is above all dialogical, with the goal of finding common ground.

We have already seen that his purpose in proposing a consistent ethic of life was to stimulate public discussion and debate in the service of building consensus on the whole range of life issues among Catholics and within the wider society (SG, 13). To this end, over the years he responded to critics on both sides of the political spectrum who disagreed with his articulation of a consistent life ethic. No doubt, this is why the emphasis seems to shift, in his various addresses, from the importance of linking all life issues to the absolute prohibition of abortion, and back, yet he always insisted that in a truly Christian ethic, "quality of life" and "right to life" issues cannot be divorced from each other.

In his various lectures on the consistent ethic of life, Bernardin persists in pushing toward the common ground which he believed such an ethic delineates and where he believed fruitful dialogue can take place (SG, 19, 108, 264). He participated in and encouraged dialogue not only between church and society, but also between groups advocating for various life issues (SG, 107), between theologians and bishops (SG, 104), and among the various academic disciplines (SG, 102), hopeful that such engagement could lead to the social changes necessary for sustaining life. As he told one audience, "Thinking and reflecting and deliberating together, I am confident that we can arrive at solutions which will improve the societal environment in which we seek to protect and foster human life and dignity in all its circumstances and in all its stages of development" (SG, 47). Such dialogue requires the kind of courage that is clearly evident in Bernardin's proposal for a consistent ethic of life.

In the Gannon Lecture, Bernardin acknowledged the potential for controversy inherent in his proposal saying, "I do not underestimate the intrinsic intellectual difficulties of this exercise [of shaping a consistent ethic of life in our culture] nor the delicacy of the question—ecclesially, ecumenically and politically" (SG, 7). Some years later, again at Fordham University, he admitted, "As I prepared [the Gannon] address, I was aware that I would be walking through a minefield."[29] Nonetheless Bernardin chose to seize the opportunity created by the public debate that the peace pastoral had already generated to push the dialogue even further. Moreover, he did so in the context of a university, "a community and an institution committed to the examination and testing of ideas" (SG, 7), thus inviting and encouraging critical scrutiny of his proposal. This required not only courage but humility—a clear sense of his own gifts and of his need for the gifts of others—as well.

Bernardin was aware that in his role as bishop and chairman of the then NCCB's Pro-Life Committee he was in a unique position to initiate and promote the development of a consistent life ethic. Yet he also knew that this was not a project he could advance by himself. Thus, he encouraged a wide range of contributors to help in the process of clarifying his notion of a consistent ethic of life and thinking about how such an ethic "can be set forth in a convincing way" (SG, 108). At Seattle University, for example, he called for "bishops who foster the debate, political leaders who enter the discussion, professors and policy analysts who can clarify categories, and members of the Church who exercise the supremely important role of citizens" to join together in "thinking through the meaning" of the consistent ethic of life (SG, 108). Humility, as much as courage and a commitment to dialogue, defines Bernardin's rhetorical style.

Without humility, in fact, dialogue, at least as Bernardin understood it, is not possible, for as he explained, "In dialogue we affirm, examine, deepen, and rectify our own defining beliefs in relationship to another person."[30] This assumes a willingness to refine and even change what we believe in the face of convincing arguments, and it requires a mutuality that is only possible when all participants in the dialogue recognize that no one person or group has a monopoly on the truth.[31] Such humility is evident in Bernardin's thinking about his primary task, as bishop, to teach. As he told one audience:

> The crucial question for me is not *whether*, as a bishop, I should teach or even *what* I should teach. My basic concern is *how* I can pass on the Church's authentic teaching in the most effective, credible way. As you know, the best teachers are those who learn from their students. In fact, the best learning environment is often one in which teachers and students search together for the truth. That is my goal when I exercise my teaching office.[32]

At his twentieth-anniversary commemoration of episcopal ordination, Bernardin admitted that he was not always so humble. His humility grew over the years, he told the attendant congregation, along with his realization that "the human condition is very complex and at times paradoxical." This led him to the conclusion that "while there is surely a wonderful clarity about our Catholic faith, just how that faith is to be lived out each day in our highly secularized, consumer-oriented society is not always so clear. So," he said, "I have learned to be a little more realistic, a little more humble in terms of my ability to set things right, to provide answers to the challenges and the problems of daily life."[33] Humility and realism, consequently, informed Bernardin's view of effective pastoral leadership in shaping an ethical agenda in the public milieu, and he called his fellow bishops to such humility and realism as well.

In attempting to "address the moral dimensions of any issue," Bernardin observed, a "problem that bishops face is their personal limitations." He continued:

A key solution is to engage in frequent dialogue with others—with experts in various fields, with respected colleagues, with trusted advisors, with the public at large. . . . Through our participation in dialogue we share our competencies and God-given personal resources while compensating for our weaknesses and personal limitations. *Our collaboration helps ensure the quality of a moral vision for this nation and makes it both credible and worthy of implementation.*[34]

Accepting our limitations and compensating for them through broad-based collaboration is essential for the credibility of the church's public position on moral issues. So, too, is maintaining a broad perspective on the whole spectrum of moral issues. "Bishops constantly encounter pressure from special interest groups," Bernardin warned. "But a bishop must keep within his perspective the whole range of issues that affect the quality of human life." He acknowledged that this can disappoint some "who expect a bishop to agree with them on every idea and strategy or who expect a religious leader to be available full time for a particular project." Nonetheless, Bernardin felt strongly that bishops need to keep in view the "whole spectrum of issues" if the church's public witness is to be effective.[35]

That the church's witness be effective and credible when it entered into public policy debates concerning moral issues was one of Bernardin's oft-repeated concerns. While he strongly defended the bishops' right to participate in such civil discourse, he also insisted that they had to "earn the right to be heard by the quality of their arguments."[36] To reiterate his observation in the Merton Lecture, "Americans tend not to be convinced simply by the dictates of authority; they want to hear persuasive arguments."[37] As we have seen, Bernardin held that the authentically Catholic "vision of the relationship between God and the world" made the church ideally suited for entering into public debate because it recognizes that the "truths of secular culture are embraced by the Truth disclosed in Jesus Christ and, thus, . . . the Church need not retreat into a defensive, authoritarian stance."[38] Quite to the contrary, Bernardin saw the church's proper stance as one of mutuality and respect that allows for truly productive dialogue within the church, and between the church and society. His great hope was that through dialogue, the church might "learn how to *work together* as a community of faith" to witness to "both the sacredness of every human life and the God of Life who is the origin and support of our common humanity" (SG, 265).

Sadly, while his faith in this possibility never seemed to diminish, over the years the possibility of its attainment did. Twelve years after delivering the Gannon Lecture, Bernardin admitted, "Unfortunately, a great deal of polarization exists within the Church today. This has created at times a mood of suspicion, even acrimony. A candid discussion of important issues—and a common witness to them—is often inhibited, so that we are not always able to come to grips effectively with the problems that confront us" (SG, 265). The solution, in his view, was to realize that within the church "there is room for considerable diversity among us," a return to "civility, dialogue, trust, and tolerance," and a redoubling of efforts to restore and rebuild the unity of the body of Christ. "Dealing with each other in a consistent, gospel-inspired way," he concluded, "will add greatly—I would say it is indispensable—to our public, collective witness to the consistent life ethic which is so desperately needed in today's world" (SG, 266).

Civility, dialogue, trust, and tolerance, as we have seen, are essential to Bernardin's rhetorical style. It is a style defined by an attitude of respect and mutuality toward his dialogue partners; by the humility to listen, learn, and even change his beliefs in the face of convincing arguments; and by the courage to address complex and controversial issues. Bernardin's rhetoric embodied these skills and virtues, which he recognized as necessary for effective and responsible participation in the public life of the United States.

Drawing on John Courtney Murray's work, Bernardin defended the right of the church to participate in public policy debates but insisted that in doing so it must observe the legitimate limits imposed by the pluralism of U.S. society and the secularity of its government (SG, 121). He maintained that part of the church's mission is to provide a public and prophetic witness to the sacredness of all life and to bring about just and compassionate social policies capable of sustaining life. At the same time, he realized that this mission is undermined when "civic amity," that is, the civic virtue of rhetoric, breaks down. Just three months before he died, Bernardin confessed that he feared the church's credibility was being eroded by "an increasing polarization," even, "at times, a mean-spiritedness [which] hindered the kind of dialogue that helps us address our mission and concerns."[39] My students' ignorance about the breadth of the church's social teachings suggests that his fear was well-founded. I suggest that if we as church are really serious about the claim, reiterated every four years since 1988 by the U.S. Catholic bishops, "that the consistent ethic of life forms a moral framework for principled Catholic engagement in political life,"[40] then we need to learn some rhetoric lessons from Cardinal Bernardin.

Conclusion: Rhetoric in the Style of Bernardin and a Practical Example

Like Bernardin's, the church's rhetorical style must be dialogical. We must develop the skill of listening in order to understand what the other is really saying. We must assume an attitude of humility that allows us to acknowledge the limits of our knowledge and the difficulties inherent in a truly consistent ethic of life. And we must have the courage to allow our engagement in dialogue to change us.

Developing a rhetoric in the style of Bernardin will increase our chances of being heard in society at large when we argue for an ethic of life. This should be of great concern especially at this point in the history of the Catholic Church in the United States. We cannot promote a "vigilant regard for the sanctity of life"[41] if the very way we bring up issues concerning respect for life causes others to stop listening to us. A dialogical rhetoric, furthermore, challenges us to broaden our perspective by admitting into consideration the full complexity of any particular issue. This is no small task, and a crucial one in shifting attitudes on various issues of life and death. Finally, engagement in dialogue has the potential to build common ground in response to issues of life and death, rather than contributing to the polarization and fragmentation that currently characterize such responses. Let me conclude with a practical example to illustrate how this might work.

As I have already written, my students are well aware of the Catholic Church's teaching on abortion (as well as contraception and the ordination of women). Many of them, in fact, are sympathetic to the Church's "pro-life" position (if not its positions on women and sexuality). Yet in the face of concrete moral dilemmas my students inevitably slip into the moral relativism that is so decried by church leaders. One student's story is illustrative.

In a reflection paper about a significant moral dilemma she had faced, my student (I call her Jane) described her decision to accompany a friend to Planned Parenthood to get an abortion. Jane, who grew up Catholic but is now attending a nondenominational, evangelical Protestant Church, described herself as strongly "pro-life." Her moral dilemma, as she saw it, was whether to hold to her conviction that abortion is always wrong because life begins at conception, or to provide emotional support to her friend who was going to have the abortion whether Jane went with her or not. Going with her friend to Planned Parenthood, Jane feared, would provide moral support to her friend's choice. Not going, however, would be abandoning her friend at a time when she was clearly in need of emotional support. Ultimately, Jane chose to go with her friend. Asked to explain her moral choice, Jane used a logic familiar to anyone who has spent time teaching undergraduates: just because she personally thought abortion was immoral, Jane wrote, did not give her the right to impose her moral judgment on another person. Projecting her reasoning into the political arena, Jane argued that abortion, though immoral, should remain legal because, given the religious pluralism of the United States and the constitutional separation of church and state, religious values should not encroach on individuals' freedom of choice.

Jane's logic reflects a false dichotomy infecting many current public policy debates, between religion and morality on the one hand and religious liberty and individual rights on the other. Media coverage following the last U.S. presidential election suggests that the divide, if not created by religious conservatives' arrogation to themselves of "moral values," is at least aggravated by it. The public rhetoric of some U.S. bishops during the election campaign in no small part contributed to this polarization. How might a consistent ethic of life have helped Jane to avoid the trap, resulting from this false dichotomy, of having to choose between her religiously informed conviction on the one hand and supporting her friend on the other?

First, it could have helped her to understand that religious values, no less than any others, can and should inform public policy debates. Those engaging in the political debate from a religious perspective must do so in language and concepts that can be understood in the religiously and culturally pluralistic public square of the United States. As Bernardin pointed out, any attempt to impose religious values simply on the basis of authority, whether biblical or magisterial, ought to be met with suspicion, if not outright rejection. Yet this ought to be true for all participants in the political debate, regardless of their particular vantage point. No argument ought to be admitted into the public policy discussion which is not comprehensible and cogent.

Second, examining her dilemma through the lens of the consistent ethic of life might have allowed Jane to articulate aspects of her friend's situation which disappear from view when the moral dilemma is reduced to a contest between a fetus's absolute "right-to-life" versus a woman's absolute "right-to-choose." A consistent ethic of life requires that the lives of both fetus and woman be kept in view. While I do not know the particular circumstances of Jane's friend, I can imagine them by drawing on the stories of other students who have confided in me about the abortions they have had.

A recurring theme in these students' stories is their fear of abandonment. Most know that they cannot count on their boyfriend's support, and many fear that their families will not support them either. More than one student, in fact, has admitted to having an abortion in the face of overwhelming pressure from her family, pressure often motivated by parents' determination that their daughter will escape the family's socioeconomic marginalization. Like their parents, most of my students are convinced that a college education holds out their only hope for an improved standard of living. Yet for these students, who most likely are the first in their family to go to college, the goal of attaining a college degree presents not only enormous financial, but also emotional hurdles. They fear these hurdles would become insurmountable were they to bring to term a pregnancy at this point in their lives. Given perennial political pressures to decrease funding for social programs, including financial aid for college students and aid to families with dependent children, such fears are not unrealistic. Faced with an unwanted pregnancy, many of my students feel that their only viable choice is to abort.

In the end, the concrete circumstances informing my students' decisions to abort may not morally justify that decision. Clearly, one issue that needs to be raised is why so many young women are in sexually active relationships when they are in no position, emotionally or financially, to take on the potential responsibilities such a relationship entails. My students desperately need help in developing a sexual ethic that is self-respecting, life-giving, and a counter-weight to the messages about sex and sexuality with which they are bombarded by the media and popular culture. In the wake of its sex scandals, the loss of moral authority of the Catholic Church to provide guidance in this regard is a real tragedy. The above examples, however, do illustrate some of the social needs that must be addressed if we want to support young women like Jane's friend in sustaining and nurturing life. Surely, here is common ground on which "pro-life" and "pro-choice" advocates can meet to promote the conditions necessary for the flourishing of both women and their children. Furthermore, the rhetoric of a consistent ethic of life allows us to articulate what I suspect Jane intuited: that ultimately her dilemma was not choosing between the fetus's "right to life" or her friend's "right to choose," but between her own moral certitude and her friend's need for consolation in the face of what seemed to her, rightly or wrongly, to be death-dealing circumstances. While Jane may not have had the language to articulate it as such, I submit that choosing not to abandon her friend was, in fact, a choice consistent with an ethic of life.

7.
MINISTERING IN A DIVIDED CHURCH

Can the Consistent Ethic of Life Bridge the Contention?

Regina Wentzel Wolfe

Introduction

One of the challenges of faithful discipleship is found in the call to be active in the transformation of society. This means attending to the manner in which we relate and respond to human life in order that all might be afforded the dignity and respect with which they are due. An always difficult task, responding in this manner today can be daunting. In the not too distant past, attending to issues of social justice appeared straightforward, understandable, and solvable. During most of the twentieth century, for a significant majority of American Catholics working toward the common good meant supporting the platform and values of the Democratic Party, values that were seen to be in harmony with church teaching. It also meant that those in pastoral ministry were catechizing and preaching to a people who were open to church teaching on, and fairly unified in their response to, issues of social justice. This is no longer the case in the Catholic Church in the United States.[1]

The past thirty years have seen a growing division and polarization among Catholics as they attend to and act on the moral and social teaching of the church in an attempt to address ever more complex issues. In this charged environment, the consistent ethic of life, which Joseph Cardinal Bernardin advanced, holds an appeal to many, including many of those in pastoral ministry who are engaged in ongoing faith formation. There is something about challenging the faithful to approach *all* life issues consistently that seems reasonable and doable. Such an approach appears to provide a means of addressing the divisions that increasingly confront those in ministry. In addition, it seems to provide a guiding principle upon which members of the faith community can reflect as they consider their own responses to and actions in the political and social processes that shape the character of society in the United States.

It should come as no surprise, then, that the American bishops adopted an approach to political life in the United States that is reminiscent of

Cardinal Bernardin's consistent ethic of life. As they have for every national election since 1976, the bishops released a statement "focused on 'political responsibility' or 'faithful citizenship' . . . that helps us consider the challenges in public life and contribute to greater justice and peace for all people."[2] "Forming Consciences for Faithful Citizenship," released by the United States Conference of Catholic Bishops (USCCB) in November 2007, acknowledges the bishops' conviction that "the consistent ethic of life provides a moral framework for principled Catholic engagement in political life."[3] The bishops note that "as Catholics we are not single-issue voters."[4] With the release of "Forming Consciences for Faithful Citizenship," USCCB continued its efforts to increase awareness of the duties of citizenship and to summarize key moral and social teachings of the Catholic Church. In addition to the statement, through its Web site the USCCB has continued to offer those in ministry a wide selection of materials—bulletin inserts, videos, homiletic aids, clip art, and so forth— as resources to foster substantive faith formation. For anyone conversant with the consistent ethic of life, even a cursory examination of the materials will elicit a sense of familiarity. The issues that concerned Cardinal Bernardin are the same as the issues that concern the bishops today though, given advances in knowledge, some are more complex, as is demonstrated in Thomas Shannon's consideration of the consistent ethic of life and genetics later in this volume.[5] The challenge to move beyond single-issue responses that Cardinal Bernardin put forward is repeated in the statement, as noted above. The resources provided by the USCCB are comprehensive and sophisticated and are readily available to those engaged in all aspects of pastoral ministry. It would appear that the consistent ethic of life has reached maturity, that its potential to provide a comprehensive approach to moral and social issues of our time is being realized.

Appearances, however, can be deceptive. Responses to the campaign and its call "to defend human life, from conception until natural death" anchored "in the fundamental moral obligation to respect the dignity of every person"[6] at best resulted in attempts to prioritize issues and at worst devolved into single-issue discussions that foster division in the church. This type of division is precisely what Cardinal Bernardin wished to overcome. The question remains, then, whether there is a possibility of reframing or revisioning the consistent ethic in order to provide members of the faith community with a comprehensive, consistent, and principled approach to moral and social issues. At this particular juncture, there is no definitive answer to that question, though Dawn Nothwehr's specification of "mutuality as the formal norm foundational to the consistent ethic of life" is a positive move in this direction.[7] Another question is whether or not it is possible to identify and adopt a strategy for presenting the consistent ethic of life that will make respectful dialogue possible and diminish, or at least bridge, the divisions that are apparent. Such a strategy would be true to the legacy of Cardinal Bernardin, who saw himself as a bridge builder.

During his lifetime, Cardinal Bernardin welcomed debate and discussion

on the consistent ethic of life and called for ongoing examination of and dialogue on the concept "in the quest for a comprehensive and consistent ethic of
life" (SG, 102). An early response to this call was a symposium held at Loyola
University Chicago over twenty years ago. It was at that symposium, which
I attended not as a theologian but as a representative of the press, that I was
first introduced to some of the challenges to the consistent ethic and concerns
about its coherency.[8] In reviewing the commentaries on the consistent ethic of
life that were presented at that symposium, I am struck by the fact that there
is still no clear resolution of the many concerns raised at that time. While
Paul Perl and Jamie McClintock have argued that it is likely that the bishops'
continued support of the consistent ethic of life has affected the attitudes of
a small number of the Catholics who attend Mass frequently, they note that
"consistent life ideology must be considered quite marginal in terms of the
number of people who subscribe to it."[9] In part this reflects the difficulty of
trying to link "a 'conservative' position on abortion with 'liberal' positions
on quite different issues."[10] Two challenges in particular present themselves.
One is the need to overcome increasing polarization. The other is the need to
challenge members of the faith community to adopt a moral stance grounded
in the consistent ethic of life as a response to the call to discipleship.

    As noted above, there remains a fundamental reasonableness to the
concept, a sense that it can provide people with a way to address issues of
justice as well as foster active, faith-filled participation in society. Why, when
it presents an appealing way of challenging the faith community to live up
to baptismal promises and the call to discipleship, does it seem to be impossible to use a consistent ethic of life effectively in faith formation in today's
church?[11] Perhaps it is the concept itself or maybe pastoral ministers are not
well versed in it. What if it were to be considered a necessary component of
the curriculum in the education of those studying for pastoral ministry? What,
if any, possibility is there of the consistent ethic of life being an integral part
of catechesis and faith formation? The answers to these questions require a
closer examination of the concept itself and of strategies for placing it at the
heart of the response of the faithful to the many moral issues confronting
the United States today.[12]

Examining the Consistent Ethic of Life

    At the aforementioned symposium, Richard McCormick spoke of the
"soft underbelly" of the consistent ethic of life. He identified six unexamined
or "unwitting assumptions" that inhibit effective pastoral application of the
concept because they "dim our view of the centrality and dignity of the human
person and infect our deliberative processes."[13] More significantly, he argued
that considerable problems and concerns are raised by Cardinal Bernardin's
insistence that at its core the concept calls for "the consistent application
of the principle 'no direct taking of innocent human life.'"[14] McCormick's

conclusion is still valid, as is evidenced by the distinction that is sometimes made in reference to anti-abortion proponents and pro-life proponents. This distinction implies that the former give priority to the issue of abortion in a manner that undermines a consistent ethic of life approach leading to less concern, or in some cases even complete disregard, for other life issues, such as war. In respect to the latter, the distinction implies the attempt to adopt a consistent ethic of life approach across all life issues, which in practice might include tolerating exceptions to the principle "no direct killing of innocent human life." Such an approach is rejected by those who hold the former position.

One option for resolving this difference is to rearticulate the principle. This is not a new idea. Timothy O'Connell speaks of "nonthreatening human life."[15] Frans Jozef van Beeck, arguing against "insisting on one absolute principle" in favor of "several convergent formulas," suggests "no intentional, self-serving, undeserved termination, by disproportionate force, of any human life."[16] Despite suggestions of these sorts, it seems unlikely that there will be any official magisterial rearticulation of this sort given more recent teachings.[17]

A second option is to consider van Beeck's suggestion that we understand the consistent ethic of life as a response to Christian faith and discipleship. In this view, "the consistent ethic of life positively draws its consistency from the Christian faith; . . . from the commitment of Christians as moral agents viewing themselves as well as humanity and the world in the light of Christ."[18] While van Beeck's suggestion has merit and certainly points to Bernardin's Christocentric vision that M. Therese Lysaught so thoroughly considers,[19] I am not convinced that it represents fully Bernardin's intention in promoting the consistent ethic of life.

A third option is to understand the consistent ethic of life as providing a moral stance from which to engage the wide range of issues that confront today's world. James J. Walter argues convincingly that it was Cardinal Bernardin's intention "essentially to develop a 'moral stance.'"[20] This approach, I believe, answers positively the question, which was posed earlier in this chapter of whether there is a possibility of reframing or revisioning the consistent ethic in order to provide members of the faith community with a comprehensive, consistent, and principled approach to moral and social issues. As Walter has ably demonstrated, "Cardinal Bernardin's consistent ethic of life structures one's fundamental understanding of moral experience, serves as a critique of others' interpretations of moral reality, and becomes a source of ethical criteria to evaluate particular actions and social policies across a wide range of moral issues."[21]

Challenging the faithful to adopt a moral stance grounded in the consistent ethic of life as a response to the call to discipleship and its corresponding responsibility to participate actively in the transformation of society would be a positive step toward reconciling the divisions that exist in the American church today. Such a moral stance not only challenges the faithful to be more consistent in their own responses to life issues, but it also enhances their ability to be in dialogue with the broader society and likewise challenge that society to be more consistent in its response to life issues. Whether or not this is achievable rests in part on the manner in which pastoral ministers are educated. Do they have a solid grasp of the consistent ethic of life? Do they have an appreciation of and tolerance for ambiguity? Do they have the ability and willingness to enter into constructive dialogue with those whom they serve, a dialogue that fosters the development of a moral stance grounded in the consistent ethic of life? Are they able to identify and employ some practical strategies for engaging with the faithful in substantive reflection on and response to a variety of life issues?

Educating for the Consistent Ethic of Life

Educating for the consistent ethic of life must be undertaken in light of the call to discipleship and the moral obligation to participate in the social transformation of society, which is grounded in baptismal promises.[22] It must also be experiential and include hands-on, face-to-face learning experiences that expose students to the concrete realities of the spectrum of issues that the consistent ethic of life addresses. Such an educational environment provides the context for an integrative approach to discipleship that in turn offers the possibility of avoiding the polarization described above. It will impact the curricular structure of the theological education of those called to ecclesial ministry. At the heart of such education is an understanding of pastoral ministry as a collaborative endeavor in service of the gospel.[23] It is beyond the scope of this chapter to examine in detail a pastoral ministry curriculum that places at its center the consistent ethic of life. However, it is important to acknowledge those aspects of such a curriculum that are necessary if a moral stance grounded in the consistent ethic of life is to be a hallmark of ongoing faith formation.

Any serious study of the consistent ethic of life must attend to the tensions inherent in it. While it is essential for those training for ministry to fully understand and be conversant with magisterial teaching, that alone is not sufficient. To be effective pastorally—that is, to be effective in challenging and supporting people to grow and develop into morally mature persons of faith—ecclesial ministers must understand the theological deliberations and discussions that surround the many morally charged issues with which humans are confronted in their day-to-day lives. This includes an appreciation for and grasp of the richness of the historical roots of both the moral tradition and the social teachings tradition with all of its resources, as well as an appreciation for and understanding of the development of doctrine and the tradition of *disputatio*. Such appreciation and understanding will go a long way in forming pastorally effective ministers who have an ability to work with the faithful as together they engage in honest and open dialogue about the complex moral issues of contemporary society.

One aspect of effective pastoral ministry to which an adequate curriculum must attend is the issue of ambiguity. Acknowledging that everyday issues and concerns are complex and that clear and straightforward responses to moral dilemmas that arise from those issues and concerns do not necessarily present themselves is important. Best practices encourage pastoral ministers to begin where people are, to help them articulate and reflect on the stance from which they approach moral issues, and when appropriate, to challenge them to reconsider and adjust their stance while not demanding the impossible of them.[24] Acknowledging people's lived experience often provides an entry point for challenging them to engage in deeper reflection on who they are and whom they are called to be. It also calls for some degree of comfort with the many ambiguities of day-to-day life.

It is important to recognize, however, that attending to ambiguity is not limited to acknowledging its presence in day-to-day life. Acknowledging the ambiguity that exists in the church and its teachings is also important to a moral stance rooted in the consistent ethic of life. As the Common Ground Initiative's "Principles of Dialogue" make clear, "No single group or viewpoint in the church has a complete monopoly on the truth. . . . Solutions to the church's problems will almost inevitably emerge from a variety of sources."[25] Taken as a whole, the seven principles of dialogue proposed by the initiative are a reminder that ambiguity exists in the church, as it does in the world. At the same time the principles provide a strategy for negotiating ambiguity and conflict while insisting on realistic and effective responses to the issues that confront today's world.

Another aspect of pastoral education for the consistent ethic of life centers on the moral theology curriculum. "Fundamental moral theology deals with aspects of morality that are common to all instances of moral living. Special moral theology, on the other hand, addresses specific experiences, for example, personal, sexual, bioethical, social, or political morality."[26] As Charles Curran notes, "this traditional division creates one significant problem. By reflecting on what is true of the person in all situations, the focus tends to be somewhat individualistic—what the individual person should be and do."[27] This can result in pastoral ministers being more adept at and comfortable with one-on-one situations that serve people individually as they reflect on and come to adequate judgments of conscience. While this is an essential part of ministry, especially in the context of sacramental reconciliation, it does not necessarily provide an in-depth understanding of the more complex and wide-ranging life issues that the consistent ethic addresses.

To be effective in assisting people in reflecting on the more complex social issues and concerns, pastoral ministers need to be conversant with them. While recognizing that there are limitations to what can be included in any curriculum, courses that examine these issues are often not offered or offered only as electives, which can easily lead to the perception that they have little significance or relevance.[28]

The family is the locus of many morally charged social issues with which pastoral ministers are often concerned and which the consistent ethic of life addresses. Yet courses that focus on marriage and family ministry are usually offered as electives and often have a low enrollment.[29] The vast majority of adults in any faith community spend the better part of their waking hours in the workplace. As even a cursory glance at the business section of the local newspaper will demonstrate, today's work environment is fraught with moral and ethical dilemmas. Here again, little if any importance is placed on studying issues of business and professional ethics as an aspect of preparation for pastoral ministry. The same can be said regarding courses that examine the role of politics and public policy, both of which impact the issues with which a moral stance grounded in the consistent ethic will be concerned.

Another aspect of a curriculum and formation program that takes the consistent ethic of life seriously is education for collaborative ministry in its broadest sense. For the most part education for collaborative ministry is understood in the context of the growing number of laypeople who have joined the ranks of ecclesial ministers. While it is essential for members of pastoral teams that are made up of both lay and ordained ecclesial ministers to work with one another in ways that are respectful and acknowledge their shared responsibility for and common purpose of serving the faithful, collaborative ministry in the context of the consistent ethic of life is broader. First, it is not limited to ecclesial ministers but includes all those who take seriously their right and responsibility to participate fully in the life of the faith community and to respond in and through the world to God's call to be active in the transformation of society. Second, it recognizes today's knowledge society, which, with the ever-increasing specialization and rapid social change that it engenders, calls for cooperation and collaboration.

Two aspects of the knowledge society are particularly relevant. First, it emphasizes teamwork, in which participants are not superiors and subordinates but colleagues who share their knowledge and expertise for a common purpose. Peter Drucker considers the symphony orchestra to be the prototype for this kind of teamwork. "The first violin may be the most important in the orchestra. But the first violinist is not the superior of the harp player. He is a colleague. The harp part is the harp player's part and not delegated to her by either the conductor or the first violinist."[30] The education and formation of pastoral ministers should foster this form of teamwork.

The second relevant aspect of the knowledge society is the prominence given to lifelong learning. This learning is both formal and informal and takes place inside and outside of the classroom. It requires people to take responsibility for their own learning and recognizes that all are both teachers and learners. It also "demands for the first time in history that people with knowledge take responsibility for making themselves understood by people who do not have the same knowledge base. It requires that people learn and preferably early how to assimilate into their own work specialized knowledges from other areas and other disciplines."[31]

The emerging knowledge society will present many challenges, most of which are yet to be identified, but the inevitable and significant changes that will accompany it will also present many opportunities. There are two obvious implications of the knowledge society for pastoral ministry. First, the relationship of pastoral ministers to those they serve is a collegial one, not a hierarchical one. Second, pastoral ministers have as much to learn from the faithful as they have to teach the faithful. One conclusion that can be drawn from these implications is that pastoral ministers must become adept at being generalists in the sense that Peter Drucker suggests: individuals "who have learned how to acquire additional specialties."[32] They should also recognize that "innovation in any one knowledge area tends to originate outside the area itself."[33] The changes and advances needed to further the consistent ethic of life are very likely to come from the laity. An important part of the education process will be to instill both a passion for lifelong learning and an openness to other voices and viewpoints.

A second conclusion that can be drawn from the implications of the knowledge society for pastoral ministry is that ministerial formation programs must focus on collaborative ministry in its broadest sense. There are some examples that point the way toward such an approach to ministry. Cardinal Bernardin himself provided one in his work on the pastoral letter *The Challenge of Peace: God's Promise and Our Response*.[34] The approach to drafting the letter was a consultative one that involved a wide variety of individuals. It acknowledged the need for assistance in understanding the complexities of the issue and invited people from a wide array of disciplines and walks of life to share their expertise. The process fostered an exchange of ideas and viewpoints that informed and shaped the document. Also of import was the cardinal's sense of shared responsibility. In an interview with John M. Whiteley about the pastoral letter, Cardinal Bernardin said, "I think that we are all responsible for the well-being of our society even though our roles may be different. So I think that it's very, very important that people become familiar with the issues and that they address those issues."[35] The cardinal's attitude and his own work and ministry provide a starting point for developing an approach to effective pastoral ministry that is collaborative in its broadest sense. Another important step is identifying and implementing strategies that will further the goal of establishing a moral stance grounded in the consistent ethic of life as a hallmark of ongoing faith formation.

Strategies for Effective Pastoral Ministry

As noted above, there are two particular challenges. One is to overcome the polarization among members of the faith community. The other is to challenge members of the faith community to embrace a moral stance grounded in the consistent ethic of life.

An obvious strategy for meeting the first challenge is to adopt the Common Ground Initiative's "Principles of Dialogue" described above. Here it is not simply a matter of presenting the principles as the ground rules for engaging in conversation, but facilitating those conversations in a manner that ensures the principles are respected. This task can be demanding, and it requires good facilitation skills. Educating for collaborative ministry in its broadest sense, as discussed above, will assist in developing those skills.

Another strategy is to identify ways in which those who disagree can work together. Todd Whitmore presents an example of how to do this in "Common Ground, Not Middle Ground: Crossing the Pro-Life, Pro-Choice Divide."[36] Whitmore suggests finding points on which the two sides can agree and responses to abortion on which they can cooperate. Citing the deeper consensus to which public opinion polls point, he notes that there is a sizable middle for whom "the effort to create alternatives to abortion is an attempt to reduce suffering."[37] He admits that the cooperation he is suggesting has its risks:

> Close cooperative activity on a daily basis with people who disagree with Catholic teaching on abortion may lead some Catholics to change their views. The risk of changing one's mind runs in both directions, however, and it is precisely Catholics who aid women in the care of children who offer the most compelling witness to Catholic teaching.[38]

Whitmore also acknowledges that examples of cooperation are few but do exist. One that other groups have increasingly used is the Common Ground Network that brought Andrew Pudzer, one of the authors of the 1986 Missouri law that restricted abortions, together with B. J. Isaacson-Jones, president of the group that challenged the law in court. As "Isaacson-Jones noted, 'it was shockingly easy to identify issues we agree on, like the need for aid to pregnant women who are addicted to drugs, the need for better prenatal care and the need to reduce unwanted pregnancy. Neither side wants women to need abortions because they don't have the money to raise a child.' "[39] While it may be hard work to implement, a strategy of this type brings people together in a way that reduces stereotyping, fosters respectful dialogue, and begins to bridge the divide. It also has the potential for deepening an appreciation for and acceptance of the consistent ethic of life.

Effectively challenging members of the faith community to adopt a moral stance grounded in the consistent ethic of life rests in large measure on the degree to which people understand it. It is important to develop effective strategies for fostering a solid understanding of the consistent ethic and its relation to the church's social teachings. A first step, as noted above, is to recognize where people are and to acknowledge their lived experience. It is strategically important, therefore, for pastoral ministers to take the time to know and understand the members of the faith community with whom they serve and work. As I mentioned earlier in this chapter, familiarization with the findings of the American Catholics in the Public Square Project is helpful as background. The real work is to be present to and interact with parishioners in as wide a variety of ways as possible and to do so in a collaborative manner. Having a sense of the community will make it possible to tailor activities to the community's specific circumstances and needs.

There are numerous ways to engage people in deepening their understanding of the church's social teaching and the consistent ethic approach to addressing contemporary social issues. Studies indicate "that parishioners are able to see, when given a chance for reflection, that there is a connection between what they believe personally and collectively as Catholics, and the ways in which they live as citizens and voters. They come to recognize a social Catholicism as something that affects their lives in the public square."[40] In light of this finding, an important strategy is to provide opportunities for such shared reflection.

Another strategy is to increase awareness of and take advantage of local resources such as Catholic colleges and universities, state-level Catholic conferences, and other institutions and groups that have as their purpose addressing social issues and furthering Catholic social teaching. For example, introducing people to state-level Catholic conferences and to the way that "these bodies work with others in political coalitions with a range of social advocacy groups" provides an "example of how Catholic values can be part of the give and take of politics."[41] It would also be a way to address the "need to more actively involve Catholic parishes and laypeople in the conference's work," a need "pointedly" noted by Edward Dolejsi, executive director of the California State Catholic Conference.[42]

The report on the American Catholics in the Public Square Project notes that "print and broadcast media facilitate the reception of episcopal and papal statements not only to the general population, but also to most Catholics. Shaping public (and Catholic) reception often requires an assessment of how the media will receive and treat such statements and announcements."[43] Sharing resources and working with Catholic colleges and universities can provide ways to overcome commonly held misperceptions about the church's teachings.

The findings of the Public Square Project suggest that a focus on homilies is another strategy that can be used to good effect. The "researchers found that the people they polled thought of social issues as important to the extent that they heard more homilies on such topics, but the association was on the whole a modest one."[44] It was modest, in part because it reflected, for the most part, the views of weekly Mass goers, who themselves represented only one-third of those Catholics surveyed.[45] It also indicated that this group was "most influenced by sermons touching on the poor and social justice."[46] Clearly, preaching for social justice does have a positive effect and should be an intentional consideration in preparing homilies. The findings should also lead to expanding the social issues that are addressed in homilies to include other issues such as domestic violence.[47]

Conclusion

Establishing a moral stance grounded in the consistent ethic of life as a hallmark of ongoing faith formation is one way to respond to Cardinal Bernardin's request "for ongoing examination of and dialogue on the concept 'in the quest for a comprehensive and consistent ethic of life'" (SG, 8, 102). It has the potential to effect substantive change in the manner in which members of the faith community respond to the many social issues with which they are confronted. It also has the potential to impact significantly the design of academic and formation programs for those preparing for pastoral ministry. Finally, it has the potential for transforming the way in which parish life is organized and structured by embracing collaborative ministry in its broadest sense.

PART 4
EXPANDING CONTEXTS

8.
FROM *THE CHALLENGE OF PEACE* TO *THE GIFT OF PEACE*

Reading the Consistent Ethic of Life as an Ethic of Peacemaking

M. THERESE LYSAUGHT[1]

Introduction

The consistent ethic of life stands as one of Cardinal Joseph Bernardin's major contributions to Catholic public discourse. Yet if one looks at Cardinal Bernardin's major works in chronological perspective, one might notice a subtle but striking fact: standing like bookends to his championing of the consistent ethic of life are two intriguingly titled documents—the then National Council of Catholic Bishops' document, *The Challenge of Peace: God's Promise and Our Response,*[2] and his own autobiography, *The Gift of Peace.*[3] Is it mere coincidence that "peace" frames Bernardin's development and forwarding of the consistent ethic of life?

I think not. In this chapter, I argue that the consistent ethic of life must be understood as essentially, necessarily, intrinsically (though not solely) an ethic of peacemaking. Bernardin himself repeatedly noted how his development of the consistent ethic of life grew out of both his work on the peace pastoral and the content of the pastoral itself. But I wish to make an even stronger claim. In this paper, I argue that the consistent ethic ought to be read not primarily as an ethic of principles, not primarily as a tool for negotiating public policy, and not solely as focused on the principle of the sanctity of life. Too often, the "sanctity of life" as a theological commitment becomes decoupled from the Christian story in which it makes sense with the ironic result that "life" becomes an idol that is championed through violence. Therefore, in order for the consistent ethic of life to fulfill its function as a way for Christians to work for the common good in the public square and to faithfully fulfill their mission of incarnating the gospel, we must attend to the substantive theological vision out of which it arose and that must continuously inform it. This paper teases out that vision.

Methodological Presuppositions

Before turning to the argument itself, allow me to state three important methodological claims that shape my reading of Bernardin's work. First, the consistent ethic of life, to be adequately understood, must be read in context. Too often the consistent ethic of life is treated as a self-contained body of work—analyses focus on the thirty-six or so "consistent ethic" talks and proceed from there. However, while Bernardin was writing and delivering the consistent ethic talks, he was writing and delivering a much larger body of work. Consequently, as with any other important intellectual and theological figure, one necessary hermeneutical lens is provided by the larger corpus of Bernardin's work as a whole. To fully understand the larger theological and moral vision, his consistent ethic talks must be read in conversation with his homilies and pastoral letters to the Archdiocese of Chicago as well as significant episcopal documents.

Clearly, one difference between the consistent ethic and his other works could be identified as that of "audience." Bernardin identified the consistent ethic as a tool for engaging public policy in a secular pluralist context. He makes this clear from the beginning in the Gannon Lecture, the first lecture devoted to the consistent ethic of life. And often, when theologians analyze, utilize, and criticize the consistent ethic, they think of it in these terms. As just one example, Alphonse Spilly, who edited the two-volume compilation entitled *Selected Works of Cardinal Bernardin*, locates the consistent ethic talks in the second volume, which is labeled "Church and Society," under the subheading "The Life of Society."

But to see the consistent ethic primarily or solely as a tool for the church to navigate its relationship to society, as a tool for public policy, is to overlook the logically prior public at which the consistent ethic is aimed: the internal public of the church, the Catholic community itself. In crafting the consistent ethic, Bernardin was seeking to provide a vision for consensus *within* the church, a consensus that could "shape the public witness of the Catholic Church" and thereby serve as a transformative force within society.[4] The social policy piece can only follow from and must necessarily build upon the prior task of ecclesial formation.

Thus, in the following pages, I do not explicitly take up the public policy aspects of the consistent ethic. While this is an important dimension of the consistent ethic, it is logically secondary.[5] The primary "public" that the consistent ethic seeks to shape is the public of the church, the ecclesial public, in its own inconsistency, in its own inability to see connections between war and abortion; sexual ethics, bioethics, and social ethics; technology, peace, and justice; "social issues" and "life issues"—or however these silos are variously named. Minimally, these are all different ways that Bernardin identifies in the consistent ethic corpus the disconnects within the Catholic community. As Bernardin notes, "We should begin with the honest recognition that the shaping of a consensus among Catholics on the spectrum of life issues is far from finished" (SG, 14).

This brings me to my third methodological claim. The consistent ethic is often interpreted as being about "principles," most specifically about the principle of the sanctity of human life or the dignity of the human person. Certainly Bernardin's own texts lend themselves to this interpretation (SG, 10-13). But I wish to argue that in Bernardin's corpus as a whole, we see the beginnings of an important methodological shift, one that he himself might not have explicitly seen or been able to claim, but which I think is there in a very powerful way. Especially if we see the ecclesial community as the logically prior and primary public for the consistent ethic, I suggest here that it ought to be understood not primarily as an ethic of principles but as an ethic of practices.

It has been a commonplace within the Catholic tradition to see "spirituality" and "ethics" as two distinct realms, one pertaining to individual, personal faith formation, the other to the impersonal realm of the "public." Bernardin himself was formed in a milieu that took this separation for granted. But those schooled in moral theology since Wittgenstein and MacIntyre know this distinction to be increasingly fragile. In reading the consistent ethic in context, we can see in Bernardin's life and work a move past this artificial distinction toward an appreciation of the practices of the Christian life as both epistemologically crucial and the necessary basis of Christian moral formation, ergo, the necessary basis of principles. Through practices we come to know and are transformed, and this knowledge and transformation are necessary for Christian action and witness in the public sphere, necessary for (in other words) ethics.

These commitments, then, delimit the scope of my remarks and shape my hermeneutic. To summarize, I maintain that the consistent ethic must be read in the larger context of Bernardin's corpus; that its prior and primary audience is the church (in an attempt to shape an ecclesial consensus); and that the ability to apply—or better, *live*—the consistent ethic requires immersion in a spectrum of Christian practices. In the following, I offer a reading of the consistent ethic of life in the context of Cardinal Bernardin's corollary writings—*The Challenge of Peace* (1983), his pastoral letters and homilies written from 1982 onward, and *The Gift of Peace* (1997). By displaying the contours of this far more extensive discourse—a corpus that preaches a powerful vision of Christians as peacemakers, formed through Christian practices in the image of a kenotic, peace-giving Christ—I hope to make the case that the development of the consistent ethic of life as an ethic of peacemaking is an intrinsic development, bringing to fruition the critical insights found within the powerful witness of Bernardin's own life and work.

The Challenge of Peace: A Genealogy of the Consistent Ethic

Cardinal Bernardin launched his championing of the concept of the consistent ethic of life on December 6, 1983, as the center point of his

Gannon Lecture at Fordham University (SG, 7-14). Invited to speak on the NCCB's pastoral on war and peace, his Gannon Lecture became the first step in attempting to forge what he called a theologically grounded broader moral vision.

But the consistent ethic did not here spring into the world *ex nihilo*. In developing the consistent ethic of life as a platform for use in the public square, Bernardin was not creating something new—indeed, he did not claim to be. Instead he rightly suggested that he was simply retrieving a vision rooted in and widely dispersed throughout the Catholic tradition. Even the phrase itself precedes him. Bernardin himself indicates that the bishops' pastoral was a key starting point for him in developing the notion of the consistent ethic (SG, 7).

If we trace this genealogy, it becomes clear that the consistent ethic emerges out of the Christian commitment to peacemaking. In this section, I begin with a brief outline of the historical forebears of the consistent ethic. One of those historical forebears is the bishops' pastoral, where they root a vision of the consistent ethic in their theology of peace. The second task for this section, then, is to display the theology of peace forwarded by the pastoral letter, highlighting components of the document that are important not only for understanding the consistent ethic but that can be followed as Bernardin's work continues.

The Consistent Ethic of Life: A Brief History

Bernardin makes clear that the main catalyst for his re-envisioning the traditional spectrum of issues was his appointment as chairman of the NCCB's Committee for Pro-Life Activities. From that vantage point, he now creatively connected what had been traditionally treated as quite disparate issues, issues where the direct linkage to "life" might not be as obvious: genetics, including genetic counseling and genetic engineering; abortion; war; capital punishment; euthanasia and care of the terminally ill; pornography; hunger; homelessness; unemployment; education of the illiterate; undocumented migrants; sexism; racism; welfare reform; working mothers and single parents; birth technologies; health-care reform; care of the disabled; care of the elderly; inhumane living conditions; inhumane working conditions; violence; exploitation; tolerance of poverty; international justice and peace.[6] In Bernardin's vision, these and any issue in which life or human dignity is threatened or diminished constitute a "seamless garment," a metaphor he later employed (SG, 15, 36, 52-54, 69, and 77).

The image of the seamless garment, most often associated with Bernardin, was not, however, his own. It originated in a 1971 interview given by Eileen Egan. Egan was, importantly, a member of the Catholic Worker movement and a prominent peace activist.[7] Not only did she help found the organization Pax Christi, in her work with the Catholic Worker, she attended to and lived in solidarity with many of those named within the consistent ethic.

The same year that Egan coined the phrase "the seamless garment," Archbishop Humberto Medeiros of Boston gave an address entitled "A Call for a Consistent Ethic of Life and the Law," where he called for an ethic that was "comprehensive in scope and consistent in substance," that connected Christian commitment to nascent life with problems of housing, education, welfare, race, warfare, and so on.[8]

In this, Egan and Medeiros were drawing not only on their own insights as to the necessary connections among these issues (or, negatively stated, the problematic inconsistencies in positions held by many Catholics); they were drawing as well on a theme sounded in the Second Vatican Council. In *The Pastoral Constitution on the Church in the Modern World* (*Gaudium et spes*), one finds an early articulation of this theme:

> In our times a special obligation binds us to make ourselves the neighbor of absolutely every person, and of actively helping him when he comes across our path, whether he be an old person abandoned by all, a foreign laborer unjustly looked down upon, a refugee, a child born of an unlawful union and wrongly suffering for a sin he did not commit, or a hungry person who disturbs our conscience by recalling the voice of the Lord: "As long as you did it for one of these, the least of my brethren, you did it for me" (Mt. 25:40).
>
> Furthermore, whatever is opposed to life itself, such as any type of murder, genocide, abortion, euthanasia, or willful self-destruction, whatever violates the integrity of the human person, such as mutilation, torments inflicted on body or mind, attempts to coerce the will itself; whatever insults human dignity, such as subhuman living conditions, arbitrary imprisonment, deportation, slavery, prostitution, the selling of women and children; as well as disgraceful working conditions, where men are treated as mere tools for profit, rather than as free and responsible persons; all these things and others of their like are infamies indeed. They poison human society, but they do more harm to those who practice them than those who suffer from the injury. Moreover, they are a supreme dishonor to the Creator. (§ 27)

Thus, the notion of the consistent ethic of life and the seamless garment were astir within the Catholic community when the NCCB inaugurated their Respect Life program in 1972, articulated by a cofounder of Pax Christi and the magisterium. By 1983, the Respect Life program had become the Committee on Pro-Life Activities, and Bernardin was at the helm. When Bernardin picked up his pen to write the Gannon Lecture, the concept of the consistent ethic had shaped the Pro-Life Committee for eleven years.[9]

The Challenge of Peace: *Peacemaking as Vision, Method, Practices, and Process*

Equally, for three years prior to his penning the Gannon Lecture, Bernardin—by virtue of his role as chair of the Bishops' Ad Hoc Committee on War and Peace, the committee responsible for drafting *The Challenge of Peace*—had been steeped in an intense process of reflection on peace, specifically a theology of peace and its relationship to traditional Catholic analysis. Bernardin makes clear that in proposing the notion of the consistent ethic of life in his Gannon Lecture, he is drawing from the final section of *The Challenge of Peace*. Here the bishops, in a section subtitled "True Peace Calls for 'Reverence for Life,'" outline a vision of a consistent ethic:

> No society can live in peace with itself, or with the world, without a full awareness of the worth and dignity of every human person, and of the sacredness of all human life (James 4:1-2). When we accept violence in any form as commonplace, our sensitivities become dulled. When we accept violence, war itself can be taken for granted. Violence has many faces: oppression of the poor, deprivation of basic human rights, economic exploitation, sexual exploitation and pornography, neglect or abuse of the aged and the helpless, and innumerable other acts of inhumanity. Abortion in particular blunts a sense of the sacredness of human life. In a society where the innocent unborn are killed wantonly, how can we expect people to feel righteous revulsion at the act or threat of killing non-combatants in war? (§ 285)

As Bernardin will later, the pastoral most explicitly wrestles with the linkage between the issues of war and abortion. But importantly, it also includes the middle ground, the "many faces" of violence within society. The issues of life and peace remain coupled throughout the section, ending as it does with Pope Paul VI's "If you wish peace, defend life."[10]

Four aspects of the pastoral and Bernardin's experience with it are important for our purposes here: the thickly displayed theology of peace the pastoral develops in chapter 1, Bernardin's own contribution to the pastoral, the pastoral's methodology, and the pastoral process itself.[11] Let me take each of these in turn.

A Theology of Peace. The Challenge of Peace opens with a "religious vision of peace" (§ 20) or a "theology of peace" (§ 25).[12] Beginning with the witness of the Hebrew Scriptures, the bishops offer a vision of peace that is first and foremost theocentric—peace is the fruit of the covenant, of right relationship with God (§§ 27, 33).[13] Covenant fidelity entails, on the one hand, forgiveness, reconciliation, and union (§ 27), and, on the other, care for the needy and helpless; as they say, "a society living with fidelity was one marked by justice and integrity" (§ 34).[14]

The bishops trace how the links between communion with God, reconciliation, care for the poor, and peace are reinforced, deepened, and extended in the New Testament witness. Here their display becomes Christological, centered on both the person of Jesus and his proclamation of the reign of God. Conversion (§ 44) and the Sermon on the Mount emerge as central to what Jesus's vision of peace looks like:

> His words, especially as they are preserved for us in the Sermon on the Mount, describe a new reality is manifested and the longing of the people is fulfilled. In God's reign, the poor are given the Kingdom, the mourners are comforted, the meek inherit the earth, those hungry for righteousness are satisfied, the merciful know mercy, the pure see God, the persecuted know the Kingdom, and peacemakers are called the children of God (Mt 5:3-10). (§ 46)

As in the Old Testament, central to the character of this kingdom is forgiveness:

> Jesus' words also depict for us the conduct of one who lives under God's reign. His words call for a new way of life which fulfills and goes beyond the law. One of the most striking characteristics of this new way is forgiveness. All who hear Jesus are repeatedly called to forgive one another, and to do so not just once, but many, many times (Mt 6:14-15; Lk 6:37; Mt 18:21-22; Mk 11:25; Lk 11:4; 17:3-4). The forgiveness of God, which is the beginning of salvation, is manifested in communal forgiveness and mercy. (§ 47)

Such forgiveness, of course, pertains not only to friends and families but most importantly to enemies, who we are called to love.[15]

Jesus models the possibility of this sort of love, forgiveness, and service to the poor, and makes it possible through the ongoing presence of His Spirit. His first act post-resurrection is to confer on his followers his "gift of peace" (§ 52), a gift that made it possible for the community to become its identity—the Body of Christ.

> The early Christian communities knew that this power and the reconciliation and peace which marked it were not yet fully operative in their world. . . . At the same time, they knew that they were called to be ministers of reconciliation (2 Cor. 5:19-20), people who would make the peace which God had established visible through the love and the unity within their own communities. (§ 53)

God's gift of peace in Christ enables the church to become a community of reconciliation that thereby witnesses to God's reconciling love in the world.

Thus, consistent with the model provided by *Gaudium et spes*, the bishops ground their theology of peace "solidly in the biblical Kingdom of God [and] then place it centrally in the ministry of the Church" (§ 25). Importantly, this Scriptural vision of a kingdom inhabited by those named in the consistent ethic says little about the sanctity or dignity of human life. Rather, it is thoroughly Christological, grounded in a sacramental sense of Christ's ongoing work as well as in the concrete contours of his life as narrated in the Gospels:

> Jesus Christ, then, is our peace, and in his death-resurrection he gives God's peace to our world. In him God has indeed reconciled the world, made it one, and has manifested definitively that his will is this reconciliation, this unity between God and all peoples, and among the peoples themselves. The way to union has been opened, the covenant of peace established. The risen Lord's gift of peace is inextricably bound to the call to follow Jesus and to continue the proclamation of God's reign. . . . In the continuing presence of Jesus, disciples of all ages find the courage to follow him. To follow Jesus Christ implies continual conversion in one's own life as one seeks to act in ways which are consonant with the justice, forgiveness, and love of God's reign. Discipleship reaches out to the ends of the earth and calls for reconciliation among all peoples so that God's purpose . . . will be fulfilled. (§ 54)

Bernardin and the Pastoral. By chairing the Ad Hoc Committee, Bernardin could not avoid a constant interaction with this "religious vision." As we will see, most of his life's work simply elaborates it. Equally important for our purposes is the last section of the pastoral, entitled "The Pastoral Challenge and Response" (§§ 274-329). This section returns to the Christological focus of part 1, opening with John Paul II's call to the church to be a community of Jesus's disciples, a community of those who are "doer[s] of the word, wayfarer[s] with and witness[es] to Jesus," following the "personal and demanding" road that may entail a "share of the cross" (§ 276).[16]

Central to this section is its description of two Christian practices, prayer and penance.[17] Again citing John Paul II, the pastoral affirms that the objective reality of peace requires conversion: "disarmament of the human heart and the conversion of the human spirit to God alone who can give authentic peace . . . Interior peace becomes possible only when we have a conversion of spirit. We cannot have peace with hate in our hearts" (§ 284). Necessary for such conversion is the practice of prayer:

> A conversion of our hearts and minds will make it possible for us to enter into a closer communion with our Lord. We nourish that

communion by personal and communal prayer, for it is in prayer that we encounter Jesus, who is our peace, and learn from him the way of peace. . . . As believers we understand peace as a gift of God. (§§ 290, 293)

This section continues on to provide a wonderful, extended meditation on the varieties of practices of prayer available to Christians and their communities—contemplative prayer, the Mass, the Eucharist, the sign of peace.

Following the discussion of prayer, the bishops boldly note the importance of penance: "Prayer by itself is incomplete without penance. . . . Because we are all capable of violence, we are never totally conformed to Christ and are always in need of conversion" (§ 297). The bishops call for a visible, tangible sign of penance, in a return to the traditional practice of Friday fasts and abstinence for the cause of peace: "Every Friday should be a day significantly devoted to prayer, penance, and almsgiving for peace" (§ 298).

This final section of the pastoral is significant for two reasons. First, it unapologetically assumes the epistemological importance of Christian practices. Prayer is deemed to be that by which we "learn from [Christ] the way of peace" (§ 290); "it fosters a vision of the human family as united and interdependent in the mystery of God's love for all people" (§ 294). Both are deemed crucial to "conversion"—to our formation, or better transformation, into "instruments of Christ's peace in the world" (§ 293). Most importantly, this final section—the section on conversion, prayer, and penance—was originally drafted by Cardinal Bernardin.[18]

The Pastoral's Methodology. This attention to practices, coupled with the "religious vision" of chapter 1, lead to the third aspect of the pastoral that I would like to highlight. Just as in the consistent ethic, Bernardin and others sought to make new connections between traditional Catholic moral theology and social ethics, moving beyond their traditional boundaries; here the bishops point toward new methodological integration.

First, more extensively than perhaps anywhere else in the magisterial corpus, traditional moral analysis of the just war principles is situated within a context of a biblical theology of peace.[19] Here the bishops continue and expand this similar sort of methodological shift found in *Gaudium et spes.* Classic philosophical reasoning, so long characteristic of the Catholic moral tradition, is now brought into conversation with thoroughgoing biblical exegesis. What is more, the pastoral opens and closes with the more traditional "theological" material, locating the philosophical, principled analysis within that context, giving it priority.

In addition, the pastoral brings together the traditional moral analysis of just war principles with communal, liturgical practices. Although prayer, penance, and the Eucharistic life of the church had long been the practical context of the Catholic moral tradition, all too often the discourse proceeded without any reference thereto. "Ascetical" theology or "spirituality" was decoupled from rigorous moral analysis. Here they are again brought into conversation, set side-by-side. And again, communal liturgical practices provide the framework for the analysis that proceeds via rational principles.

Does the pastoral integrate Scripture, principles, and practices in a totally satisfactory manner? Not at all. But it is critically important that they are all tied together into one document, a document meant for multiple audiences—the Catholic community as well as all those interested in the wider public debate. For both indicate a necessary and crucial methodological shift in the Catholic moral tradition and empower its development.

The Pastoral as a Process of Peacemaking. The last aspect of the pastoral worth noting is, of course, the process of making it happen. Bernardin himself noted that "the process of discussion, writing and witness" may have been "the most important long-range consequence" of their efforts.[20] The pastoral itself was the product of a three-year process of study, writing, meeting, discussing, arguing, consulting, revising, and responding to the cultural context. It entailed engagement with not only the members of the National Council of Catholic Bishops itself, but equally with officials in the Reagan administration, bishops from across the Catholic communion, the Vatican, U.S. Catholics, and the American public as a whole. As Bryan Hehir notes, "The first year of the committee's work was largely given over to a series of 'hearings' in which a number of people were invited before the committee to share their expertise and experiences."[21]

This itself was no easy process. As Jim Castelli's wonderful account of the writing of the peace pastoral in *The Bishops and the Bomb* displays, the production of the document required in no small part dialogue, reconciliation, and redemptive suffering. In shepherding the process—in particular, in shepherding the potentially fractious Ad Hoc Committee—Bernardin saw firsthand the depths of the divisions within the Catholic community. Castelli's account demonstrates the nature of those divisions, the hostile rhetoric and politics attendant to both sides. One of Bernardin's main contributions to the pastoral was to engage in the kind of practical work necessary to overcome these divisions and move toward a document that was approved by 96 percent of the bishops in the NCCB. In other words, producing a document on peace required the practice of peacemaking.

And, of course, this should make sense. The method of dialogue was embraced by Bernardin and the bishops not only as a shrewd political tool. Bernardin notes in a later address that John XXIII, Paul VI, and John Paul II identified the method of dialogue as itself a way to peace.[22] Only by being formed in the practices of peace would they be able to embody it, achieve it, and offer a credible witness to it. As has been said, the means *are* the end.

This then is the ground that is laid by 1983 when Bernardin launches the consistent ethic of life as a program of the Committee for Pro-Life Activities. From the Second Vatican Council and a Catholic Worker peace activist, the concept of the consistent ethic meets, in *The Challenge of Peace*, a Christologically displayed theology of peace tied centrally to the practices of the Christian life through a dialogic process that itself was an exercise in reconciliation and peacemaking. As we shall see, these elements then shape Bernardin's work until the end.

"Christ Lives in Me": Bernardin's Writings from 1983 to 1996

Bernardin delivered his addresses on the consistent ethic of life from 1983 to 1996. In some years he delivered as many as six such lectures, and in others only one. He delivered no lecture on the consistent ethic of life in 1992. But during this period, he wrote far more. From 1983 to 1996, his "selected works"—at least as collected by Alphonse Spilly—comprise two volumes, over two hundred documents, over 1,250 pages. I will not here provide an exhaustive analysis of all 1,250 pages! In fact, what follows is merely a sketch, a sampling to indicate that the themes developed in *The Challenge of Peace* continue in his other work. Through material from his pastoral letters and some of his homilies, I hope to at least suggest that the themes and practices of peacemaking outlined above resonate thickly through this other corpus.[23] And they do so, as he is creating and forwarding the consistent ethic program.

I begin with his 1985 pastoral reflection on Christology entitled " 'Christ Lives in Me': A Pastoral Reflection on Jesus and His Meaning for Christian Life," for it captures well the relentlessly Christocentric focus of his theological vision. By 1985, the consistent ethic of life (as a program) was two years old, and Bernardin had been taking no small amount of heat for it. It is significant that in his introduction he makes the following claim: "It seems clear that the internal and external problems and tensions confronting the Church today cannot ultimately be solved on the level of ecclesiology alone. We must have recourse to Christology to understand the inner reality of the Church and to work for its authentic renewal."[24]

The subsequent fifty-page reflection is a personal, heartfelt, and compelling account of the significance of the person and work of Christ for individuals, for ecclesial identity and formation, and for the work of the Church in the world. No summary can substitute for reading it oneself, but let me point to three key aspects of it.

Central to his argument is the *identity* of Christians and of the church with Christ. Through a wonderful display of the early church witness, he builds to the claim that Christians are to be "more than just 'like' Jesus. They are to *put on* Christ. . . . They are to *become* Christ, to be *other* Christs. They are to carry on Christ's work and help bring it to completion."[25] The Church, likewise, is Christ's Mystical Body; "it is Christ present in the world."[26]

The bulk of the letter moves through a meditation on what it means to call Jesus "the Way, the Truth, and the Life" to a consideration of the sacramental life of the church as crucial for making real the above-mentioned identity, giving specific attention to Eucharist, penance, and an extended reflection on prayer.[27] At the end of this section, he turns his attention to "following Christ in today's world," moving from Christ, through Christian practices, to mission in the world. Here he delineates this mission under the headings of "presence to others," "our obligation to the poor," and the "quest for peace": "While outreach to others takes many forms, I shall highlight three: being 'present' to friends and neighbors, helping the poor by promoting justice, and being peacemakers. . . . Following the Lord Jesus leads one to become involved in these and other social issues."[28]

He continues later:

> To speak of social issues may seem to have little to do with the theme of prayer and participation in the Church's sacramental life as bases for our relationship with Jesus. But there is a direct and necessary connection. As prayer and the sacraments are the foundation of our relationship with Jesus, so that relationship is—or should be—the ground and context for our lives, including our efforts to address and remedy the social evil of our times.[29]

To attend to these social issues, these social "evils," is a way of continuing Christ's redemptive mission in the world. But if it is so, our work must likewise be Christoform: "As Jesus triumphed over sin and death, we also can overcome evil and death by being united with him in faith and love. We 'overcome' evil, of course, precisely as he did—by redemptive suffering. The Cross is central to the Christian life."[30] Christ, prayer and sacraments, service to the world. These are his constant themes.

Again and again, the particulars of Jesus's life and witness are proclaimed in his sermons. In the third sermon he gave in his new role as cardinal-archbishop of Chicago (August 29, 1982), this time to the people of the archdiocese, gathered in Grant Park for his first Mass, he provides a deeply personal witness to the Jesus who frequents his sermons:

> All this amounts to a great challenge. In meeting this challenge we must open our hearts to Jesus Christ. We must not hold back any part of ourselves from the power of God's Holy Spirit. If we open wide the doors of our whole lives, holding nothing back from God, Christ will surely enter. Then we will be fitting heralds to announce God's word to others.
>
> As a priest and bishop I have continued to try to open wide the doors of my heart to Christ. I have found again and again that, when I stopped resisting, stopped trying to be completely in charge of my life and placed my trust in the Lord, things have gone better for me. As your new archbishop, I want each of you to know how important Jesus Christ is to me. I believe in him and all that he has taught. He is the Way to my salvation. I love

him with all my heart, and the central desire of my life is to be intimately united with him. Then I will experience his great love for me in the very depths of my being. I know that in this way my life will become one with his.

I wish to affirm you and encourage you, as you also search for the Lord in your daily lives and seek to grow in intimacy with him. Do you ever feel misunderstood, lonely, discouraged, wounded, abandoned? Then you need to experience Jesus' love, compassion, and healing power. He is not far away. He is right there beside you, waiting for you to turn to him and place yourself in his hands.

. . . If each one of us continues to strive for union with Jesus, we can go forth from this, our first Mass together, "as those who serve." We can build bridges of faith and love between ourselves and all those around us.[31]

Union with Jesus, the particular Jesus of the Beatitudes and Matthew 25, is the basis for becoming servants to the world, disciples who will serve precisely the people named in the consistent ethic.

Again and again, he connects the person of Christ to the issues of the consistent ethic. In a Passion Sunday homily (1983) he offers a meditation on Jesus, drawing on Luke 19:37-40:[32]

But he rides into our midst anyway. And even though our welcome may sometimes be less than enthusiastic, still he warns us that if we fail to recognize him for who he is, the lifeless stones themselves will cry out in greeting. Perhaps the reason our cheers sometimes ring hollow is that we recognize deep down the reality of our situation, that as Lord of Life, he has sway over every aspect of what we do and are. Nothing is excused. Nothing is exempt. Nothing is locked to his entry. Politics, economics, human endeavors of every kind: all are unbarred to his gaze. And this means that those voices which would limit the man on the donkey to what is specifically "religious" understand neither who he is or what he claims.[33]

Politics, economics, human endeavors of every kind—this is the stuff of the consistent ethic. It is Jesus's lordship over all that opens these areas up to Catholic witness in the public realm. In one last homily he reminds the Catholic community that the essence of this lordship is love, a love that includes enemies (SG, 98-101):

We gather this evening in love, not in hatred, for "love never wrongs the neighbor. Hence love is the fulfillment" of the gospel and the law. May the God of love, the creator of life, continue to show his care for us. May the Lord Jesus walk with us in our efforts for justice and peace. May he give us the very fullness of life. May our loving embrace of one another this evening reach out to include all our brothers and sisters in all stages of human development and all circumstances. (SG, 101)

In his pastoral letter on liturgy, "Our Communion, Our Peace, Our Promise" (February 1984), he shifts his attention more exclusively to communal liturgical prayer, still unfailingly linking it to peace and service to the world.[34] The letter moves step by step through the components of the liturgy, commenting as needed on each. When he gets to Communion, he explicitly refers to *The Challenge of Peace*, reminding his hearers of the bishops' injunction "to make the sign of peace at Mass an authentic sign of our reconciliation with God and with one another. This sign of peace is also a visible sign of our commitment to work for peace as a Christian community. We approach the table of the Lord only after having dedicated ourselves as a Christian community to peace and reconciliation."[35] He continues:

At this table we put aside every worldly separation based on culture, class, or other differences. Baptized, we no longer admit to distinctions based on age or sex or race or wealth. This Communion is why all prejudice, all racism, all sexism, all deference to wealth and power must be banished from our parishes, our homes, and our lives. This Communion is why we will not commit the world's resources to an escalating arms race while the poor die. We cannot. Not when we have feasted here on the "body broken" and the "blood poured out" for the life of the world.[36]

Christology continues as the basis of ecclesiology and Christian witness in his pastoral letter on the church, "The Family Gathered Here Before You" (1989). Here he identifies five "constant elements of Church life," which include proclamation of the gospel, celebration of the sacraments, work for Christian unity, work in the world, and "direct service . . . rendered in love." It is this last one that I would like to highlight here:

In St. Luke's Gospel, Jesus describes his mission in an opening discourse in the synagogue at Nazareth. Quoting from the book of Isaiah, he says: . . . To be faithful to Jesus' mission, the Church must care for people, especially for those most in need. Its service to humanity includes instruction, healing, peacemaking, and authentic and full human liberation. These activities are not peripheral to the Church's mission, but are at its very heart. We read in St. Matthew's Gospel that the care of the least of Jesus' brothers and sisters is the ultimate criterion by which we shall be judged (Matt 25: 31-46).[37]

His point of raising this passage is to turn it to critique the church itself. He challenges the church to be inclusive and break down barriers of class, gender, age, felony status, sin, and (dis)ability. He challenges economic disparities within the church. He calls the church to become the embodiment of loving, reconciled human relationships to that it is both true to its identity and can then witness it in the world.[38]

In his homily on Thanksgiving Day 1983, he articulates a "recipe for holiness," a recipe he finds notably displayed in the Beatitudes.[39] What are the ingredients of this Beatitude recipe for holiness? Importantly, peacemaking is among them:

> It calls for a poverty of spirit. . . . The recipe calls for sorrow. . . . Another ingredient is humility. . . . The recipe also calls for peacemaking. Peacemaking does not mean simply reaching some general agreement that peace is a good thing. It is much more than merely expressing a vague hope that peace might come some day. This recipe, instead, calls for concrete, practical peacemaking; for the doing of deeds that will promote peace with justice in our relationships, neighborhoods, and world, deeds that will prevent war in our time. This is one of the most important ingredients in the recipe for holiness.[40]

Here he harkens back to the bishops' pastoral in its rooting of Jesus's peaceableness in the Beatitudes and enjoins living the Beatitudes as a practice of prayer: "Think of the Beatitudes as a workable recipe for holiness in our world. Life as envisioned by Jesus in his Beatitudes—the Lord's own holiness lived out in our lives—is the most perfect gift we can bring to God. It is the best prayer we can offer."[41]

The Gift of Peace

Clearly, then, what emerged from *The Challenge of Peace*—a theology of peacemaking and reconciliation rooted deeply in the scriptural witness to Christ, necessarily fostered through Christian practices—continues to be a focus in Bernardin's writings going forward, and in fact deepens. This trajectory is crystallized in his simple yet profound and powerful autobiographical reflection, *The Gift of Peace.*

The Gift of Peace is a deceptively simple book. On its face, it seems a somewhat random series of autobiographical reflections—the story of how he was falsely accused of sexual abuse; his struggle with terminal pancreatic cancer; and a brief opening reflection on how he took up the practice of daily prayer. But he clearly includes these three stories between the covers of one, small book because he saw them as deeply interconnected. I would argue what we find here is not a simple story of his spiritual journey; it is more fundamentally a treatise on the relationships between Christian practices, spiritual conversion, and social action.

The narrative is very intentionally written and very intentionally opens with the section entitled "Letting Go." Here he recounts his story of learning to attend to prayer, a story that frames his whole account. Bernardin reprises the testimony he gave in his homily at the opening Mass to the Archdiocese of Chicago mentioned above, witnessing to his lifelong project of attempting to "throw open wide the doors of his heart" to Jesus and to turn over control of his life to God.

For Bernardin, the key to learning to let go was the practice of prayer. Having risen to the rank of archbishop in the 1970s, he had like so many professionals become "very busy, and I fell into the trap of thinking that my good works were more important than prayer."[42] Confronted and counseled by his own priests, he comes to adopt the habit of praying for one hour each morning, or rather "giv[ing] God the first hour of my day, no matter what, to be with him in prayer and meditation where I would try to open the door even wider to his entrance."[43]

Here we see the Cardinal embark on a particular practice—the practice of prayer—a traditional Christian practice. It is through and only through this practice that he develops a particular disposition, attitude, skill, virtue—he names this as "letting go," but we could equally well call it "openness" to God and others, liberation from those things which possess us (pride, possessions, power, fear), trust in God, learning to understand God as the Lord of life, and so on. In his life he had long believed these things in theory, but he acknowledges that he had not really believed them in practice because he had not lived as if they were true.

These virtues, these dispositions prove critical for the last two major events of his life. The first of these is the false accusation of sexually abusing a seminarian. He introduces this chapter of his life with a meditation on "emptying oneself"—"emptying myself of everything—the plans I consider the largest as well as the distractions I judge the smallest—so that the Lord can really take over."[44] He quotes the Pauline hymn of the kenotic Christ ("Though he was in the form of God, he did not deem equality with God something to be grasped at. Rather, he emptied himself and took the form of a slave . . . humbling himself, obediently accepting death, death on a cross" [Phil. 2:6-8]) to convey what he means by "emptying oneself." Here he returns more explicitly to the Christological themes outlined above—Jesus' experience of suffering and continuing presence to us—as well as his emphasis on discipleship as suffering "*in communion with* the Lord."[45]

I will not rehearse the details of this part of the story here (I would encourage all to read it), but a few key elements are important. As with many situations that incite us to violence, the accusation came out of nowhere and was devastating. His world was, in many ways, turned upside down. The accusation struck at one of the key centers of his identity—his chastity. Since

Bernardin was cardinal archbishop of Chicago, the news meant that instantly millions of people knew this charge and most likely believed it to be true. He was angry, bewildered at who could possibly launch such a false charge against him, and deeply humiliated. "As never before," he notes, "I felt the presence of evil."[46] Here a destructive power was at work, bearing down on him, threatening everything he held valuable—his life's work, his deepest convictions, his personal reputation, his position as cardinal of Chicago.

Yet at the same time he felt equally sustained by the conviction "The truth will set you free" (John 8:32). He knew almost tangibly the presence of the God he had come increasingly to know in prayer. And the habit of prayer he had learned through ordinary days and years now becomes crucial. Before facing hordes of reporters the day after the accusation becomes public, he prays the rosary early in the morning, meditating on the Sorrowful Mysteries, and later spends an hour by himself in prayer and meditation. While he feels very much akin to Jesus's aloneness in the garden during his own Agony, he equally knows that it is God's grace, strength, and presence that enables him to face the reporters, to stand calmly in the face of evil, and to speak the truth in love and peaceableness.

Moreover, from the beginning, he finds himself overwhelmed with a sense of compassion for his accuser. A few days after the filing of the charges, he notes, "I felt a genuine impulse to pray with and comfort him."[47] He almost immediately writes a letter to the man, asking if he might visit him to pray with him. The man's lawyers never deliver the letter. The case eventually unravels on its own, and the charges are eventually dropped as the "evidence" proves to be fabricated. Bernardin could have simply rejoiced in his vindication, or he could have brought countercharges for defamation of character. But this is not the road he chooses. Rather, eleven months after the suit was dropped, he again tried to contact his accuser. This time he was successful. In the end, he meets with him and—beyond what would be wildly imaginable—was reconciled with him.[48] They become friends, such that six months later, when Bernardin is diagnosed with pancreatic cancer, one of the first letters he receives is from his former accuser. It is a powerful story of forgiveness and reconciliation.

Bernardin makes clear that it was only by becoming open to the presence and grace of God in his life, an openness given by God and cultivated through the practice of prayer, that enabled this story to unfold as it did. Through the practice of prayer, Bernardin learns to love God and to let go of the god of self-love. He developed the virtues necessary to be able to love one who is clearly his enemy, the person who he states has inflicted upon him the most damage, in the most vicious manner, that he has ever experienced. What does such love look like? It is nonviolent—the cardinal made clear to his advisors and attorneys at the outset of the crisis that there will be no scorched-earth countersuit to beat the enemy down. It is compassionate—it feels the pain of the other, even of the enemy. It is reconciling—it seeks not to obliterate the enemy but to overcome the enmity between them through reconciliation. It reaches out to the enemy, in order to both create community with the enemy and to do the work of God's love in the world.

To this extent, it is Christoform—Bernardin makes clear that such is the nature of Christian love, rooted in the person of Jesus. Through his practice of prayer he has come to know Jesus as a fully human person, one who both experienced pain and suffering and yet "transformed human suffering into something greater: an ability to walk with the afflicted and to empty himself so that his loving Father could work more fully through him."[49] And it is this Jesus that he meets through his practice of prayer that increasingly becomes the One who shapes his life.

This experience becomes the prelude to the final chapter of his story, the story of his struggle with terminal pancreatic cancer complicated by painful spinal stenosis. In his narrative, we watch as he uses the tools of medicine to resist the growth of cancer in his body. We watch as he wins a short-lived remission, and then how the cancer returns with renewed virulence. But importantly, the autobiography of his illness is not primarily about his illness; it is instead about how his illness leads him into a new world of ministry, meeting, being present to, and praying for literally hundreds of others who struggle with cancer. Again, with his diagnosis of cancer, Bernardin transforms his life and actions into one of powerful public witness. He models not only a position of need—an unusual position to be taken by a leader in our culture—but he transforms his tragedy into a powerful new ministry, ministering to other cancer patients and others who are sick in an entirely new way. Modeling to the world what it looks like to reach out to "the least of these" in society (to live the consistent ethic of life, we might say), he bears witness to the possibility of radically different social relations. In the end, he comes to be reconciled even with his cancer and death, learning from Henri Nouwen to refer to death as his "friend."

From start to finish, *The Gift of Peace* bears witness in one actual Christian life to the theology and practice of peacemaking articulated in *The Challenge of Peace*. From shepherd to lamb, Bernardin embodies in his life the peace preached in the pastoral—a peace that is the fruit of consistent God-centeredness and communion with Jesus; a peace learned through practices of prayer and sacrament; a peace tied to ongoing conversion of heart; a peace gained through forgiveness and sacramentally mediated reconciliation; a peace that leads to justice and the consistent ethic of life, to work that values the lives of all persons, in this case, one's enemies and cancer patients.

"O Lord, Make Me an Instrument of Your Peace" The Consistent Ethic as an Ethic of Peacemaking

That we find this Christological, sacramental, lived embodiment of reconciliation and peacemaking in the life and works of Joseph Cardinal

Bernardin should come as no surprise. He was an affiliate first order Franciscan oblate who carried with him the prayer of St. Francis and who had the practice of saying it at the beginning of meetings—particularly meetings he knew would be contentious or difficult.[50] "O Lord, make me an instrument of your peace."

But how does this broader context of his life and works help us reread, recast, reorient the consistent ethic of life? Echoing Bernardin, "The logic of the consistent ethic cuts two ways not just one: It challenges pro-life groups and it challenges justice and peace groups" (SG, 107). While the challenge to justice and peace groups is to revision traditional issues in social ethics as "life" issues—which I think has been a creative and helpful move—the challenge to "pro-life" groups is to understand "life"' issues as equally "peace" issues.[51]

As Bernardin notes, "The substance of a Catholic position on a consistent ethic of life is *rooted in a religious vision*" (SG, 14, emphasis added). One of the key tasks going forward for the consistent ethic is to articulate that religious vision in a thickly theological way. In the liturgy pastoral, he asks his readers to "move beyond the pithy statements [of the pastoral] to a study of the rich heritage they seek to reflect." Likewise, I hope this display makes clear that we need to move beyond the "principle" of the sanctity of life to the rich theological heritage it attempts to capture. For too often, it functions—even for religious adherents—with the thinnest of theological content. The principle of the sanctity of life—if it draws only on one line from Genesis and maybe the Incarnation—is theologically inadequate.[52] The *principle* of the sanctity of human life or the dignity of human life must necessarily be attached to a very particular body of content, a particular vision, a particular set of narratives that control the parameters for the application and interpretation of that principle. Prior to our ability to deploy the principle of sanctity of life, then, it is necessary to display thickly the religious vision out of which it arises.

For Bernardin, that vision is deeply Christological—everywhere except the consistent ethic of life. Here I would take issue with him. In the Gannon Lecture, in I think his attempt to bring the peacemaking conversation into conversation with the pro-life community, he casts the pastoral—and the peacemaking tradition—in terms not entirely faithful to the pastoral. He notes:

> The central idea in the [pastoral] letter is the sacredness of human life and the responsibility we have, personally and socially, to protect and preserve the sanctity of life. Precisely because life is sacred, the taking of even one human life is a momentous event. Indeed, the sense that every human life has a transcendent value has led a whole stream of the Christian tradition to argue that life may never be taken. That position is held by an increasing number of Catholics and is reflected in the pastoral letter. (SG, 10)

But is it? The theology of peace of chapter 1 of the pastoral is not a principled pacifism and not a pro-life pacifism. Rather, it's a Christological pacifism, rooted in a vision of the kingdom of God as captured in the Sermon on the Mount and in discipleship to our Lord who met death on the cross. And while the final section of the pastoral does invoke the sanctity of human life, it does so in a context of liturgical practices that are centered not on the dignity of human life but on the centrality of the cross.

Moreover, Bernardin's own witness challenges his own presuppositions. Without a doubt, the world in which Cardinal Bernardin was trained did not make explicit connections between Jesus and the public square, prayer and social policy. Bernardin was formed in a milieu in which moral theology was one discipline and "spirituality" was separate. Trained in natural law, for Bernardin legitimate public engagement on the part of the church required a publicly accessible language and rational discourse capable of convincing all people of goodwill. Christian participation in public life requires consistency, coherency, and compelling intellectual engagement, arguments that persuade and convince. As he notes in the Gannon Lecture: "Attitude is the place to root an ethic of life but ultimately ethics is about principles to guide the actions of individuals and institution" (SG, 12).

I would suggest, however, that his journey is one that overcame his past. I would like to think that he had, perhaps, a nonthematic awareness of the problematic separation of "spirituality" and "ethics," and of the constitutive role of practices for Christian moral discernment and action. For we do not find *dis*continuity. At the end of his life, Bernardin was in the process of writing a pastoral letter on the liturgy. He did not live to finish it. But even in draft form, it speaks to his confidence in the formative necessity of Christian practices.[53] Liturgy, he notes, is "who we become." Liturgy, moreover, is of a piece with public action. He continues:

> Following on the example of the early churches described in Acts, we should name the deeds, the works of the church this way: Our liturgy and all our life of prayer and rite; every aspect of our work of formation of children and adults as Catholic Christians; the building up of our communion as sisters and brothers in the body of Christ and the striving we make toward justice the service of any in need. These are not so many separate departments of parish or diocesan life. *They are and must be seen as one whole.* (emphasis added)

Neither ought liturgy, moral theology, spirituality, nor systematics be seen as separate disciplines, with distinct and mutually exclusive methodologies. They are and must be seen as one whole, each informing the other.

And in the end, Christian practices emerge as the basis for serving the common good. In speaking of a diocesan-wide process he had initiated a few years earlier he notes:

After reflection and much consultation, I came to the conclusion that during the next several years our energy should be focused in part on the liturgy with special attention to the Sunday Eucharist, to preaching and to the celebration of the sacraments. I came to this conclusion after reflecting on how we might best be an evangelizing people. I was concerned that as Catholics we needed to become more enthusiastic about our faith and freely share that faith with others. We must invite all people to hear the message of salvation, work in our culture for the dignity of the human person, and the common good of all. If this were to happen, however, we first had to renew and strengthen our liturgical life. . . .

That liturgy, prayer, and social ethics are of a piece cohere with his growing conviction that the primary public of the consistent ethic is the church. As he notes in his Seattle lecture:

However the idea must be linked to a community—a constituency—which holds and embodies the vision. Within our own Catholic tradition, we recognize that a vision without a community is not capable of influence. A vision tied to a committed community is the first prerequisite of serious social impact. This is why we try to build that community and invite others into the discussion. (SG, 214)

And essential to the building of this community are practices of dialogue and reconciliation, key elements of the ethic of peacemaking. At the end of what I believe was his last consistent ethic address, he offers a critical yet hopeful account of the church, in the course of which he lays the groundwork for his common ground initiative. I quote it at length because I find it so powerful:

Eleven years ago, the pastoral letter on war and peace spoke of a "new moment" in the nuclear age. The letter has been widely studied and applauded because it caught the spirit of the "new moment" and spoke with moral substance to the issues of the "new moment." I am convinced that there is an "open moment" before us on the agenda of life issues. It is a significant opportunity for the Church to demonstrate the strength of a sustained moral vision. . . . But to take advantage of this new, "open moment," we must learn how to work together as a community of faith. Unfortunately, a great deal of polarization exists within the Church today. This has created at times a mood of suspicion, even acrimony. A candid discussion of important issues—and a common witness to them—is often inhibited, so that we are not always able to come to grips effectively with the problems that confront us. So what do we do?

As I conclude, I would like to suggest how we might begin to answer that question. The reality is that those who take extreme positions are often the most noisy—they get most of the attention. Those in the middle—the majority—are often quiet. I submit that we must make a greater effort to engage those in the middle and, in the process, establish a common ground—a new space for dialogue—that will make it possible for us to reach those who are alienated or disillusioned or uninformed for whatever reason.

To establish this common ground—this space for authentic dialogue—a broad range of the Church's leadership, both clerical and lay, must recommit themselves to the basic truths of our Catholic faith. The chief of those truths is that we must be accountable to our Catholic tradition and to the Spirit-filled, living Church that brings to us the revelation of God in Christ Jesus. Jesus who is present in sacrament, word, and community is central to all we do. So our focus must constantly be on *him*, not on ourselves.

This rules out petty criticisms and jealousy, cynicism, sound-bite theology, inaccurate, unhistorical assertions, flippant dismissals. It rules out a narrow, myopic appeal to our personal or contemporary experience as if no other were valid. It acknowledges that our discussions must take place within certain boundaries because the Church, for all its humanness, is not merely a human organization. It is rather a chosen people, a mysterious communion, a foreshadowing of the kingdom, a spiritual family, the body of Christ. When we understand the Church in this way, we will be able to see the full beauty and relevance of our heritage as it has developed under the influence of the Holy Spirit from the apostolic age to the present. It will also help us to become more tolerant of one another.

In sum, what we need in the Church today is a realization that there is room for considerable diversity among us. When there is a breakdown of civility, dialogue, trust, and tolerance, we must redouble our efforts to restore and build up the unity of the one body of Christ.

Dealing with each other in a consistent, gospel-inspired way will add greatly—I would say it is indispensable—to our public, collective witness to the consistent life ethic, which is so desperately needed in today's world. (SG, 265-66)

Were the church to achieve this vision of consensus and unity, how would Christian peacemakers engage in the public square? *The Gift of Peace* provides the program—by witness. In *The Gift of Peace*, Bernardin worries neither about arguing and justifying particular Christological claims nor that they will be illegitimate. He simply embodies them and allows the power of their witness to do the work of persuasion. Likewise, to recast the consistent ethic as an ethic of peacemaking might require that it navigate the public sphere not primarily via rational arguments (although that is not impossible) but rather through the changed lives of Catholics and Christians embodying, putting on Christ.

This is the work that remains to be done—to better display how the consistent ethic could reflect Bernardin's deeply held theological and lifelong convictions about peacemaking and to continue to develop his methodological insights toward a more theologically satisfying practice of moral theology, one no longer separated from dogmatics, ascetical theology, liturgical theology, and so on. If we could do this, we would see that what connects these disparate "issues" is not necessarily "life" but rather the vision of the gathered, reconciled community found throughout—a community of peace and love, reconciled to each other across the myriad of boundaries that slash our world in its ongoing violence, a community that practices penance, prayer, and service as a way of discipleship, following the Jesus captured most powerfully in the Sermon on the Mount and the cross. Whether this community is the community mentioned in *The Challenge of Peace* (§ 285), envisioned in Bernardin's championing of the consistent ethic, the church displayed in his pastoral writings, or the community he created through his ministry to the sick at the end of his life, they all coexist in the hope that one day, eschatologically perhaps, they will all compose one seamless garment of God's kingdom.

9.
FROM ONTOLOGY, ECOLOGY, AND NORMATIVITY TO MUTUALITY

The Attitude and Principle Grounding the Ethic of Life

DAWN M. NOTHWEHR, O.S.F.

Introduction: Sound Theology and Sound Ethics

Cardinal Joseph Bernardin's teaching was so powerful, demanding attention from his detractors as well as his supporters, because it was "theologically impeccable" and "pastorally sensitive."[1] It is evident from his written documents, speeches, and homilies that he stayed abreast of current theological developments, though he was not able to pursue them all in an equally comprehensive manner.

With that in mind, I propose that developments in Christian feminist theology and ethics encompass and further specify the Cardinal's understanding of theological ontology, ecology, and normativity. In fact, the relationship he saw between God and humans (and indeed with all creation), I suggest, is best identified as the feminist notion of mutuality.[2] Further, because mutuality (in its four forms) is at the heart of all relationships (cosmic, gender, generative, and social) that allow for the maximum flourishing of all creation, I submit that, as a formal norm, it provides the "attitude" and the "principle" in which Bernardin seeks to "root an ethic of life" (SG, 12). Therefore, this chapter provides a summary definition of the four facets of mutuality that includes a short explanation of the theological grounding for each. I then illustrate how utilizing mutuality as a formal norm brings consistency to the Consistent Ethic of Life (CEL). The chapter concludes with a discussion about what ontology, ecology, and normativity bring to the CEL and what the CEL brings to ontology, ecology, and normativity.

Christian Ontology

Behind Cardinal Bernardin's articulation of the concept of the CEL lies a response to the age-old question concerning ontology: "What is the origin and state of being of the universe?"[3] Invariably, Joseph Cardinal Bernardin began his explanation of the CEL by making several ontological claims:

Life is a precious gift from God which must be protected and nurtured from the moment of conception until natural death. This is why the direct taking of innocent life—whether of an unborn child through abortion, an aged person through euthanasia, or noncombatants in war—is always grievously sinful. This is why those actions or situations that diminish life—such as poverty, inadequate nutrition and health care, chronic unemployment—are also moral issues.[4]

The distinguishing mark of the Christian ontology that underpins Bernardin's claims is the belief that the world has a beginning and that theology (revelation) "provides a fuller experience of total reality than transcendental reflexion on which [philosophical] ontology is based."[5] In short, Christians hold that God the Creator of the universe is a very distinct kind of being apart from (though related to) the cosmos. God is eternal and the Creator of the universe, and God is not part of the universe nor is the universe a part of God.[6]

Traditional Christian ontology was grounded in God's Self-revelation to Abraham and Sarah and through them, ultimately and most fully, to us in Christ.[7] A Christian's belief in God and response to God's Self-revelation is the result of God's initiative, not a search for nature's origins and order. However, while reverencing the ultimate mystery of God, Christian theologians were persistent in asking questions of what they understood as revealed truth. Over the centuries some of these responses were established as doctrines and expressed in the councils and creeds of the church.[8] One such doctrine (creation) claims God is the one Creator and humans are created in God's very image and likeness.

Ontology in Cardinal Bernardin's Articulation of the Consistent Ethic: God and Human

Though nothing published by Bernardin specifically elaborates on his notion of God as Creator, his understanding of the character of God is accessible in many sources. For example, "All of life is charged with God's presence—good times and bad, sickness and health, day and night, summer and winter whether we are alone or with others. It makes no difference when or where."[9] Or on another occasion:

God—our God—lives with us. His very name is "God-With-Us." Our every concern is his concern. Our every breath is filled with his Spirit. To find him we only need to look around us: in *this* city, in *this* person. Remarkable as it is, he is present even in *this* heart, even though it is mine!

To be a disciple of the new age is really a very simple task. All we need to do is recognize that everything, including our hearts, belongs to him and acknowledge his presence as we discover his love all around us.[10]

Bernardin's God is both immanent and transcendent; the Creator is above, yet present with creation. What matters to us, matters to God. Similarly, what Bernardin says about the human person is influenced by how he understands God to be concerned about human well-being. When explaining the CEL, Bernardin says this concerning the human person:

> Catholic social teaching is based on two truths about the human person: human life is both sacred and social. Because we esteem human life as sacred, we have the duty to protect and foster it at all stages of development from conception to death, and in all circumstances. Because we acknowledge human life is also social, we must develop the kind of societal environment that protects and fosters its development. (SG, 78)

Human persons are understood in Catholic moral theology as beings of inviolable dignity, because they—male and female—are created in the *imago Dei* (Gen. 1; 2). The relationship between God and humans, and humans with one another, was formalized in the Covenant with Israel and finally in the New Covenant—through the incarnation, life, ministry, death, and resurrection of Jesus Christ. Indeed, Catholic theological ontology holds that God is the one who initiates and humans are those invited to respond to and live in relationship with God and one another, as well as with the entire creation. Bernardin's method of coming to this understanding of the God/human relationship is best described by the "dialogical model" James Walter presents in chapter 1 of this volume.

Ecology in Cardinal Bernardin's Articulation of the Consistent Ethic

It is precisely this relational ontology that provides Bernardin's starting point for the CEL, and that points us to ecological questions.[11] Both implicit and explicit relationships and linkages are asserted in Bernardin's discussion of the CEL. Explicitly, the relationship of humans with God that makes human life sacred; the relationship of humans—each created in the *imago Dei*—with other humans of inviolable dignity requires that they protect and nurture one another both personally and through the social structures they create. It is within the highly complex and interconnected life that is human that the various morally significant issues pertaining to that life arise: abortion, euthanasia, death penalty, poverty, inadequate nutrition, war, stewardship of the environment, and more.

Stewardship of the environment does find a place in Bernardin's litany of issues, but it is never elaborated upon.[12] While we can only speculate how he might have elaborated the notion of ecological relationships as a dimension of the CEL, there is an intriguing resemblance between the cardinal's lists of related issues and those issues raised by the eight themes cited in the U.S. Catholic Bishops' 1991 pastoral on environmental ecology, *Renewing the Face of the Earth*. Equally striking is the U.S. bishops' challenge to "explore the links between concern for the person and for the earth, between natural ecology and social ecology."[13] This exploration, the bishops charge, is to follow these eight themes: (1) a God-centered and sacramental view of the universe, (2) respect for human life, (3) respect for all creation, (4) affirmation of global interdependence and the common good, (5) an ethics of solidarity, (6) understanding the universal purpose of created things, (7) an option for the poor, and (8) a conception of authentic development.[14] Unfortunately, the cardinal did not live to see a more mature eco-theological reflection on those themes by scholars such as Leonardo Boff and others, who utilized the categories of "social ecology," "mental ecology," and "environmental ecology" to account for the ecological dimension of the various issues that the cardinal understood as related. However, it is possible for *us* to see a correlative relationship between Bernardin's linkages and what Boff identifies as ecological relatedness.[15] The ontological truth of a radically connected universe holds vast and profound implications for the sacredness and the sociality of life—human and nonhuman alike. What is at play in Bernardin's CEL and the U.S. Bishops' pastoral is a relational ontology that is supported by both theological and scientific evidence. However, the weight of the evidence shows us that what Bernardin saw during his lifetime were the analogous relationships between the various morally significant issues of life.[16]

Normativity in Cardinal Bernardin's Articulation of the CEL

In his Gannon Lecture, Bernardin stated, "Attitude is the place to root an ethic of life, but ultimately ethics is about principles to guide the actions of individuals and institutions" (SG, 12). Bernardin indicated a four-step process that progressed from the more abstract principle to practical application (SG, 18-19). Now as James Keenan notes elsewhere in chapter 4 of this volume, virtues that are universal point to the rules, principles, or norms that govern our praxis (actions) and that enable us to live virtuously. So, a norm that is at the core of an ethics of life must be a notion that functions both universally and specifically.

Generally, moral norms are defined as "the criteria of judgment about the sort of persons we ought to be and the sort of actions we ought to perform."[17] For Christians, the sources of norms include concrete embodied human experiences, Scripture, natural law, regulations or laws of the church, experiences of the value of persons and their social relationships, as well as the ongoing life of discernment as faithful People of God.[18] As Daniel C. Maguire asserts, moral norms hold the moral memory of the community's collective experience and wisdom.[19] Beyond the individual's wisdom, the community's wisdom can add breadth and depth, illuminating personal and communal insight into moral decision making, providing stability and consistency in judging right or wrong, good or bad. Moral norms carry no sanctions as such, but they do challenge individuals and communities to be accountable to others for the common good.

For Christians, moral norms serve to carry a standard through the ages that enables the faithful to live the moral life in their own time and place. These moral norms are usually categorized in two groups: "formal norms" that relate to character (virtues/vices) and "material norms" (behavioral principles). Our concern here is with formal norms characterized as moral absolutes.[20] According to Timothy O'Connell, "formal norms" are those that

> describe the form, the style, the shape that one's life should have in a particular area of ethical concern. Although material norms try to grapple with the concreteness of the situation, with its material, in order to assess various values, formal norms try to point out the form, the successful moral agent will possess. . . . Formal norms proclaim the goal to which every script ought to conform, the dream every script ought to incarnate. Or, again, although material norms tell us what we should do, formal norms tell us who we should be.[21]

Formal norms have an absolute character because they express values that are common, beyond the distinctiveness of gender, culture, or history, and are inclusive of enduring notions of divine revelation, as well as that which is universal to the human person.[22] Formal norms express the character of what ought to be, but they do not express the exact content of the behavior required to achieve that standard.

Cardinal Bernardin posited the principle of "the sanctity of life" as the basis for the CEL.[23] As this principle has been probed over time in Catholic moral discourse, it has become clear that at the heart of the content of this principle stands a theological relational ontology. That theological relational ontology is the specific kind of relatedness between God and human beings, and indeed, all of creation. God is the source and end of all life. However, human life is unique; it bears the *imago Dei*; it is God's gift; and humans were created for a special relationship with God, that is, in turn, their destiny. Thus, we have one tenet of Bernardin's theological ontology—namely, human life has an *in se* inviolable character.[24] However, it is also true that humans cannot survive and thrive in isolation apart from God, other people, or their physical environment.

Bernardin also states that the goal of practicing a CEL is the common good (SG, 241). Precisely what the cardinal understood by the common good is best presented in his own words:

> When considering the common good, it is far too easy to fall into the trap of seeing the common good as somehow opposed to individual rights and freedoms. This is a false dichotomy since individual concerns are inherently contained in consideration of the common good. The common good is not concerned with the good of the community in a way that sets itself in opposition to the rights and freedoms of individual persons. In fact the common good of the community is harmed when individual rights and freedoms are not respected. On the other hand, the individual is harmed when narrow self-interests and pursuit of purely private gain are pursued without reference to the needs and interests of the community as a whole.
>
> As described in the Second Vatican Council in the *Pastoral Constitution on the Church in the Modern World*, "The common good . . . is the sum total of all conditions which allow people, either as groups or as individuals, to reach their fulfillment more fully and more easily." [§ 26] Thus, there is a dynamic relationship between the individual and the rest of society in promoting the common good. This relationship is reflected in the law of the Church, which says that "in exercising their rights, individuals and social groups are bound by the moral law to have regard for the rights of others, their own duties to others and the common good." [*Dignitatis humanae*, § 7; see also canon 223][25]

Thus, one *ought* to practice the CEL to bring about and sustain the common good. Also, we have here in Bernardin's characterization of the common good another dimension of his theological ontology—the relatedness of all humans and their responsibility for one another. Yet, because humans require certain conditions for their physical health and well-being such as clean air, potable water, arable land, and a livable climate, beyond that primary statement of the common good, and by extension, ecological considerations also impact the "sanctity of life" and press us to include reverence for nonhuman life and, in fact, for the entire cosmos as "life issues."[26] And so we need to ask: "How is the common good best achieved?" On the one hand, what is the decisive principle that governs the relationship of *all parties* involved in any one of the issues Bernardin names—death penalty, abortion, civil and human rights, stewardship of the environment—that gives us the conditions for the maximal thriving of all? And, on the other hand, what principle allows (even requires) consideration of the reality that every aspect of *each* human life is distinct (though unified)[27] and thus gives a *particular* character to the various issues, one from the others?

"Is," "Ought," Normativity, Mutuality, and the CEL

If it is the case that humans are created, not as objects that God possesses and owns, but rather as subjects who bear the inviolable image of God, *then*—as it is known from the human side—the origin and state of being of the universe is utterly relational. The relationship between God and humans (and indeed with all creation) I suggest is in fact one of mutuality.[28] Indeed, recent advances across numerous academic fields recognize the facticity of mutuality, and even its ontological status.[29] As feminist and ecological theologians have shown, acknowledging mutuality as a foundational formal norm along with love and justice in the Christian ethical framework has the effect of limiting what qualifies as genuine love and genuine justice. Further, because mutuality (in its four forms) is at the heart of all relationships (cosmic, gender, generative, and social) that allow for the maximum flourishing of all creation, I submit that as a formal norm it provides the "attitude" and the "principle" that Bernardin seeks to "root an ethic of life" (SG, 12).

Mutuality: A Formal Norm Reclaimed

Developments in Feminist and Ecological Theology

Rosemary Radford Ruether, Elizabeth A. Johnson, Carter Heyward, and Beverly Wildung Harrison are the primary pioneers in situating mutuality as a formal norm for Christian social ethics, and indicating that it is a corrective and a complement to the traditional construal of the norms of love and justice.[30] These thinkers broke through the dualistic and hierarchical theology (recall the classical model in James Walter's chapter in this volume) and ethics that legitimated the kind of relationships that were often harmful, abusive, or which discounted women, women's perspectives, and that of all "others," even to the extent of denying them full personhood and moral agency. More recently as I have shown elsewhere, theologians such as Denis Edwards offered additional warrants for mutuality as a formal norm.[31] Edwards argues that the power of the Holy Spirit is that of relatedness, and he suggests that the ontological relatedness of all creation presses for a more tangible qualification of what constitutes adequate notions of love and justice.[32]

Certainly, mutuality is a necessary condition for genuine love or justice. When mutuality accompanies love and justice, a vast qualitative difference in each virtue is determined, namely, the dynamic of power becomes limited to "power-with."[33] There is evidence for the normative status of mutuality and that it functions along with love and justice in the Christian ethical framework to create the optimal flourishing of all—a flourishing set within in the interdependent context of the whole of creation. I now turn to that discussion, beginning with a summary definition of mutuality.

What Is Mutuality?

Mutuality is a formal norm that can be conceptualized in a manner similar to our understanding of justice, and it is similarly complex. Analogous to those theories of justice that ascribe to it a tripartite nature—contractual, distributive, and social—we find four forms of mutuality: cosmic, gender, generative, and social.[34] The basic definition of mutuality is "a sharing of 'power-with' by and among all parties in a relationship in a way that recognizes the wholeness and particular experience of each participant toward the end of the optimum flourishing of all."

The first form of mutuality is *cosmic mutuality*, that is, "the sharing of 'power-with' by and among the Creator, human beings, all earth elements, and the entire cosmos in a way that recognizes their interdependence and reverences all." Evidence for cosmic mutuality is advanced from particularly astrophysics, ecology, and quantum physics, and it names the foundational kinship of everything in the entire cosmos. This radical relatedness can be understood as a "relational ontology" set in place in the beginning by the Holy Spirit's inspiring and creating activity.[35] Beyond that, ecofeminist theory holds that the natural environment asserts itself as a living aspect of "our bodies, our selves"— it "answers back" when humans defile nature.[36] Humans violate the ecosystem to their own detriment. Cosmic mutuality is also grounded in the fact that the most effective social analysis takes into account how any form of power impacts the most disadvantaged, not forgetting all elements of the ecosystem, in the interest of attaining the well-being of all.[37] Traditional Christian ontology is retrievable to the extent that the relatedness of the created order and the social order is stressed in light of the biblical witnesses. The deep relatedness between God and creation, known as panentheism,[38] has been recognized for centuries as orthodox. The fact that God *is* Creator, Vivifier, Redeemer, only in relation to creation shows, in a certain analogous sense, need on God's part for relationship to the cosmos.[39] Of particular interest for us is the claim that the proper role of the Holy Spirit in the world is that of the giver of life and the creator of communion.[40] Thus, acknowledging the kinship of all creation through the Spirit's life-giving and communion-building activity requires us to count nonhumans as our neighbors as well.[41] This evidence all points to cosmic mutuality.

Gender mutuality, a second form of mutuality, is defined as "the sharing of 'power-with' by and among women and men in a way that recognizes the full participation of each in the *imago Dei*, embodied in daily life and through egalitarian relationships." Gender mutuality is grounded in the fact that women and men are both bearers of the full *imago Dei* (Gen. 1:27) and they are both capable of full mature moral agency. For the baptized, the Holy Spirit inspires life *en Christ*, meaning they are part of a discipleship of equals (Gal. 3:28) that foreshadows the eschatological "New Heavens and the New Earth."[42] It was the Holy Spirit who prompted Jesus's "*kenosis* of patriarchy" that significantly precludes sexism in any form. This Spirit-inspired action is important, because Jesus's life, ministry, and teachings are normative for the Christian life. The four feminist pioneers mentioned above, also advance biogenic and sociocultural evidence supporting gender equality to challenge classical dualisms and physicalist interpretations of natural law.[43] In addition, the social sciences show that social, political, or economic structures can be organized to purposefully empower or disempower women (or other marginalized persons). Finally, all erotic, sensual, embodied knowledge (including sexuality) is a means of God's revelation of Self to us through one another.[44] All of this points to gender mutuality.

The third form of mutuality, *generative mutuality*, is "the sharing of 'power-with' by and among the Divine, human persons, and all creation in the ongoing co-creation and redemption of the world." Insofar as each human person bears God's image and likeness within her/his own flesh, each enjoys mutuality with God as co-creator and co-redeemer.[45] The paradigm of the Incarnation itself, Christ Jesus as both human and divine, part of the material world, also lends support to that notion.[46] Indeed, insofar as each creature images God, each participates in the co-creation and redemption of the world. Significantly, "The Spirit can be thought of as God present in countless ways that are beyond the human."[47] In fact, the nonhuman, but particularly animals such as our pets or farm animals, have a great capacity to teach us the meaning of co-generativity. Co-creative and co-redemptive processes include human and divine cooperation in the Life Giving Spirit, bringing communion among humans and all of creation, initiating human friendship with God (Aquinas, *ST* I-II, 1-5, and II-II, 23-27), and being present in the *koinonia* of the baptized.[48] Indeed humans, empowered and inspired by the Holy Spirit, participate in completing the redemption of the world begun by Jesus, by struggling in daily life to "transcend themselves and . . . become what is new."[49] All of this data signals that generative mutuality exists among the Divine, human persons, and all creation.

The final form of mutuality is *social mutuality*, and I define it as "the sharing of 'power-with' by and among members of society in a way that recognizes the fundamental dignity of each and the obligation to attain and maintain for each what is necessary to sustain that dignity." Perhaps Beverly Wildung Harrison explains social mutuality best when she states:

> Jesus was radical not in his lust for sacrifice, *but in his power of mutuality*. . . . . His death was the price he paid for refusing to abandon the *radical activity* of love—of expressing solidarity and reciprocity with the excluded ones of his community. . . . Radical acts of love—expressing solidarity and bringing mutual relationships to life—are the central virtues of the Christian moral life.[50]

Indeed, Jesus is the bearer of the liberating Spirit who led him to heal, dine with the outcasts, form a community, and preach the reign of God.[51] Living as Jesus lived, with a commitment to mutuality, enables us to bear God into the world. As the Pentecost sequence proclaims, the Holy Spirit is the "Father of the Poor" who inspires acts of justice, and orchestrates liberation through the release and the taking up of power in relationships. Countless persons, both named and nameless, who have freely suffered for the sake of mutuality, exemplify the reality that at times, fidelity to mutuality requires that we make sacrifices for the cause of radical love in order to consciously create and sustain relationships, or right wrong relationships.[52] The chosen sacrifice of mutual love always has an eye toward a more fully lived experience of mutuality, i.e. "right relationship."[53]

The Holy Spirit animates and empowers people, enabling them to choose to share in a common power with those less powerful or oppressed, not forgetting the earth and otherkind. But, the role of the less powerful must also be stressed. Given the constitutive sociality of the human person, the less powerful are obliged to assert their claim to "power-with" in order to maintain their human dignity. This evidence suggests *social mutuality* is needed between the powerful and the powerless of our world. Thus, we have completed a summary definition of mutuality in its four forms.

Normative Status of Mutuality

Ruether, Harrison, Heyward, and Johnson all hold that mutuality (as defined above) is a formal norm for Christian ethics.[54] For Ruether mutuality describes the form and style of human relationships among God, humans, earthcreatures, the earth itself, and the entire cosmos. She views mutuality as a moral absolute in that without it, the dynamics of power readily become oppressive and abusive. She illustrates how the concept of mutuality is accessible through reason in the natural sciences such as astrophysics, quantum physics, and ecology. From a Christian perspective, mutuality characterizes and forms the reign of God. Overall, mutuality expresses what it means to have a healthy thriving relationship with all things and all beings.

Carter Heyward employs psychological data to explain that no healthy relationship lacks mutuality. Heyward also points to astrophysics, quantum physics, and ecology as ways people come to know and understand mutuality through reason. She cites biblical sources that reveal a God of mutual relations, particularly exemplified in Jesus. Further, she illustrates how lack of mutuality in sexual relationships leads to abuse and oppression. Heyward understands mutuality as an exceptionless formal norm.

Harrison agrees with Ruether and Heyward, but raises some additional arguments. With her eye always toward the dynamics of power in the economic, political, and social arenas, she sees the capacity for mutuality as the common power residing in each person and as a function of the *imago Dei*, grounded in the sociality that is innate in humanity. Because God's relations with humans are mutual and normative, Harrison claims that we must engage in mutual relations with others.

Based on human experience, especially the affiliation patterns of women, Elizabeth A. Johnson observed that mutuality is normative. Primarily, she understands all of God's relations *ad intra* and *ad extra* as mutual, and she holds the life of God as exemplary for human life. Thus, she forcefully argues that because this is the case, human relations must also be normatively mutual.[55]

Mutuality: What a Difference It Makes!

Our four feminists and Edwards would agree that mutuality makes a great deal of difference shaping an ethical framework and in the outcome of moral discernment.[56] Living in mutuality is a process animated by the Life-Giving and Communion-Building Spirit, and not a static situation.

Set within a dynamic worldview, a feminist ethic of mutuality has implications for the CEL, first of all, concerning our *appreciation of truth and truth claims*. According to Edwards, truth seeking is part of the ongoing "Becoming" of all creation: "It is the Spirit who is the immanent principle that empowers the self-transcendence of the universe towards Christ. . . . The Spirit is at work in the evolutionary emergence whenever something radically new occurs in the unfolding of the universe and in the story of life."[57] Such self-transcendence is necessary to attain the "attitude" that Bernardin's CEL requires. It opens people to a genuine self-knowledge and self-respect that also requires them to respect the ontological sacredness and radical relatedness to all others and their needs.

Within the context of a genuinely healthy and wholesome self-love, parties in mutual relation are oriented to the needs of the other and maintain intentionality directed to the well-being of self and the other(s).[58] Mutuality thus requires a *praxis view of truth* in which the truth is conditioned by the intentions of the relationship.[59] What is true is related to the action-oriented intention of the speaker.[60] The CEL does not deal in abstractions, but in concrete details of human life. What is theoretically possible may not always be so in the concrete embodied material reality of a given time and place, or concrete reality may require revision of moral theory.

Mutuality is a relationship in which each party has a distinctive particularity and history. Sustaining the relationship requires a *perspectival view of truth* in which all standpoints determined by culture, gender, history, economics, politics, or other factors are taken into account. Indeed, this view presses humans to also consider nonhuman perspectives when considering truths about issues such as endangered species or polluted rivers.[61] For mutual relations it is necessary to recognize that language is limited in the meaning it can bear. As Wittgenstein has argued, human language can bear only one or two perspectives at once.[62] What is true needs to be understood in a context. One dimension of reality is the particularity of the moment. As with any ethic, the CEL requires an adequate knowledge of reality (*ex objecto*) that is characterized by a relational ontology.

From Gadamer and Ricoeur, there is evidence that knowledge of any text is also an interpretation of the text. In sustaining a mutual relation, this *interpretive view of the truth* needs to be acknowledged lest there be false absolutizing of unintended information or action.[63] How do we attend to the texts of the poor, the elderly, the marginalized, the enemy, or the nonhuman world? What truths do we miss if we ignore them? The CEL requires us to attend to everyone and everything in their particularity, as moral subjects.

A fourth kind of truth is *dialogic truth*. As one acts, speaks, and interprets with another there are moments when the "I" and the "Thou" combine to form the "We."[64] It is in those moments that mutuality reaches its apex. Do we listen deeply to those with whom we disagree? On numerous occasions Bernardin expressed his desire that there be respectful dialogue among the diverse perspectives on the issues, and he identified that dialogue as "consistent and gospel-inspired."[65] Edwards shows that the Spirit has a differentiated personal presence to each creature, "a presence that creates a bond of communion with each."[66] In effect, then, each creature can contribute something unique toward a more complete understanding of the truth. Or, are we, like Martin Buber, attentive to the dialog invited by trees, horses, cats, or rocks?[67] If we are not open and ready for these kinds of truth, and the moment of true mutuality that happens in the "between" of dialogue, we live in a false reality, assuming that what are indeed only elements of truth to be the full truth.[68] A true consciousness is a dimension of the attitude that the CEL requires.

A second set of implications mutuality holds for the CEL is that *mutuality shifts ethics' understanding of the moral subject by focusing on the sociality of the human person*. Edwards shows that "human beings have their own unique relationship to the indwelling of the Holy Spirit. In the communion of the one Spirit they are kin to all of the creatures" and to one another.[69] No action can be evaluated as if the person acted in isolation. Moral actions need to be considered in light of the context of the situation. We are always in a situation of response to others.[70] Our actions make sense only in relationship to others, including nonhuman others. The structure of a relationship is key to its moral value. It is this kinship (social, mental, and environmental ecology) that links the various issues Bernardin includes in the CEL.

Mutuality also *expands the idea of the moral subject* from one bearing an abstract status (a human nature) to one who develops, experiences, and transforms value and who is, in turn, developed and transformed by valuing. The moral capacity of the self, the motivation for sacrifice and justice is understood in terms of mutuality in relationships. Indeed, a theological and relational ontology, expressed as the *imago Dei* and in the sacramental character of creation, undergirds the CEL. This suggests that everything and everyone has moral standing.

Further, mutuality *focuses on reciprocity in moral agency*. In the situations of mutuality, the moral subject constantly exchanges valuing and being valued. We are enabled "to grasp our dependence on each other and our social institutions and relations for our moral self-regard and moral power."[71] We are formed by our context, and in turn, we create and shape contexts. The CEL suggests that all contexts are somehow sacred insofar as they create and nurture life, since everyone and everything has its origins in God.

A third set of implications mutuality holds for the CEL is that *mutuality modifies what is understood as the "good."* Normative mutuality *moves the starting point for ethical reflection to a radically inclusive place,* where literally everyone and everything is included. Edwards holds that God companions each creature with love that respects the identity of each, its possibilities, and its proper autonomy. Thus, the Spirit is grieved (Eph. 4:30) when humans destroy, abuse, and disregard the experience or needs of any part of the web of life.[72] The moral horizon here is the vision of the "New Heavens/New Earth." The present history and the future shape the twofold context for the vision. "Goods" based on atomistic individualism and patterns of competition, adversarial relations, exploitation, authoritarianism, or paternalism are ruled out because they diminish or deny the fundamental mutual relation that exists between God and humans and that needs to exist between humans, and with all of creation. In relationship with others we gain the necessary orientation for how our own conception of the "good" affects others whose lives and well-being are intertwined with ours. Relationship is the ontological reality that no one person ever stands alone. In light of all of this, the CEL is an ethic of mutuality.

Human good needs to fit in with all other "goods" in the cosmos with an eye toward the maximum flourishing of all—not just human thriving. This means mutuality requires an integration of independent and responsible acts as well as interdependent and relational activities. It means that in achieving the "good" what must be overcome is whatever isolates, completely separates, and arouses disinterest and atomistic individualism. There is one good that permeates both private and public spheres; mutuality empowers by including everything and everyone in the social/political/economic equation.[73] This understanding makes the CEL possible in that there is no one or no thing that stands outside of a relationship. Thought of in this way, the CEL is also an ecological ethic.

Every human conceived is in need of relationships. When needs and rights are not met and honored, injustice accompanied by self-doubt, mistrust, or resentment occurs. The practice of justice in society also, therefore, needs to include mutual practices of reconciliation.[74] When an impasse in relation results because both parties do not recognize mutuality, an ethics of care does not abandon the effort. Rather, it moves the moral agent while still caring for his or her own health and well-being to consciously choose to confront the deeper (often social-psychological) blockages and to try again and again. The moral agent, practicing an ethic of mutuality, may then knowingly choose to love sacrificially in order to act-the-other-into-life, moving toward greater mutuality. The Spirit is most certainly present in such an encounter. As Edwards has shown, "the Spirit is the mid-wife that groans with creation in its labor pains (Rom. 8:22) as it transforms and gives birth to all things new."[75]

Relationship between Love, Justice, and Mutuality

Two formal norms, love and justice, have traditionally been viewed as foundational for all Christian ethics. While at times either love or justice has been more heavily stressed, both have been perennially presented as measures of Christian morality. As Daniel C. Maguire points out, it is significant that throughout the canon of Scripture, love and justice are viewed as coordinates of the same plane. He states:

> "Sow for yourselves justice and reap the fruit of steadfast love" (Hos. 10:12). The dichotomy between love and justice is spurious. The two are naturally related. Justice goes before love, insisting on the minimal prerequisites for survival. But then it makes common cause with love upon discovering that surviving without thriving is not surviving at all.[76]

Mutuality: A Corrective and Complementary Norm

It is precisely in the consideration of what behavior constitutes "thriving" that the need arises for mutuality as a formal norm to complement and correct love and justice in the Christian social ethical framework. Failure to consider mutuality as a norm has left many significant questions unexplored or inadequately considered.

Critique of Love

At many points in Christian history, sacrificial love has been stressed to the neglect of mutual love. In a number of Christian traditions, any love of self was suspect, and *agape* at times came to be understood as void of a healthy self-love, pride in one's own goodness, or any self-interest. In Catholicism, it seems that the tendency to understand love as nearly exclusively sacrificial is a bequest of some forms of medieval passion mysticism.[77] As Christine E. Gudorf claims, we cannot presume that Christian love is disinterested or set apart from other love as self-sacrificing. "All love involves sacrifice and aims at mutuality. . . . Much love is mutual; all love is directed at mutuality. It could not be any other way, for we find love rewarding."[78] Mutuality functions as a corrective to a one-sided emphasis on sacrificial love.

Critique of Justice

Justice has long been considered a complex multifaceted reality.[79] For example, the influential Aristotelian and Thomistic theories of justice state that

justice has a tripartite nature—commutative, social, and distributive.[80] Some
contemporary ethicist's renderings of that theory assume reciprocal influence
of varying degrees in each form of justice.[81] However, generally, theories of
justice can be classified in three categories: Rationalist[82] and natural law theories, analytical and positivism theories, and utilitarian and other theories.[83]
Mutuality functions as a complement and challenge to natural law theories in
that it requires a more critical view of hierarchy than is commonly found in
natural law traditions, entailing the elimination of relationships of unilateral
submission and subjugation. Mutuality functions as a corrective to the posi-
tivists in that it shifts the criterion for justice from pure legalism to include
the concrete and dynamic needs of the other as basic to thriving. Mutuality
functions as a corrective to utilitarianism in that it requires consideration of
the good/needs of all beings and elements of the universe in relation to one
another, not merely the greatest good for the greatest number.

Distinctiveness/Relationship: Love, Justice and Mutuality

Love. For our purposes in distinguishing love, justice, and mutuality, the differentiations made by Ruether and Heyward concerning love
are most revealing. Ruether stresses the necessity of a healthy self-love and
the perception of equality among the lovers/beloved as conditions for love,
which she describes as "[seeking] the total welfare and personal growth of
the other."[84] Heyward agrees with Ruether and emphasizes (as does Ruether
invoking the prophetic tradition) the unity of the three classical aspects of
love (eros, agape, philia) in practical action rather than focusing on concepts
of love. Feminists turn to these distinctions, qualifications, and emphases to
counter many long-standing interpretations of sacrificial love, which in the
world of women frequently translated into unhealthy self-denial and passive
subordination.[85]

Beginning with Valerie Saiving Goldstein's watershed article on the relationship of sacrifice and sin in the moral lives of women and men, modern
feminists have roundly rejected notions of love that see only sacrifice in the
Christian notion of agape.[86] Feminists prefer a definition of love that is conditioned by the formal norm, mutuality. Our feminists repudiate traditional
and unqualified definitions of love, referring to the classical Greek notions of
agape, eros, and philia rooted in the philosophy of Aristotle and Plato.[87]

Rooted in the Hebrew and Christian Scriptures, the feminist notion
of love involves, first, a healthy self-esteem that is grounded in knowledge
of God's unconditional love for each person (1 Jn. 4:19) and a relational
anthropology.[88] This self-esteem includes a balanced self-confidence that
acknowledges one's gifts and talents, but also one's limitations and failures
to be assertive. Self-love requires that one meet one's basic needs (not wants)
to the highest degree possible, and within the bounds of justice, such as
food, clothing, shelter, health care, basic education, and rest.[89] No healthy
love of self can be sustained outside of some sort of communal affiliation,

because humans are naturally social beings. Here is where love of neighbor finds its source and its end. Created in the image and likeness of a God who is in mutual relation *ad intra* (Johnson), but who "is also a person" (Buber), humans are related to one another in the kinship of humanity and the common Parenthood of God. Love of neighbor is to be as an intense desire for the good of the other as one's love for oneself (Matt. 2:39-40). All of this further defines the social dimension of the human person to which Bernardin constantly refers when discussing the CEL and the moral obligation to provide structures that protect and foster human development.

Jesus extended the boundaries of what love requires to also include love of enemies and anyone in need (Matt. 5:46; Lk. 6:32-34; Matt. 5:43; Lk. 10:29-37). In making that extension, Jesus moved to the deepest challenge of love—namely, to the place where the common ground, even of foes, is their humanity itself. It is in the attempt to love the enemy that the Christian finds her greatest strength, in the "power to be powerless" (cf. Mk. 10:35-45). From a feminist perspective this means that if the Christian is not to be ruled by the power-over that is of the enemy, s/he must move to a stance of power-with, relinquishing power-over, but also asserting the common humanity s/he and the enemy share. Once the enemy is viewed as an equal, true affection can be given to her/him. The move that has been made constitutes a change of stance from "power-over" to "power-with." I recognize that my "enemy" and I share a common humanity as well as the limits of sin and finitude, and with this shift my attitude changes to that of mutuality.

It is in the "love of enemy" where the relation between love and mutuality perhaps becomes most clear. As Ruether has pointed out, there can be no real love between those who do not understand themselves as equals in some form. This does not mean, as in the case of Aristotle, that only social/political/economic peers can love. It does mean that the basic dynamic and attitude toward power in the relationship of love need to be characterized by "power-with." The dynamic that names the exchange constitutes mutuality; what is exchanged is love (affection). This exchange is more accurately called mutual love. Only when one chooses self-denial toward a goal of greater mutuality (out of mutual love) is sacrifice healthy. All other motives for self-denial can be traced back to selfishness or sloth or, worse, self-hatred. Love, then, is the exchange of affection between acknowledged equals, toward the maximum well-being of the other(s), in the context of mutuality. Here we find that mutuality provides the attitude and the principle for the CEL by qualifying the most adequate form of love as mutual love.

Justice. Earlier, I gave a general critique of positivist, utilitarian, and natural law theories of justice, which represent the key criticisms feminists raise against them. The four Christian feminists in this study fundamentally agree that the most adequate theory of justice is found, instead, in the biblical justice outlined within the Hebrew and Christian Scriptures.[90]

These feminists emphasize the relational nature of justice and contrast their understanding of justice, which focuses on ethics of care, with concepts of justice focusing on ethics of rights.[91] Heyward's definition of justice, for instance, centers on the Hebrew notion of *hesed*: compassion, caring, or fidelity.[92] The interhuman compassion that is *hesed* is possible only through knowledge of God, who is a God of covenant and mutual relations.

Johnson cites Carol Gilligan's ethic of care, which suggests that justice is done when relationships are converted from either total dependence or independence to interdependence.[93] Utilizing the image of a web, Gilligan suggests that all humans are related to one another and the entire universe. Perfect justice happens when everyone and everything is responded to and included in a manner that serves the maximum thriving of all; no one is hurt or left out. Justice, then, is not only a matter of equality, but also a matter of interconnection. Justice becomes a matter of power-with grounded in the common power of mutual relation, rather than power-over rooted in coercion. It is mutuality that forms the strands of the web that hold everyone and everything in relation. Here it is the principle, justice as proper interconnection, that brings consistency to the CEL.

Mutuality. Mutuality requires justice to address rights and needs. Traditionally, self-interest was viewed as the root motivator of society's ills and in many cases as the fundamental justification for hierarchical, coercive social structures.[94] In the face of the persistence of self-interest, rights language, which tends to focus on individuals, delineates minimum standards and boundaries that must not be violated. The traditional role of justice is to supervise and protect those boundaries. When the good is understood in terms of relationality, however, justice needs to address persons in the context of the groups to which they belong—for example, their common humanity or as one being among other creatures of the cosmos. Mutuality, which views the person as part of social-historical relations, requires justice to consider those social-historical relations to correct historical wrongs as well as immediate infractions, and to restore and reconcile relationships.[95] Or, as Cardinal Bernardin claimed, "Because we acknowledge human life as social, we must develop the kind of societal environment that protects and fosters its development."[96]

Mutuality, Love, and Justice: Foundational Formal Norms

Our special attention to mutuality here does not suggest that we replace love and justice in the Christian moral framework. Rather, the norm of mutuality serves as a complement and corrective to love and justice. In relation to love and justice, mutuality is the prior recognition of the power common to all, in all of creation and in relation to the divine, to make reciprocal claims on one another.

Mutuality brings justice to love. It does so in two ways. First it liberates and affirms the person in meeting her/his own needs. Indeed, as we have seen, mutuality requires that the partners in a relationship be whole, distinct individuals. Mutuality challenges moral agents to integrity of character.[97] For the Christian, the *imago Dei* and the unconditional mutual relation with God lie at the heart of such integrity. From a stance of inner justice, a healthy self-esteem, the person is able to move outward to others with an affection rooted in their common power. In maintaining personal integrity, justice plays the role of calling the person to honesty; to deal with her/himself as a whole embodied being—physical, emotional, spiritual, mental—in all its strengths and weaknesses. On this personal level, the challenge mutuality brings to love is similar to the dynamics that are at work in the love of one's enemies, only here, the "enemy" may be within. Those aspects of every person that bring alienation in any form and which militate against personal wholeness are challenged forth for confrontation and healing. Positively, the call of justice that mutuality brings to love is for the perfection of the self—for the self to inclusively embrace what one/it is.[98]

A second way that mutuality brings justice to love is in the way it requires one to love one's neighbor. In light of what was just stated, the motivation for love of neighbor can be made more clear if one addresses this question to herself: "Am I a neighbor?" The test of that question is honesty within one's self and the challenge to cease projecting outward what is not whole within. If one views oneself as like another, one must first see the common power and common limitations one shares with the other. Mutuality dictates that all humans share a common power in relationship by virtue of the *imago Dei*. By not being a "neighbor," in a real way I deny my own humanness. If this is so, I am not capable of a human love or an inner justice, and I am plagued with disease that requires healing. Only after healing takes place can I be free enough to be influenced and motivated to be a neighbor. As a neighbor, I can give and receive mutual love and choose to serve others in dignity with integrity.

Justice tempered by mutuality saves love from condescension in that mutuality requires a reverence for the common dignity that is shared and/or an appreciation of the relatedness of all creation to the divine and to one another. Mutuality requires that the boundaries of any relationship be set together by all involved in the relationship. A noteworthy example of this dynamic can be seen in Jesus's approach to others in many of the healing stories.[99]

We have seen how mutuality serves justice and love. Mutuality and love also serve justice. Justice restrains mutuality from "value free" agreement that could point a relationship in a direction that detracts and harms the common good by failing to direct individual needs toward the well-being of all.[100] Justice keeps mutuality real by holding forth concrete needs that must be filled in order to satisfy human dignity and the common good. Love prevents mutuality from regressing to a utilitarian exchange, a mere reciprocity, by holding up *communio* as the *telos* of relationship. In love, justice, and mutuality, then, we have the formal norms that constitute a more adequate value framework for Christian ethics than the traditional structure that includes only love and justice.

The Probative Value of Mutuality and the CEL

As we have seen, mutuality identifies the attitude and the principle (virtue)—that is, the "ought" that follows from the "is" (relational ontology) that undergirds the CEL. Human flourishing and the well-being of the cosmos requires that moral action and ethical discernment account for this ontological truth, this radical relatedness of everything and everyone, if it is to be adequate. Such an accounting is sought and attempted in Bernardin's CEL.

Conclusion

What are the implications for understanding mutuality as a central norm for the CEL? We can see that mutuality does make a difference in our perception of truth, the moral subject and the moral good. As Edwards reminds us, "Theology and science can meet in a view of reality as relational—in a relational ontology."[101] The verity of mutuality and even its ontological status are widely recognized in all academic disciplines. Together these understandings form and inform our moral vision of whom we ought to be and what we ought to do in relationship with self, God, others, and the cosmos.

What Do Ontology, Ecology, and Normativity Bring to the CEL?

Bernardin's CEL depends on the ontological claim that "life is a gift from God." As we saw above, Bernardin understands God as both the giver of life and the one who is present with humanity in all of life. Denis Edwards's ecological theology explicates the mystery of this God and shows how a radically relational Triune God creates "a world that is relational to its core."[102] Edwards also makes explicit the relationship between God and the creation, as well as the relationship between all created beings. Indeed, the Life-Giving Spirit as the Power of Becoming has a personal relationship with each being, and this reality grounds the sanctity and dignity of human life. The Life-Giving Spirit as the Ecstatic Gift of Communion provides the basis for the sanctity of the social dimension of human life and the obligation to sustain human dignity by creating and sustaining just social structures.

From the ecological view, Bernardin's claim that there is a linkage between the various life issues is sustained. There is a radical interdependence that exists among all beings and at many levels (social, mental, and environmental), yet particularity and diversity are required for integral relationships to thrive. It is even possible (and necessary) to account for relationships of pain and suffering from an ecological and ecotheological perspective.[103]

While ontology addresses the source of all being and ecology shows the reality that all beings are related, mutuality specifies and defines the foundational formal norm that makes the "common good" for all beings possible. Mutuality as a formal norm limits the legitimate exercise of power in a relationship to "power-with." As I have shown, the probative value of mutuality, when used with love and justice in an ethical framework, broadens and deepens the ethical horizon and moral imagination to deal more thoroughly with the complexities of relationships.[104] By considering ontological and ecological questions, it becomes possible to specify mutuality as the formal norm foundational to the CEL insofar as it (1) accounts for the linkage Bernardin sees between the various life issues and (2) delimits the kind of power in relationships that determines the common good.

What Does the CEL Bring to Ontology, Ecology, and Normativity?

The CEL draws ontological considerations into ordinary moral discernment because that is where Bernardin begins. In practice, this starting point shifts the consideration from legal or social dimensions *only* to also include ontological dimensions. Consider this: the death row inmate (even if not innocent) can no longer be seen *only* in terms of the fact that she killed someone unjustly (generative mutuality).[105] It is highly probable that she is economically poor, a woman of color, not well educated (social mutuality), and a victim of sexual or spousal abuse or both (gender mutuality). Rather, she now needs to be viewed as one who is given life by God, and who bears the *imago Dei* (cosmic mutuality). She is my sister, whose actions affect me (generative mutuality) because we are related at the ontological level—our common humanity, having a common Creator, and live in a common world. While numerous distinctions exist, the ontological reality of mutuality provides a sobering attitude and principle from which to discern moral action. As the author of the book of Wisdom proclaimed so long ago, "Your immortal spirit is in all things" (Wis. 12:1), giving life and creating communion.

10.
THE CONSISTENT ETHIC OF LIFE AND DEVELOPMENTS IN GENETICS

Thomas A. Shannon

Introduction

In 1983 at Fordham University, Cardinal Bernardin gave the first of his presentations on what he called a consistent ethic of life (CEL). This project developed and carried forward ideas initiated by Eileen Egan, a pacifist and member of the Catholic Worker movement; Cardinal Medeiros of Boston; and Pat Coltz and Catherine Callaghan, the founders of Feminists for Life.[1] Bernardin developed an approach to Catholic ethics that sought both to unify and to address ethical problems from the perspective of respect for life. Because this framework addresses a broad range of ethical issues, it is, therefore, a conscious move away from single-issue ethics or politics. Of critical interest is whether one principle, even one as central and basic as respect for life, can bear all the methodological weight placed onto it.

The Context

Cardinal Bernardin gave his first talk on the CEL thirty years after the discovery of the double-helix structure of the DNA molecule by James Watson and Francis Crick. Though their claim that they had discovered the secret of life might be slightly over the top, nonetheless the discovery of the four-letter alphabet and the way in which the letters pair up opened the door to all of the discoveries in genetics in the last fifty years. Cardinal Bernardin wrote about a decade after the discovery of the technology of recombinant DNA. This technology provided a way to sever strands of DNA and then insert these strands into different organisms, thus producing the first transgenetic organisms in history. This technology helped us learn that DNA is DNA and that this core molecule is common to all of organic life. DNA can be moved around from organism to organism, and it will function in the same way.

Cardinal Bernardin gave his initial address about a decade before the initiation of the Human Genome Project, the multibillion-dollar project to map the human genome, a project completed in 2004. This map gives the location of the genes that make up our genetic structure; it is the biological outline of what makes us human. Some interesting things were learned from this project. We have many fewer genes than previously thought—perhaps only 20,000 or 25,000, as opposed to the 150,000 genes that were projected. The human genome has only about 300 more genes than the mouse genome. We differ from orangutans by about only 0.8 percent. We know that DNA of the human genome is common to all organisms. What is interesting is what differences a variety of arrangements make. The map is also helping us to locate the gene or genes responsible for a variety of diseases and anomalies, which, of course, has significant applications for prenatal diagnosis and gene therapy.

Cardinal Bernardin gave this first address about ten years before the birth of Dolly, the first cloned mammal, and about twenty-one years before the first documented report of a cloned human embryo in 2004. This research has raised a variety of questions about the role of in vitro fertilization (IVF) for the nonreproductive purpose of generating embryos for research and to obtain stem cells from them. Additionally IVF combined with the technologies of genetic engineering provide the technical basis for a variety of interventions—therapeutic or enhancing—on the human embryo.

Implications

Because of Cardinal Bernardin's untimely death, he was not able to address the critical issues of our time that contemporary genetics raised. On the other hand, IVF seems to be the only issue with some relation to the field of genetics specifically addressed in the corpus of the consistent ethic of life. I recognize that one cannot address everything, and many agenda, such as peace and war, economic issues, and racism, were on his and the hierarchy's plate during this time period. Also many were suspicious of the cardinal's approach because they felt that it distracted the church from its vigorous opposition to the practice of abortion. Finally, this orientation is not fully developed. Other essays in this volume ask: is it an attitude, a vision, a methodology, a set of principles?

What is clear, though, is that while the consistent ethic of life was being developed and tested through a variety of articulations in various speeches and articles, many critical developments in genetics were moving ahead, sometimes at the breakneck pace of seemingly a major discovery a day. These developments were discussed neither specifically nor thematically by the cardinal, though there are general allusions to genetics. This omission may represent a missed opportunity, the limits of any one person to speak cogently to a variety of particular issues, or perhaps may reveal a weakness of the methodology. A whole area of modern life and science was not systematically addressed from this perspective by its author.

The task of this essay is threefold: (1) to present several thematic perspectives in contemporary genetics, (2) to review the content of the corpus of the cardinal's writings, and (3) to test the significance and relevance of the consistent ethic of life as a means of the moral evaluation of contemporary genetics. The core question, then, in this essay is to determine whether or how the CEL might function in this area.

The Consistent Ethic of Life and Genetics: Context, Problems, and Methodology

General Issues in Genetics[2]

To enter the world of contemporary genetics is to enter a rapidly changing, increasingly complex, and progressively problematic world. Those who have had recent undergraduate or graduate courses in genetics may recognize some of the terms they hear, but unless they graduated within the past month, much of what they hear is new. What chance, then, do those of us have without even this modest background? The basic problem is that even though we may not have any background in biology or genetics, developments in this field impact each of our lives, and we need to grapple in particular with the realities of new genetic information that is here to stay. I discuss here four themes that are of particular importance: genetic information, reductionism, control and freedom.

To say that we have had an information explosion in genetics and modern biology is an understatement. We have moved rapidly from the discovery of the basic structure of the DNA molecule by Watson and Crick in 1953 to learning how to recombine elements of different molecules in the 1970s, to the realities of gene therapy, cloning, and the completion of the map of the human genome in the last decades. The first layer of complexity here is simply trying to keep track of and then process all this information, which is one of the most difficult elements in the whole field of genetics. A second layer is recognizing that this information simply cannot somehow be withdrawn or repressed. For better or worse, this information is public, and we will have to deal with the consequences of our knowledge. A third layer is the relation between knowledge and action. That is, can certain kinds of experiments or applications of knowledge be prohibited? We clearly have a tradition of freedom of speech. Is or should there be a similar freedom of action? Many seem to agree that human cloning should be prohibited, but others think it is simply another reproductive technology. Resolving this question will be a major struggle of the future.

A key element in scientific problem solving is the reduction of a problem to its elemental parts and then resolving each of these in turn. Thus, the method of science is reductionistic. It seeks to solve complex problems by solving smaller parts of the whole first. Another name for this method is Ockham's razor, a principle that says do not multiply entities without necessity or that the simplest solution is frequently the best. As a methodology in science, reductionism is critical and indeed responsible for much of the success of modern science. But a problem arises when a shift is made, and frequently it is made uncritically or unconsciously, from reductionism as a method to reductionism as a philosophy. Reductionism as a philosophy states, in its most popular phrasing, that only the elements of a problem that can be quantified in some fashion are the ones that can be taken into account. Thus, while reductionism as a method focuses on the role of particular genes in producing a behavior, reductionism as a philosophy says that only the genes need to be studied to understand a behavior.

Another phrasing of reductionism as a philosophy affirms that the only reality that exists is material. While this may be correct, it is not correct because the reductionist method in science is successful or because the reductionist method functions because of quantification. Ignorance of or disregard for this distinction between reductionism as a method and philosophy is responsible for apparent conflicts between science and religion or ethics.[3]

One capacity that modern genetics has given us to a much larger degree than ever before is enhanced control. We can select for certain genetic profiles, we can transplant genetic information from one species to another, we can make predictions about the future health status of an individual, and we are trying our best to custom design crops and animals; some fear that designer humans will be next. The ethical/religious term that helped us to think about control is "stewardship."

The term "stewardship" came out of a particular cosmological and biblical framework. Biblically, the term originates in the Genesis narrative of the Garden of Eden in which Adam and Eve are placed. In this garden, they are given certain responsibilities and obligations. Essentially they are to care for the garden that God has created. Embedded in this narrative is the reality that the garden is not theirs and that their care for it is to be exercised within the ethical framework given them by God. Precisely stated, they are to be stewards, ruling on behalf of God. Therefore, they had limits, and they answered to a higher authority. From a cosmological perspective, the universe was a static universe designed according to a plan, and this plan specified where everything was to go and how it was to act, thus forming the general ethical framework for understanding the limits of stewardship. This cosmological perspective was integrated into philosophical and theological discussions and formulations for centuries. It specified a universe of boundaries and limits, and within such a universe, the ethical standards were reasonably clear and well grounded—indeed literally grounded in the universe in which one lived and breathed.

In such a universe, stewardship was not only an ethic easy to validate—it was the only ethic available. Within the worldview of those in this framework, limits were obvious and binding, and actually there was no other choice. There were no other competing frameworks; only very limited interventions were possible, and human powers had very finite and obvious limitations. Stewardship made sense because within the static, hierarchical cosmology and theology of both ancient and medieval Western civilization, it was the only option.

Several interlocking events shook this framework to its very foundation and produced a new reality in which the steward and stewardship language are strangers in a very strange land. The first was the Protestant Reformation, which challenged the authority of the ecclesiastical establishment of Rome and replaced it with personal responsibility for one's salvation (faith alone) and private understanding of the Scripture (Scripture alone). The role of authority in interpreting Scripture, imposing limits, and defining responsibility was weakened as responsibility for that was more and more taken over by private conscience. Second, the Industrial Revolution, fueled by the concurrent rise in capitalism, showed that human capacity and creativity could be expanded enormously by power sources and money. Limits now seemed to be limits of the imagination—and one's cash or credit reserves. Third, the theory of evolution forever shattered Aristotle's great hierarchy of being and the social structure implied by it with the insight that the reality of today is the result of a series of random interactions that had no guiding principle. Stability was replaced by process, and one existed at a point in a continuum that had no determined future. Finally, jumping ahead several centuries, we have the reality of genetic engineering that gave us the possibility of engineering or designing the designer.

One response, using somewhat familiar religious language, has been proposed by Philip Hefner, now retired from the Lutheran School of Theology in Chicago.[4] He has proposed the term "created co-creator." This term affirms that indeed we are created by God, though that creative process is framed in an evolutionary context. But the "created" dimension of that term suggests some set of limits. We are not on our own; we are not totally independent. We stand in a relation of creaturely dependence on God. The "co-creator" dimension of the term directly acknowledges our capacity for creativity. But again there is a qualification in that we are "co" creators. That is, our creativity starts from what is, from the limits that are factually imposed by lack of knowledge and capacity. The lacks are changing all the time, but their reality does remind us that we do have limits. Perhaps the analogy for human creativity that emerges from this phrase is that of the human as a working partner in cooperation with God. We can take initiatives as a partner does, but such initiatives are to be in harmony with our other more senior partner—God. But here again an argument has to be made to justify the harmoniousness of our actions with what we know of God.

Stewardship, while having an important and useful past, thus encounters difficulties in light of our contemporary understanding of the cosmos and in light of our increased technical capacities. Alternative understandings of the basis of our responsibilities in the world need to be developed.

Freedom

If any value is celebrated in the United States it is surely the value of freedom. Indeed, our very origin as a country began in a declaration of independence that gave us the freedom to establish our own country. We assume and celebrate freedom of thought, movement, expression, style, religion, and politics. We rebel against impositions of lifestyles and rules not of our choice. But in this we have an interesting view of freedom. Freedom consists of choosing: choosing between alternatives, choosing a lifestyle, choosing a partner, and choosing a political candidate. The critical reality of freedom is the act of choosing. Once we have chosen, we are finished. The fact of choice is the beginning and end of the story. That I chose something is the only justification needed for my choice.

The problem with this version of freedom is that it does not permit an evaluation of what is chosen. It doesn't make any difference what we choose; what is important is that I choose. Then my choice is my choice, and once made, my choice is not to be questioned. But how would this work, for example, if my choice were to have a female child and I continued to choose abortion until I had a female fetus? Or if I chose to fertilize in vitro a human sperm and a chimp egg and to implant it into a chimp surrogate mother; or if I chose to clone humans to obtain embryonic stem cells? Each of these choices has significant consequences that are independent of my choice, as do the vast majority of choices that I make. Thus, the question must at least be asked: is the fact that I choose an action sufficient justification for that action, or should I at least be required to give some accounting of why this particular choice is a good or a better choice? Our choices arise out of value frameworks and set other values in motion, and in the field of genetics these values have significant social consequences. Parents who attempt to custom design a child through choice of eggs and sperm as well as rejection or acceptance of certain genetic profiles set up particular expectations for that child. They may also be contributing to a disruption of the ratio of males to females, or may unwittingly select a profile that could turn out to be utterly inappropriate for changes in a culture or environment. People who argue that research in stem cells should receive funding priorities take away research money from efforts at prevention of disease—that is, there will be less money to conduct antismoking or healthy lifestyle campaigns.

The options we will be given from the power of modern genetics are going to implicitly challenge our dominant understanding of freedom as choice. We are going to be forced to examine our choices and evaluate them. This will be a very difficult task because culturally we do not accept people challenging or questioning our choices. "It's my choice" will continue to be the battle cry, but a battle cry under challenge from the significance of the consequences that flow from our choices.[5]

Consequences for the Consistent Ethic of Life

A specific problem arises for the CEL from the perspectives I have raised in genetics. The problem is that the CEL typically returns to the one principle of the inviolability of innocent human life as the key ethical principle for analysis of all cases. In part this is because the principle is an important one. Another element is that, from a political and ecclesial perspective, the CEL is to a certain degree being held hostage by the pro-life movement. Clearly Bernardin was head of the Pro-Life Committee of the then National Confer-

ence of Catholic Bishops, and he was committed to the agenda of the committee. But he was also aware of and committed to addressing other social
problems and sought to highlight their significance by linking them to the
ethics of life perspective. Thus he sought to move off single ecclesiastical and
political ethical issues and to be more inclusive in his vision. This perspective was reflected as well in his later Common Ground Initiative that sought
dialogue between different groups in the church.

Both the CEL and the Common Ground Initiative were met with
strong resistance. Several cardinals challenged the very idea that there could
be dialogue in the church on a variety of issues, as the Common Ground
project suggested.[6] Others continued to emphasize the priority of the pro-
life, antiabortion issue over any other issues. A current example of how the
CEL continues to be held hostage to the pro-life movement is demonstrated
in three recent events in American Catholic life.

First were the various debates over whether Catholic politicians who
did not support antiabortion legislation could receive Communion or, in the
more extreme forms, should be excommunicated. The first salvos were fired
by Archbishop Raymond Burke of St. Louis who declared that Catholic legislators who continued to support procured abortion or euthanasia may not
present themselves to receive Holy Communion. To receive Communion, the
legislators had to publicly renounce their support of these practices. Burke
was soon joined by Archbishop Hughes of New Orleans. Such a move had
been previously made by Bishop Wigland of Sacramento and Bishop Carlson
of Sioux Falls with respect to politicians in their dioceses. Other bishops
issued similar letters or statements. In June 2004 Cardinal McCarrick of
Washington, D.C., head of a task force on Catholic Bishops and Catholic
Politicians, issued an interim report at the spring meeting of the United States
Conference of Catholic Bishops (USCCB). The document recognized that
individual bishops have the authority within their dioceses to set guidelines
for receiving Communion, that there was room for different judgments on
how to proceed, and that no national guidelines would be established.[7]

Second is the focus on single-issue voting in which all elections become
referenda on abortion or other narrowly drawn pro-life issues such as euthanasia or embryonic stem cell research. For example, Cathy Cleaver Ruse, in
discussing some of the 2004 election outcomes in the Life Issues Forum on
the USCCB Web site, stated that although the election was supposed to be
about "terrorism, the economy, and Iraq," she notes that the more pressing
issue was moral values, as if these three issues had nothing to do with moral
values. The real moral values are then noted in this formulation: "These new
Senators will provide a stronger margin in the Senate on issues like abortion,
human cloning, and embryo-destructive research. Their most significant
impact, however, may be on judicial nominations."[8] This is a far cry from
the kinds of issues noted in "Faithful Citizenship: A Catholic Call to Political Responsibility," the 2003 statement of the bishops that was to serve as a
framework for discussing the moral issues in the forthcoming election. The

2007 statement "Forming Consciences for Faithful Citizenship" advances this expanded moral vision by including genocide, torture, racism, and targeting of noncombatants together with abortion and euthanasia as direct threats to the dignity of human life.[9]

Third were discussions surrounding the November 15, 2004, election of Bishop William Skylstad to the presidency of the USCCB. An article in *The New York Times* noted that Skylstad is "considered a liberal within the church because he sometimes emphasizes issues like poverty, the death penalty and war, as well as abortion." William Donohue, the president of the Catholic League, framed Skylstad's election this way: "There is this fight, between the social justice and the pro-life sides of the Catholic Church." And Austin Ruse, president of the Culture of Life Foundation, noted, "There is increasing resistance to the leftism of the staff at the USCCB, like the way some on the staff try to equate the life issues with the minimum wage."[10] Thus, the CEL agenda is kept hostage to the pro-life agenda.

The problem with this single-issue approach is not only a constricted moral vision. The more critical problem is that such a constricted moral vision either misses or simply ignores many other critical social ethical dimensions that are precisely related to the so-called pro-life stance. For example, discussions of the common good seldom factor into the arguments of the pro-life lobby. Yet the common good is a core value of the social ethics tradition of the church and has a critical role to play in bioethical discussion, in particular as noted most recently by Lisa Sowle Cahill.[11] The assumption that rejecting abortion and embryonic stem cell research because they violate innocent human life resolves all of the issues connected with these problems is simplistic at best.

In the next sections of this essay, I consider two examples that simply will not leave the public arena and need significant reflection, much more than would be provided by a simple prohibition on abortion.

Two Current Issues in Genetics: The State of the Questions

Research into genetics is complex, expensive, and exciting. Clearly there is much promise in this field, but there are also many complications.[12] First are the many promises that are made, or suggested, about the benefits of the research. One element here is exaggeration and inflation of claims, or as it is called by some, gene hype. One of the most extreme examples was the claim by a senior scientist at the beginning of the genome project that the success of the project would lead to solving the problems of poverty and homelessness. While everyone can appreciate the ridiculousness of this claim, other claims are not seen as exaggerations or as significant promissory notes. What we have yet to recognize is the immense and substantive gap between discovery and cure. This is not an argument against stem cell research per se. It is a call to recognize inflated claims that are used to justify commitment of money to a process that is highly experimental and untested. The claim is not the reality, but one would not always know that from listening to discussions of various discoveries. One must be much more critical of the claims that are made and ask for a clear presentation of the research supporting such claims.[13]

Second, commitment to either embryonic or adult stem cell research in particular is a commitment to business as usual in the medical community. That is, a commitment to stem cell research is a commitment to high-tech, very expensive rescue medicine. Clearly that is the dominant mode of medicine practiced across much of the United States, particularly in the wealthier areas, and high-tech medicine is certainly where the money is to be made. Pursuing stem cell research continues this practice and continues to draw large sums of money from other possible uses as well as competition between states for scientists and research dollars.[14] Thus, the stem cell debate is also an opportunity to discuss and debate priorities in research and health care, a discussion sorely needed in this country. High-tech rescue medicine holds a place of honor in American medicine, and with good reason given the tremendous contributions that it has made. But it is not the only form of medicine, the only method of intervention, or the only method of cure. Uncritical pursuit of genetic interventions will continue the lopsided nature of American medicine and siphon research money from other appropriate areas.

Third, as E. Richard Gould points out, a commitment to secure property values in human body parts such as embryonic tissue commits us implicitly to specific health policies. First, we will seek out cures for diseases and turn "away from discovering the underlying social and environmental causes of diseases." Second, we would commit ourselves to a health policy "that holds that health status is improved by access to newer and better treatments." Finally, this policy would suggest that "disease ought to be viewed as an individual problem specifically as a problem of the individual's genetic code, instead of as a social problem."[15]

The very difficult social question is: is this the way to continue to go with research and medicine? Should we continue down the track of high-tech rescue medicine with its emphasis on intervention and cure, or is it time to have a substantive conversation on other models of medical practice and medical intervention? Stem cell research is a clear example of another promissory note in modern medicine with the payment to be picked up at the cost of other interventions and research into human well-being, as well as the delivery of health care itself. Such research is also a clear, but unacknowledged, commitment to the status quo in modern medicine.

Fourth, who will benefit from stem cell research? The rhetoric is that all will benefit. But in the meantime, the benefit will go to two groups. One: those who are insured and whose insurance will cover the treatment. Two: those who can afford to buy it. Because of the millions of Americans who are uninsured or underinsured, or whose insurance will not cover such experimental protocols, the vast majority of citizens will not have access to whatever benefits come from this therapy. Additionally, depending on how the science goes, researchers may focus on single-cell genetic diseases because these are easier to identify and target. But again this narrows the field of application considerably. While it may be the case that research on single cell genetic diseases using material derived from stem cells provides the possibility of cure for many who might otherwise be without a remedy for their disease, nonetheless this is still a significant directing of the scarce resource of research money to a small population. Even should the therapy prove successful, the number of people who stand to benefit from it are a small subset of the whole population, and perhaps even a small subset of all those with genetic diseases. Even on traditional cost-benefit or utilitarian analysis, this may not be the best strategy to pursue.

Fifth is the cost of such treatment in both experimental and therapeutic stages. This kind of research is time consuming and labor intensive. While computers and other automated systems aid tremendously, the main part of the work is both theoretical—understanding genetic structures and planning the research—and practical—carrying out the experiments and studying their results. Well-equipped labs with sophisticated equipment in addition to a highly trained staff are the basic entry requirements for this kind of work. And if much of the research will be funded by private capital because of current federal difficulties over the use of human embryos, one can be sure investors will want a return. As mentioned, that return will take the form of expensive therapy. Patients whose incomes are not in the upper 5 percent would not be able to pay for such therapy—as they are not able to pay for many other therapies in our current medical system. Even those who have good insurance plans will have difficulties because of the continued restriction on what will be covered by such plans and a growing reluctance to fund experimental therapies. Again the number of possible beneficiaries narrows.

In an early paper on justice and the Human Genome Project (HGP), Karen Lebacqz suggested that one way to achieve justice would be through some form of price controls on any medications or interventions resulting from HGP research since this research is supported in part by public funding.[16] Thus, while private capital investments are an important source of funding for the HGP, significant monies are derived from, for example, the National Institutes of Health. My point is not that such funding is wrong or improper; rather, it is to suggest that there is an obligation in justice to acknowledge these public sources of funding, and a relatively easy way would be to follow Lebacqz's suggestion of some form of price controls.

Granted, as developments in research improve and therapies are developed, the price of these therapies will also decrease, at least in theory. We need to keep in mind that one of the most problematic areas in contemporary health care is the continuing escalation of costs. Given the tremendous investments that have to be made in genetic research and given that, after several decades of intensive research, no gene therapies have been successfully developed, it is highly unlikely that such interventions, as important and successful as they may be, will be inexpensive or that companies and investors will not seek returns on their investments.

The issue of directions in and research on genes thus raises an important social justice question that needs to be incorporated into the CEL. There are critical relations between the individual good and the common good, priorities in contemporary medicine, and the availability of therapies that need substantive analysis. The CEL will be a useful approach here, but to be a critical part of this analysis, its scope must be broadened by incorporating a methodology that can focus on social analysis and a way to help adjudicate between a variety of competing goods and values.

Another area of importance in genetics is prenatal genetic testing.[17] There, a variety of routine diagnostic options are presenting a routine diagnostic intervention in the last several decades that will, in my judgment, become more significant and problematic. The methods range from taking a family history to analyzing blood taken from the mother, from preimplantation genetic diagnosis in which cells from the fertilized egg are analyzed before implantation to the use of ultrasound to visualize fetal development. The most common method is amniocentesis, a screening of the chromosomal status of a twelve- to fourteen-week-old fetus by analyzing fetal cells withdrawn via needle aspiration from the amniotic fluid surrounding the fetus in utero. This diagnostic technology will become even more common and more problematic for at least two reasons. First, most likely the search for gene function will first focus on effects caused by single genes. The simple reason for this approach is that they are easier to identify, and therapies for single-gene diseases may be easier to develop. Second, the rise in malpractice premiums will guarantee that every means of defensive medicine will be used to reduce the likelihood of malpractice claims based on the physician's not providing every relevant test to ensure fetal well-being. The information from the HGP will be combined with the various types of prenatal diagnoses, primarily the routine use of the technology of amniocentesis, to create a social and medical context in which each pregnant woman will be pressured to use these diagnostic technologies, regardless of medical indications and the pregnant woman's desires.

Additionally, prenatal testing raises several problems, some associated with the technology and others associated with the procedure's being done in a Catholic health-care facility.

With respect to amniocentesis itself, the first set of problems is informational and therapeutic. The informational problem is that we have the capacity to diagnose more anomalies than we understand. That is, our diagnostic capacity outstrips our interpretative capacity. Given the sophistication of the technology, we will be able to identify more and more abnormalities, but we will have little idea of their significance or implications, if any at all. The immediate consequence of this is more confusion for already distraught parents who have committed themselves to this pregnancy but now learn that on chromosome 10, for example, there is this little difference, but its significance is unknown.

What does one do with such information? Worry is clearly one answer, though a highly unsatisfactory one. A possible solution is for the physician not to inform the parents of information that appears to be insignificant, but this raises two more problems: what is insignificant information, and are parents entitled to all information that is learned from this test? Given the current climate of patient autonomy, withholding information is clearly problematic. Another solution may be for the physician to specify with the parents exactly what information they want: information relevant to the specific reason for the test, for example, or all information from the test. In this approach the physician could explain in advance that not all the information from the test might be clinically relevant.[18]

Another dimension of the problem has to do with the diagnosis of genetic diseases that are so-called late-onset diseases such as breast cancer and Huntington's disease.[19] These diseases do not present until later in life, and until then the individual will be symptom free and have a good quality of life. Yet the parents, at the time of diagnosis, know that there will be problems ahead, regardless of future therapeutic developments. This is a new and added burden, and one without a clear frame of reference for thinking through how to handle it; therefore, it's a problem with no satisfactory resolution, particularly if such diagnostic technologies are used prenatally. There could be tremendous pressures on parents to abort a fetus with a gene for breast cancer or Huntington's even though symptoms will not occur until much later in life.

The therapeutic problem is that regardless of the information received, not much will be able to be done. That is, our diagnostic capacities outstrip our therapeutic capacities. The major downside of the HGP is that interventions for genetic disease are a long way off. Trials for gene therapy are in the very beginning stages; many problems have already presented themselves, and many trials have been discontinued. Therapies even for single-gene diseases are not on the radar, and if the disease is multigenetic, as the majority of diseases are, the wait will be even longer primarily because of the difficulties associated with identifying the interaction of various genes in the causality for a disease, just to give one example. Couples who receive a positive diagnosis for a fetal disease have poor options: abortion, avoid pregnancies in the future, use donor gametes to avoid the disease in the future, or proceed with childbirth and let the disease run its natural course. If the last option is chosen, additional problems may be social disapproval for not having "solved the problem" through an abortion; strains on the family in terms of time, money, and interpersonal relations; and finally the reality that funds and social services for treating the disease are in increasingly short supply and seem destined to continue to diminish. Additionally since the disease was diagnosed prenatally, it may qualify as a preexisting condition for that particular disease and, therefore, disqualify the child from the insurance coverage that the parents have.

The key value that is challenged by these various technological capacities is that of human dignity or the sanctity of the life of the individual, particularly when this value is seen from the broader perspective of the CEL. Two key issues emerge: abortion and health care. Abortion can be presented as a quick and inexpensive solution to a difficult medical problem or as a solution to the so-called quality of life problem: no one should be forced to live under the circumstances presented by this disease. Such responses, though deeply imbedded in American culture, stand in sharp contradiction to the CEL.

Second, the CEL forces an examination of social policies and insurance plans that provide less care and fewer resources for those born with various diseases. Those who commit themselves to the care of a child born with a particular disease or set of handicaps find themselves financially isolated and often socially alone. The cost of care for many infants born with various birth anomalies can be very high, and many families will find their resources severely compromised by such financial costs, even though they are willing to bear them. This is particularly true if the prenatal diagnosis shows the presence of a late-onset disease such as breast cancer or Huntington's disease and is defined as a disqualifying preexisting condition for the disease.

Catholic health-care institutions and social service agencies face the same financial difficulties that other public institutions do, but, I would argue, they have a particular obligation to step forward in such situations to be as responsive as possible. The specific problem is that more resources seem to go to the prevention of abortion than for the long-term support of a child, and that abortion seems to be the only issue around which many unite and the issue that garners large financial and institutional support. Yet the problem of long-term support for people with a variety of needs is a critical one because of the genuine shortage of resources and the growing realization that market interventions themselves will not resolve the present health-care crisis. Catholic institutions can make a critical difference in health care and particularly in genetic counseling by making it known that they will make every effort to provide medical resources for a child, and perhaps more importantly, that they will support legislation mandating that the larger community provide financial and social services. The clear message of the CEL should be that this family will not be alone in their time of need. Again the social ethic dimension of the CEL presents itself as the more important component of the orientation. While some may affirm that abortion is generally an inappropriate response to this situation, doing so is made difficult if a family has access to few resources. Thus for the CEL to be effective and meaningful, the social element must be given a priority by both Catholic health-care facilities and Catholic social services. This ethic will be difficult to practice, but if the CEL is to be meaningful, this approach offers the only way to go.[20]

While these problems emerging from the technology of prenatal diagnosis itself and the provision of long-term care are difficult and complex, they almost pale in comparison to the institutional problems that present themselves when such procedures are proposed in a Catholic health-care facility.

The problem is that even at Catholic hospitals, requests for such procedures will only increase—together with the consequences of such requests. First, as more information from the HGP works its way into the medical and popular literature, more people will propose using this information. Second, as the malpractice climate increases, more physicians will recommend any and all tests that will make them less liable for a lawsuit. Third, insurance companies might see prenatal diagnosis as a cost-effective way to eliminate future care costs. The cost of a prenatal diagnosis and abortion is nothing in comparison to the costs associated with various diseases. Pressure from a variety of places may thus fuel a demand for prenatal testing, regardless of whether there may be a medical indication.

Related to these three concerns is what I would term the public relations problem of prenatal diagnosis, which is simply and directly the association with abortion. Many people refer to these procedures as "search and destroy" missions. Also there is, in this country as well as internationally, a growing use of these technologies primarily for sex selection, not exactly a medical indication, to say the least. While one can argue that the good news is that fewer than 5 percent of such procedures result in abortions, for some even that number is too high because any abortion for any reason is morally unacceptable. While no institution can ultimately determine what individuals will do with information that is provided to them, staff members can certainly influence how individuals perceive a situation and understand what options they might have. Some might argue that because of the possibility of an abortion after amniocentesis, Catholic facilities should not do this service. On the other hand, a Catholic facility has the opportunity to provide such services in a much different atmosphere than other facilities. It also has the opportunity to demonstrate its commitment to the CEL by bringing the individual into a wider community of care and support. For example, a genetic counseling service at a Catholic hospital could help the couple by introducing them to other couples who have a child with the same disease as theirs will have. This approach will help give parents a realistic sense of how to respond to such a situation. Providing a sympathetic and supporting community in a Catholic hospital may make a very critical difference in the decision individuals make.

A third aspect of the problem is mergers, already a neuralgic aspect in Catholic health care. What to do when the non-Catholic facility with which one wants to merge, manage, or co-manage routinely provides such services? What to do when a women's clinic wants to lease space within an inner-city Catholic hospital? Recent discussions in Catholic circles suggest a very strict interpretation of the principle of cooperation and concern about scandal should a Catholic facility be associated with a facility that provides sterilization or abortions. Seeking any kind of compromise here seems close to impossible.

Prohibiting such mergers, even though there are problems associated with them, may commit a greater evil by not providing health care for the poor. The genuine scandal may be that any Catholic Christian presence in the inner city is now absent. A strong, committed Catholic presence grounded in the CEL can do more good than the maintenance of institutional purity. Clearly Catholics do not want to support or be perceived as supporting abortion clinics, but neither should they abandon or be perceived to be abandoning those who need care the most, whether from poverty or distress over an infant with a severe disease. The line may be difficult to maintain, but commitment to those in need should be the primary commitment. Again this issue demonstrates the need to engage the CEL in a more social orientation.

Problems such as those identified here will only grow in intensity and complexity as technology progresses and more people demand technological interventions in their lives. Some demands may seriously challenge the Catholic ethic, but we must also think of the good of children and of families and constantly try to implement quality health care by expanding the content of the CEL. Such an ethic will let people know that they are not alone and that they will not be isolated because of decisions they make on behalf of their child. Implementing this ethic will make all the difference for many people.

Methodology and the CEL

Though not strictly related to the problems of genetics, the methodology of the CEL as proposed by Bernardin is at the heart of many issues that are important in genetics. The problems discussed above are part and parcel of the current scene in medicine and genetics. They will not go away. Pressure to continue research in genetics and even to mandate prenatal diagnosis will only increase. Continuing to say simply that the appropriate response is to more strongly and vociferously resist abortion and embryonic stem cell research will not only not help resolve these issues but in fact will take our attention away from critical and necessary social analysis of the problems directly associated with these issues.

As Patricia Beattie Jung noted in chapter 5 of this volume, two methodologies are in use in magisterial documents. The first methodology is primarily deontological or principle-based and relates to sexual activity broadly understood. When there is any reference to some life issues, such as abortion or euthanasia, or sexual matters, such as contraception or homosexuality, the method is deontological. Absolute principles, rights, or values are invoked and give rise to absolute norms that permit no exceptions. This approach is frequently grounded in a vision of natural law that affirms a particular teleology in biological acts that is inbuilt by the Creator and cannot be violated. The methodology looks at each act separately and typically a-contextually and, with respect to the norm or principle, a-historically. Thus all acts of artificial contraception are absolutely prohibited, in vitro fertilization using the egg and sperm of a heterosexual married couple is prohibited, any sexual act between a heterosexual married couple that does not eventually result in intercourse open to procreation is prohibited, all direct abortions are prohibited, and absolute rights of the fetus from fertilization onward are asserted. There are no exceptions to these norms and, as we used to say, no parvity of matter in the area of sexuality—that is, all sexual matters are objectively morally grievously wrong. Behavioral consequences follow—sin, excommunication, the possibility of condemnation by the hierarchy if one dissents, and possible exclusion from the sacraments.[21]

Additionally this approach focuses largely on the individual or the individual case. The deontological approach isolates the case from a larger social setting. While the setting is not necessarily normative with respect to resolving cases, neither should it be dismissed as having no relevance. Historically, circumstances have been important in resolving moral issues, and the deontological approach downplays this aspect too much.

The second method emerges from the social ethics tradition and recognizes the centrality of norms and rules, but these are always applied in a particular context with attention paid to circumstances and consequences. These norms are typically generated with reference to their historical development, the various social contexts in which they arose, and with much attention to their consequences. Natural law arguments are not always at the center of this method. Rather, one looks to the social ethics tradition, expert opinion, and philosophical, political, and social analysis to determine the appropriate range of actions. The methodology used by the American Catholic bishops in developing their pastoral letters *The Challenge of Peace* and *Economic Justice for All* model this approach to great advantage. Both letters began with a long process of consultation with experts from a variety of perspectives. This process was then followed by a lengthy analysis of relevant Scriptural and ethical resources. The next stage was a detailed analysis of the relevant social, economic, and political contexts. Finally a set of conclusions was drawn. While some principles that could not be violated were identified, the letters acknowledge that not all would agree with the conclusions the bishops drew. This method explicitly accepts the moral appropriateness of disagreement. Few, if any, behavioral consequences followed from disregard of the teachings of these letters. Some even wrote counter-letters.[22] In this context it is instructive to recall that William F. Buckley was never chided for his public rejection of the teaching authority of the magisterium stated on the famous cover of *National Review* after the promulgation of *Mater et Magistra* by John XXIII in 1961: "Mater, sí; magistra, non" (Mother, yes; teacher, no).[23] The American bishops have publicly stated that they cannot understand how the war in Iraq could meet the criteria of just war doctrine. Assumedly this would mean that Catholics should at least have some moral qualms about supporting the war, much less participating in it. Yet even Catholic politicians who support this war and those who voted for them have not received even the most modest chiding.

With respect to sexual morality, the norms in play have also emerged from a historical context, were responsive to particular social and political situations, and were attentive to consequences. Additionally, sexual acts cannot be understood simply in themselves. They emerge from the context of the individual or participants, their intentions, their relationship, and the consequences of their actions. These acts also need to be considered within the context of the relationship as a continuing process. Individual acts have meaning and significance with reference to the totality of the relationship, and to isolate one act and make it bear the entire weight of moral analysis is like determining that any one action of a couple is a defining point for their relationship. In short, the same set of personal, social, political, and moral realities are present in the sexual arena as are present in the arena of all other aspects of life. The same methodology should be used for both. This approach would give consistency to the analysis, would offer coherence of analysis, would ensure that all relevant moral evidence and argumentation would be brought to bear on a problem, and would affirm the necessary complexity of reality.

In particular we need to think of the particular "principle that prohibits the direct taking of innocent human life" (SG, 12). Earlier in this lecture, Bernardin noted that "there should always be a *presumption* against taking human life, but in a limited world marked by the effects of sin there are some narrowly defined exceptions where life can be taken" (SG, 10). The example he gives is war, but one could also include capital punishment and self-defense. Granted Bernardin's intent is to narrow the exceptions, but a more critical point is why are the only exceptions in the social arena? One can read, for example, *The Challenge of Peace* as an almost tortuous and painful justification of deterrence policy that in fact is theoretically prohibited by Catholic doctrine because deterrence policy intends to do what is morally prohibited: the destruction of millions of innocent civilians, even though such deaths are alleged to be indirect. Why was there, for example, not a qualified condemnation of deterrence as suggested by Gordon Zahn rather than the qualified acceptance of it? Gordon Zahn suggested this in numerous conversations about *The Challenge of Peace*. The moral implications of deterrence theory are not softened by the qualified moral approval given it by the bishops. Clearly the methodology recognizes the complexity of the morality of deterrence and provides the best moral analysis it can while recognizing simultaneously that not all moral questions can be neatly resolved.

The situations of individuals and couples in relationships are also complicated, and their moral dilemmas also cannot be tied up neatly with deontological ribbons. We must begin to accept that such decisions are not made in a vacuum or a-contextually. People wrestle with their moral choices and seek to do what is morally correct. But such an outcome cannot be defined beforehand in an a priori method that eliminates moral evaluation and decision making. Otherwise we will live in a kind of moral schizophrenia that affirms that some areas of our lives are simply less morally significant than others.

The CEL, if it is to be viable, must address this methodological issue present in all discussions of moral issues in Catholicism today. If it remains focused only on the presumption of the inviolability of innocent life (which may also be a consequence of its being held hostage by the pro-life movement), a wide number of ethical issues will not be given the detailed analysis they demand. Some problems will clearly be off-limits, or those analyzing them will be dismissed as liberals or anti-life. In either event, the significance of these and similar problems will simply be marginalized. Problems will be approached from the perspective of theory rather than experience or context, and the status of the value of the common good may not receive the attention it deserves. The CEL needs also to focus on the realities of life in all its aspects, rather than have its primary mission to be consistent.

Interestingly, there is some movement in this direction in some of the CEL presentations, ironically in ones that have not been previously published. The most complete articulation of this is given in an address in 1988 to the Catholic Conference of Ohio. First, the cardinal identified three challenges: the technological challenge suggesting that our choices will be dictated by technology not human wisdom; the peace challenge asking how to keep peace when our weapons can destroy the whole of humanity; and the justice challenge of "how to build a society which provides the necessary material and moral support for every human being to realize his or her God-given dignity" (SG, 166). These challenges, for Bernardin, raise a broader challenge: "how to respond to multiple challenges under the guidance of a coherent moral vision" (SG, 166). For the cardinal this challenge also implies being linked to a community with a moral vision. The goal of the CEL is threefold: "The Consistent Ethic provides a framework within which a range of policy issues may be pursued in a coordinated fashion. It also provides a method for establishing priorities among these many issues. Finally, it provides a method for resolving conflicts at the tactical level when some issues are in conflict" (SG, 168). Consequently, the CEL has a role in public advocacy by coordinating a spectrum of issues, by providing a grid for evaluating political platforms and the positions of candidates, and by addressing broad policy issues that have a variety of specific moral concerns.

The cardinal recognized that given the pluralistic nature of our society, the move from moral analysis to public policy is complex. Additionally, given our Constitution, there is a legitimate secularity to this process, but this does not remove religious perspectives from the public debate. Additionally Bernardin acknowledged that "it is not the function of civil law to enjoin or prohibit *everything* that moral principles enjoin or prohibit" (SG, 182). What is required to generate a consensus, Bernardin argues, is a "process of debate, decision-making, then review of our decisions and their impact on human lives, including the most vulnerable among us" (SG, 183).

While Bernardin is careful to argue that in viewing the range of life issues, the CEL should not discourage attempts to eliminate abortion, he is careful to note that "many of us—men in particular—have not stepped back enough from the legal and political debate about abortion to be able to hear the real concerns, the trials, and the anguish of women who face life issues in a way that men never will" (SG, 187). This broadening of vision about a pro-life position is complemented in another address: "We are convinced that we cannot have a just and compassionate society unless our care extends to both sides of the line of birth: We must protect the basic right of unborn children to live and, at the same time, promote the associated basic human rights of nutrition, housing, and health care which enhance the lives we have saved" (SG, 202).

What is interesting is that while these comments are not inconsistent with underlying themes of the CEL, they are much more inclusive in scope and more similar to the methodology in *The Challenge of Peace*. And while continuing to affirm that abortion is the primary moral issue in the country, Bernardin also provides an additional moral framework—by explicitly focusing on the context of the women who have abortions. In these later, unpublished addresses, there is an interesting turn of analysis and vision. That turn strikes me as much truer to his original intent—and to the methodology he helped develop in *The Challenge of Peace*.

Conclusion

From the beginning of his addressing the CEL, Bernardin called for four dimensions of that consistency: a single principle with diverse applications, distinction among cases, relating commitment to principles to our public witness, and the relationship between moral principles and concrete political choices (SG, 18-20). In my evaluation, what is critical for the success of this approach is a consistent methodology across the range of cases. Bernardin wants a CEL that is governed by one principle that he argues is almost exceptionless—the protection of innocent human life. This principle is problematic on several levels. It is a presupposition; the status of the embryo is subject to moral debate; and, when the principle is applied socially, the complexities of the circumstances tend to diminish the clarity of the principle and its precise application. On the other hand, if we seek a CEL that is consistent methodologically, one will be more attentive to the social and political context of the choices, the nuanced way in which one's moral principles help negotiate a resolution of the moral landscape, and a more coherent vision of the moral life. Granted that in this position principles are not privileged a priori, but if we move in this direction and recognize the historicity and contextuality of moral analysis, we might come closer to realizing the four above-mentioned goals that Bernardin articulated because all moral problems will be approached equally and evaluated with a methodology that appreciates the complexity of the issues and their resolution. I would, therefore, suggest a shift in emphasis to a consistent ethic of justice. Such a move would address two issues. First, the focus on the individual or individual case currently thought to be resolved by deontological principles would shift to see that case embedded in a social context. Second, the common good could be raised as a significant factor in moral evaluation. This move seems in harmony with the methodology of *The Challenge of Peace* and the direction taken in the unpublished lectures of Bernardin.

One of the main consequences of the Human Genome Project with its spin-offs in research and clinical applications has been a focus on the individual or the individual genotype. Given that the intent of gene therapy is to either reverse the effects of a genetic disease in an individual or prevent such effects in the individual and his or her descendants, that is what we would expect. And this individual orientation is at the heart of the debate over cloning human embryos to be used in therapy. The purpose is to develop stem cells from the patient so that when they are reinserted, they will not be rejected—truly a therapy custom designed for the individual. To attempt to resolve this issue solely on the basis of the personhood of the embryo stays within the individualistic framework of the therapy itself.

A social justice approach would begin by questioning the goals of genetic medicine, its place in the current health-care system, its costs, and its effectiveness. It would also raise the issue of the common good with respect to developing these kinds of therapies. Are these the diseases on which to focus, or are there other diseases that have more social consequences or are more socially significant? Additionally a justice approach would challenge the focus on genes in isolation from the environment. If one mistakenly assumes that all diseases are genetic in origin, then the individual is the cause of his or her illness and the environment has no role in one's health status. This approach could be very critical of current directions in genetic medicine and helpful in resolving some critical health-care problems.

If one remains in the deontological mode implied by earlier versions of the CEL, questions such as the ones posed here tend not to be addressed because the initial focus and energy are on the status of the embryo. While that question is not unimportant, to make it the primary question, the first question, or the center of the moral analysis starts the analysis in the wrong place. If one begins with justice questions or with the social context, as exemplified in Patricia Beattie Jung's chapter in this volume, one will also examine the context of the question and how that context affects the common good. Within that framework, other questions can then be examined. Additionally, starting with the justice question may in fact result in more people joining the conversation.[24] This approach may thus generate a common ground from which other moral analyses can occur, such as examination of the moral status of the embryo. Also the justice/common-good approach could generate an argument that individually tailored therapies should not have priority; rather the focus should be on therapies that serve the common good. The outcome may be the same, but one has not argued the case based on the personhood of the fetus. One could also argue the case for genetic medicine as part of a package of different approaches to public health and here, for the sake of the benefit of the common good, one might argue for the use of early human embryos as part of the development of that orientation. Here one would have to carefully argue the case for the common good in relation to the status of the embryo, but one would contextualize this argument in a way that might be open to more dialogue.

The CEL, as positive a contribution as it is, is limited, ultimately, by its reflecting the methodological divide in U.S. Catholicism—deontological vs. social justice—and by being held hostage by the power of the pro-life movement that defines certain questions off-limits or as not part of the pro-life agenda. Ultimately the deontological approach in the CEL trumps many other questions and analyses and effectively ends the debate before other critical issues can be considered. Beginning with a social justice analysis will bring more people into the conversation, will be more inclusive in its analysis, and will provide a framework in which all questions will have a fair hearing. Thus, I suggest we shift from a consistent ethic of life to a consistent ethic of justice.

NOTES

Introduction

[1]On August 25, 1983, Archbishop Bernardin was installed as archbishop of Chicago, and the following February he was elevated to the College of Cardinals.

[2]For a history of the development of the pastoral letter, see Jim Castelli, *The Bishops and the Bomb: Waging Peace in a Nuclear Age* (Garden City, N.Y.: Image Books, 1983).

[3]The Gannon Lecture Series had begun three years earlier in 1980 and was named in honor of Rev. Robert I. Gannon, S.J., president of Fordham University from 1936 to 1949. The purpose of the series was to bring distinguished individuals to Fordham University to deliver public lectures on topics of their expertise. This series continues to the present.

[4]See National Conference of Catholic Bishops, *The Challenge of Peace: God's Promise and Our Response* (Washington, DC: United States Catholic Conference, 1983), §§ 285-87.

[5]Humberto Medeiros, "A Call to a Consistent Ethic of Life and the Law," *Pilot*, July 10, 1971, 7. For a brief description of this statement, see Richard A. McCormick, *Notes on Moral Theology 1965 through 1980* (Washington, D.C.: University Press of America, 1981), 399.

[6]McCormick, *Notes on Moral Theology*, 399.

[7]Kenneth A. Briggs, "Bernardin Asks Catholics to Fight Both Nuclear Arms and Abortion," *The New York Times*, December 7, 1983, 1.

[8]Spilly, vol. 1, xxii.

[9]Joseph Bernardin, *The Gift of Peace* (Chicago: Loyola Press, 1997).

1. What Does Horizon Analysis Bring to the Consistent Ethic of Life?
James J. Walter

[1]See David Tracy, *The Achievement of Bernard Lonergan* (New York: Herder and Herder, 1970), 8.

[2]For examples where Bernardin describes the consistent ethic as a "vision," see SG, 16-20, 28-31, 35-39, 41-46, 49-55, 103-8, 118-21, 137-41, 149-53, 166-71, 182, 187, 191-99, 202-3, 213-14, 260-65, and 290-99. Martin Kenny, in his licentiate dissertation at Weston Jesuit School of Theology, also claims that Bernardin's consistent ethic attempted to develop a "moral vision." See Martin Kenny, "A Critique of Joseph Cardinal Bernardin's Proposal of the Consistent Ethic of Life" (licentiate diss. in sacred theology at Weston Jesuit School of Theology, 1997), 20. Also, see chap. 2 of this volume, where Ronald Hamel discusses in depth Bernardin's notion of "vision."

[3]For examples of the consistent ethic as a "framework," see SG, 50-54, 73-76, 104-8, 118, 151-53, 168-70, 180-87, 250, 264, 276, and 289-96.

[4]For examples, see ibid., 109-16 and 117-24.

[5]Almost every page of Cardinal Bernardin's speeches makes reference to the necessity for "consistency" in the ethic that he proposes.

[6]For example, see SG, 102-8 and 117-24. Also, see chap. 3 of this volume, where Thomas Nairn discusses Bernardin's understanding of moral analogy.

[7]Though Bernardin does not use the word "dialogical" to describe his stance, this word certainly renders his intent to "cast our case in broadly defined terms, in a way which elicits support from others." For examples, see SG, 21-25 and 117-24. In addition, Bernardin's constant reference to culture and what is going on in culture not only indicates that cultural facts are relevant to his analysis at the level of the object pole, but these references also clearly manifest his desire to dialogue with various groups within society.

[8]See Bernard Lonergan, *Method in Theology* (New York: Herder and Herder, 1972), 235-44.

[9]These models are based on David Tracy, *Blessed Rage for Order: The New Pluralism in Theology* (New York: Seabury Press, 1975), 24-63.

[10]See Matthew Lamb, *Solidarity with Victims: Toward a Theology of Social Transformation* (New York: Crossroad, 1982), 61-99, and Francis Schüssler Fiorenza, *Foundational Theology: Jesus and the Church* (New York: Crossroad, 1984), 5-55.

[11]Lamb, *Solidarity*, 62.

[12]For a more complete discussion of the stances that have been proposed within the Christian traditions, see James Sellers, *Theological Ethics* (New York: Macmillan, 1966), 31-68.

[13]Adolf von Harnack, *What Is Christianity?* trans. T. B. Saunders (New York: Harper and Brothers, 1957), 70-74.

[14]Karl Barth, *Church Dogmatics*, II/2, trans. G. W. Bromiley et al. (Edinburgh: T. and T. Clark, 1957), 509-49.

[15]Sellers, *Theological Ethics*, 55-65.

[16]Charles E. Curran, "The Stance of Moral Theology," in *New Perspectives in Moral Theology* (Notre Dame, IN: Fides, 1974), 47-86.

[17]See SG, 85-90, 102-8, 117-24.

[18]See in particular chap. 3 of this volume in which Thomas Nairn analyzes Bernardin's notion of "analogy."

[19]See SG, 102-8. Though the analogical character of Bernardin's vision is present, albeit implicitly, throughout all his speeches, he begins to make explicit reference to it only in his later speeches.

[20]For example, see ibid., 15-20. Bernardin also uses his vision as a way (heuristic device) for testing public policies, party platforms, and candidates. See ibid., 15-20, 102-8, and 117-24.

[21]See ibid., 102-8 and 117-24.

[22]See ibid., 117-24.

[23]Ibid.

[24]See National Conference of Catholic Bishops, *The Challenge of Peace: God's Promise and Our Response* (Washington, DC: United States Catholic Conference, 1983), especially the footnotes to part 2: "War and Peace in the Modern World: Problems and Principles," 39-62.

[25]I have utilized some of the material in this chapter that I originally wrote for a "Consistent Ethic of Life" symposium at Loyola University Chicago. That original material was published as "Response to John Finnis: A Theological Critique," in Thomas G. Fuechtmann, ed., *Consistent Ethic of Life* (Kansas City, MO: Sheed and Ward, 1988), 182-95.

2. The Consistent Ethic of Life: A Corrective Moral Vision for Health Care
Ronald P. Hamel

[1]Cardinal Joseph Bernardin, "Making the Case for Not-For-Profit Health-care," in *Celebrating the Ministry of Healing: Joseph Cardinal Bernardin's Reflections on Healthcare* (St. Louis: Catholic Health Association, 1999), 83.

[2]William F. May first used this expression in his book, *The Physician's Covenant* (Philadelphia: Westminster Press, 1983), in order to describe the task of ethics. By "vision," he meant insight, illumination of understanding as one of the primary tasks of ethics. But in providing insight, ethics is also "corrective." It does not merely describe the world as it is, but "challenges . . . the world distorted through the bias of institutional structures or through the prism of human imperfection and vice" (13-14). In its stead ethics offers "a knowledgeable re-visioning of foundations and ends," "a fresh and liberating vision of the world," one that enables change in behavior (15).

Stanley Hauerwas, among others, also employs the concept of "vision." In the Introduction to his book, *Vision and Virtue*, he writes:

> We are as we come to see and as that seeing becomes enduring in our intentionality. We do not come to see, however, just by looking but by training our vision through the metaphors and symbols that constitute our central convictions. How we come to see therefore is a function of how we come to be since our seeing is necessarily determined by how our basic images are embodied by the self—i.e., in our character. Christian ethics is the conceptual discipline that analyzes and imaginatively tests the images most appropriate to score the Christian life in accordance with the central conviction that the world has been redeemed by the work and person of Christ. (2)

A bit later Hauerwas writes,

> The moral life is fundamentally the life of vision, for the task is to see accurately the nature of the world, self, and others without illusion. . . . Such truthful vision, however, does not come without discipline. The self must be transformed if we are to attend honestly to how we are to live justly in a contingent world (2).

See Hauerwas, "Introduction," in *Vision and Virtue* (Notre Dame, IN: Fides Publishers, 1974), 1-8. See also "The Significance of Vision: Toward an Aesthetic Ethic" in the same volume, 30-47.

[3]The term "corrective moral vision," as used in this essay, is akin to James Walter's use of "ethical stance" in the previous chapter of this volume. Walter defines ethical stance as "a coherent combination of value judgments about the world, God, and self" (see p. 9 above).

[4]See SG, 7-14, 15-20, and 102-8.

[5]Bernardin's emphasis on human dignity is very strong in two of his addresses in particular. The first predates his first consistent ethic of life lecture by nine months; see Joseph L. Bernardin, "Ethical Dimensions of Healthcare Administration," in *Celebrating the Ministry of Healing: Joseph Cardinal Bernardin's Reflections on Healthcare* (St. Louis: Catholic Healthcare Association, 1999), 1-8. Here he points out that religion and health care share a "singleminded commitment to the dignity and worth of human persons" (2). This commitment must constitute the "energizing vision of healthcare" in contrast to a utilitarian view of the person. Hu-

man persons, he argues, ". . . are the one stable element in terms of which all other judgments are made. The dignity and value of human persons is a basic value, not to be traded against some other values, not to be entered in some subtle calculus that seeks the greatest good for the greatest number" (4).

The second address occurs almost a year after the first consistent ethic of life lecture: "A Vision of the Human Person and Ethical Choices," in *Celebrating the Ministry of Healing*, 19-26. Here Bernardin delineates two visions of the human person—a pragmatic humanism and a personalist humanism—maintaining that it is the latter that must underlie ethical choices in medicine.

[6]Bernardin, "Ethical Dimensions of Healthcare Administration," 19-26; "Medicine and Religion: Toward Healing and Peace," in *Celebrating the Ministry of Healing*, 9-18.

[7]It is interesting that Bernardin would employ this division. It reflects the typical division in Catholic moral theology between medical/sexual issues and social issues. The methodologies employed in the two domains are very different. This is often seen as problematic as evidenced by several essays in this volume, particularly that by Patricia Jung. Although he advocated a consistent ethic, Bernardin was never able to bridge the two methodologies.

[8]For further discussion, see Bernardin's "Ethical Dimensions of Healthcare Administration," 1-8, and "A Vision of the Human Person and Ethical Choices," 19-26.

[9]In his refocusing from "who decides" to "what is being decided about," Bernardin seems to limit the "what" to fetal life when one might argue that the "what" also includes the mother and the fullness of her situation. Bernardin does go on to speak about the plight of women who seek an abortion, but, again, that does not seem to enter into the "what."

[10]For a discussion of how Bernardin proposes this will be paid for, see SG, 246.

[11]For further development, see SG, 246-47.

[12]Bernardin, "Making the Case for Not-For-Profit Healthcare," 86.

[13]Ibid., 84.

[14]Ibid., 86.

[15]Ibid., 87.

[16]Ibid., 86.

[17]Ibid., 87.

[18]Ibid., 88.

[19]Ibid. See also Bernardin, "The Challenges Facing Catholic Healthcare Ministry," 97-98.

[20]Richard McCormick is one among several moral theologians who question the traditional interpretation of the principle that forbids direct killing of the innocent. See Richard A. McCormick, "The Consistent Ethic of Life: Is There an Historical Soft Underbelly?" in *Consistent Ethic of Life*, 96-122, and Lisa Sowle Cahill, "The 'Seamless Garment': Life in Its Beginnings," *Theological Studies* 46 (March 1985): 64-74, esp. 70ff.

[21]Richard A. McCormick, *Corrective Vision: Explorations in Moral Theology* (Kansas City, MO: Sheed & Ward, 1994), vii. McCormick borrows the phrase from May, *Physician's Covenant*.

[22]Although not discussed in this essay, one of the important pieces of Bernardin's consistent ethic of life is the need for dialogue. There is a sense in which Ber-

nardin sees this as one of the key strategies for individual, institutional, and social change. For him, learning goes both ways. See, for example, SG, 14 and 107-8.

[23]Interestingly, Cardinal Bernardin's final word on health care, his pastoral letter *A Sign of Hope*, does not directly address the consistent ethic of life, though undoubtedly his perspectives in the pastoral were shaped by the consistent ethic.

3. The Consistent Ethic of Life as Moral Analogy
Thomas A. Nairn, O.F.M.

[1]See Albert Jonsen and Stephen Toulmin, *The Abuse of Casuistry: A History of Moral Reasoning* (Berkeley: University of California Press, 1988), 252.

[2]David Burrell, *Analogy and Philosophical Language* (New Haven, Conn.: Yale University Press, 1973), 243.

[3]See George Klubertanz, *St. Thomas Aquinas on Analogy: A Textual Analysis and Systematic Synthesis* (Chicago: Loyola University Press, 1960), 116-45.

[4]Ralph McInerny, *Aquinas and Analogy* (Washington, DC: Catholic University of America Press, 1996), 128-29.

[5]Ibid., 8.

[6]Ibid., 128.

[7]Klubertanz, *St. Thomas Aquinas on Analogy,* 117.

[8]Ibid., 126.

[9]Ibid.

[10]Jonsen and Toulmin, *Abuse of Casuistry*, 252. The authors are quoting Gabriel Daniel, *Entretiens de Cléanthet Eudoxe* (1694), 358.

[11]David Tracy, *The Analogical Imagination: Christian Theology and the Culture of Pluralism* (New York: Crossroad, 1981), 408.

[12]Ibid.

[13]William Spohn, *Go and Do Likewise: Jesus and Ethics* (New York: Continuum, 1999), 55.

[14]Jonsen and Toulmin, *Abuse of Casuistry*, passim.

[15]Ibid., 66.

[16]Ibid., 252.

[17]Ibid., 256.

[18]Ibid., 322.

[19]Aristotle, *Nicomachean Ethics* 2.2.1104a.

[20]See Thomas Aquinas, *Summa theologiae* 1-2, q.94, a.4.

[21]See Burrell, *Analogy*, 243.

[22]Ibid., 30.

[23]Ibid.

[24]Ibid., 23.

[25]Ibid., 242.

[26]Ibid., 243.

[27]Ibid.

[28]Ibid.

[29]Ibid., 250.

[30]Ibid.

[31]Ibid., 249.

[32]James Keenan, "The Return of Casuistry," *Theological Studies* 57, no. 1 (March 1996): 127.

[33]Albert Jonsen, "Of Balloons and Bicycles—or—The Relationship between Ethical Theory and Practical Judgment," *Hastings Center Report* 21, no. 5 (September-October 1991): 16.

[34]See Richard McCormick, "Notes on Moral Theology," *Theological Studies* 46, no. 1 (March 1985): 50-52.

[35]See, for example, the interview of Cardinal Bernardin by Charles Isenhart in the *National Catholic Register*, June 12, 1988.

[36]For a further treatment of this understanding, see Patricia Beattie Jung's treatment in chap. 5.

[37]See Christine Gudorf, "To Make a Seamless Garment, Use a Single Piece of Cloth," in Patricia Beattie Jung and Thomas A. Shannon, eds., *Abortion and Catholicism: The American Debate* (New York: Crossroad, 1988), 294. Such questions take the issue of abortion out of its usual context, with the usual slogans, and help re-frame the many issues involved.

[38]Stephen Toulmin, "The Tyranny of Principles," *Hastings Center Report* 11, no. 6 (December 1981): 38.

[39]See Jonsen and Toulmin, *Abuse of Casuistry*, 252.

[40]Burrell, *Analogy*, 243.

[41]Ibid.

[42]Cardinal Bernardin used this formulation twice before in his lectures, in his 1986 address to the Consistent Ethic of Life Conference (SG, 118) and in an address to the Good Friday Club in Chicago in 1989 (SG, 181).

[43]For a fuller discussion of Cardinal Bernardin's understanding of respect, see Elisabeth Brinkmann's analysis in chap. 6 of this volume.

[44]Actually, the cardinal used the term once in 1987, when he responded to a symposium of scholars assembled at Loyola University in Chicago. At that time, however, he hinted at the reason he discontinued using the term: "While the phrase 'the consistent ethic' . . . seems to resonate with the ethical instincts of many Catholics, its systematic and analogical nature makes it difficult for individuals to apply it consciously or reflexively in their civic and political choices" (SG, 145).

[45]Burrell, *Analogy*, 24.

4. Virtues, Principles, and a Consistent Ethic of Life
James F. Keenan, S.J.

[1]William Frankena, *Ethics*, 2nd ed. (Englewood Cliffs, N.J.: Prentice Hall, 1973), 65. See also Frankena, *Thinking about Morality* (Ann Arbor: University of Michigan Press, 1980), 55, 89-93.

[2]Bruno Schüller, "The Debate on the Specific Character of Christian Ethics," *Readings in Moral Theology, No. 2* (New York: Paulist Press, 1980), 207-33.

[3]James Gaffney, "On Paranesis and Fundamental Moral Theology," *Journal of Religious Ethics* 11 (1983): 23-34.

[4]Alasdair MacIntyre, *After Virtue* (Notre Dame, Ind.: University of Notre Dame Press, 1981).

[5]William Bennett, *The Book of Virtues* (New York: Simon and Schuster, 1993).

[6]Stanley Hauerwas, *A Community of Character* (Notre Dame, Ind.: University of Notre Dame Press, 1981).

[7]Peter Geach, *The Virtues* (Cambridge: Cambridge University Press, 1977).

[8]Gilbert Meilaender, *The Theory and Practice of Virtue* (Notre Dame, Ind.: University of Notre Dame Press, 1984).

[9]Jean Porter, *The Recovery of Virtue* (Louisville, Ky.: Westminster/John Knox Press, 1990).

[10]Diana Fritz Cates, *Choosing to Feel: Virtue, Friendship, and Compassion for Friends* (Notre Dame, Ind.: University of Notre Dame Press, 1997).

[11]Joseph Kotva, *The Christian Case for Virtue Ethics* (Washington, D.C.: Georgetown University Press, 1996).

[12]Anne Patrick, *Liberating Conscience: Feminist Explorations in Catholic Moral Theology* (New York: Continuum, 1996).

[13]William Spohn, *Go and Do Likewise: Jesus and Ethics* (New York: Continuum, 1999).

[14]Courtney Campbell, "Principlism and Religion: The Law and the Prophets," in *A Matter of Principles*, ed. Edwin Dubose, Ron Hamel, and Laurence O'Connell (Valley Forge, Pa.: Trinity Press International, 1994), 182-208; Marcio Fabri dos Anjos, "Bioethics in a Liberationist Key," in Dubose et al., *A Matter of Principles*, 130-47.

[15]Tom Beauchamp and Ed Shelp, eds., *Virtue and Medicine* (Boston: D. Reidel, 1985).

[16]David Solomon, "Internal Objections to Virtue Ethics," in *Midwest Studies in Philosophy, Volume 13: Ethical Theory, Character and Virtue*, ed. Peter French et al. (Notre Dame, Ind.: University of Notre Dame Press, 1988), 428-41.

[17]James J. Walter also prompts us to read Bernardin's contributions in light of a basic stance, that is, a vision that *precedes* norms, in chap. 1 of this volume. Bernardin himself weighed in on the relationship between virtues and norms: "It is a person's good character that produces practical moral decisions based on beliefs, experience and sensitivity, more than on rules and principles" (Joseph Bernardin, "Why Virtues Are Basic to the Common Good," *Origins* 23, no. 19 [October 21, 1993], 337, 339-41, at 340).

[18]In his work regarding the Common Ground Project and the pastorals, "The Challenge of Peace" and "Economic Justice for All," Bernardin often turned to virtues, particularly civility and hope. On civility: "Our style of religious witness should constantly be a testimony to the theological virtue of charity, which, in turn, produces the civic virtue of civility" (Joseph Bernardin, "The Catholic Moral Vision in the United States," in *Joseph Cardinal Bernardin: A Moral Vision for America*, ed. John Langan [Washington, D.C.: Georgetown University Press, 1998], 144-57, at 149; see also in that volume Bernardin, "Religion and Politics," 48-59). He invoked hope in the peace pastoral, arguing it was the virtue he was most frequently to summon; see Spilly, vol. 1, 85-86, 576; 2:20, 53.

[19]James F. Keenan, "There Are No Private Lives," *Josephinum* 3 (1996): 76-84.

[20]James Drane, "Character and the Moral Life," in Dubose et al., *A Matter of Principles*, 284-309.

[21]James F. Keenan, "Proposing Cardinal Virtues," *Theological Studies* 56, no. 4 (1995): 709-29.

[22]Joseph Kotva, "An Appeal for a Christian Virtue Ethic," *Thought* 67, no. 265 (June 1992): 158-80.

[23]Lawrence Solum, "Virtue Jurisprudence, A Virtue-Centered Theory of Judging," *Metaphilosophy* 34 (2003): 178-213, at 178 and 184, respectively. In many

ways these claims are in concert with Thomas Aquinas's writings on prudence; see James F. Keenan, "The Virtue of Prudence (IIa IIae 47-56)," in *The Ethics of Aquinas*, ed. Stephen Pope (Washington, D.C.: Georgetown University Press, 2002), 259-71. See also Pamela Hal, *Narrative and the Natural Law: An Interpretation of Thomistic Ethics* (Notre Dame, Ind.: University of Notre Dame Press, 1994), 39ff.

[24]James F. Keenan, "Virtue and Identity," in *Creating Identity: Biographical, Moral, Religious* (*Concilium* 2000/2), ed. Hermann Häring, Maureen Junker-Kenny, and Dietmar Mieth (London: SCM Press, 2000), 69-77. I cannot here discuss the important debate between Jean Porter and Lisa Sowle Cahill: Jean Porter, "The Search for a Global Ethic," *Theological Studies* 62 (2001): 105-22; "A Tradition of Civility: The Natural Law as a Tradition of Moral Inquiry," *Scottish Journal of Theology* 56 (2003): 27-48; Lisa Sowle Cahill, "Toward Global Ethics," *Theological Studies* 63 (2002): 324-44. Whereas I agree with Porter about the way norms and principles originally are articulated, I think that this does not preclude the question of universal claims.

[25]James F. Keenan, "Parenting and the Virtue of Prudence," *Church* 10, no. 1 (1994): 40-42. See also Keenan, *Virtues for Ordinary Christians* (Kansas City: Sheed and Ward, 1996).

[26]See Florence Caffrey Bourg, *Where Two or Three Are Gathered: Christian Families as Domestic Churches* (Notre Dame, Ind.: University of Notre Dame Press, 2004).

[27]See here the important essay by Elisabeth Brinkmann, chap. 6 of this volume.

[28]Here again we see the relevance of James Walter's contribution in chap. 1 of this volume.

[29]"For the man of good character judges every situation rightly; i.e., in every situation what appears to him is the truth. Every disposition has its own appreciation of what is fine and pleasant; and probably what makes the man of good character stand out furthest is the fact that he sees the truth in every kind of situation: he is a sort of standard and yardstick" (Aristotle, *Nicomachean Ethics* 3.1113a12-34).

[30]Joseph Mangan, "An Historical Analysis of the Principle of Double Effect," *Theological Studies* 10 (1949): 41-61. Erroneously, Beauchamp and James Childress claim Thomas as the original proponent of the principle in *Principles of Biomedical Ethics*, 185.

[31]Josef Ghoos, "L'Acte à double effet, etude de théologie positive," *Ephemerides Theologicae Lovanienses* 27 (1951): 30-52.

[32]John Kekes, *The Examined Life* (Lewisburg, Pa.: Bucknell University Press, 1988).

[33]Martha Nussbaum, *The Fragility of Goodness: Luck and Ethics in Greek Tragedy and Philosophy* (New York: Cambridge University Press, 1986), 299.

[34]Martha Nussbaum, "Non-Relative Virtues: An Aristotelian Approach," in *Midwest Studies in Philosophy*, 44.

[35]Albert Jonsen and Stephen Toulmin, *The Abuse of Casuistry* (Berkeley: University of California Press, 1988), 54.

[36]James F. Keenan, "The Concept of Sanctity of Life and Its Use in Contemporary Bioethical Discussion," in *Sanctity of Life and Human Dignity*, ed. Kurt Bayertz (Dordrecht: Kluwer Academics, 1996), 1-18.

[37]Thomas Slater, *A Manual of Moral Theology I* (New York: Benziger Brothers, 1908), 302. The ownership of life issues was raised again in considering "muti-

lation" of self (at 303): "As we have not the ownership of life, so neither are we the owners of our limbs." Slater's stance was repeated throughout modern times. For instance, at the beginning of his presentation on the Fifth Commandment, Henry Davis wrote forty years later about the duty to preserve life: "By Natural law, man enjoys the use not the dominion of his life. He neither gave it nor may he take it away. God only is the author of life" (Henry Davis, *Moral and Pastoral Theology II* [London: Sheed and Ward, 1945], 141).

[38]Pope Pius XI, *Encyclical Letter on Christian Marriage* (Boston: St. Paul Editions, 1930), 32. Commenting on this encyclical, the Redemptorist moralist Augustine Regan added, "His successor Pius XII made many pronouncements and statements during his long pontificate. . . . He reiterates as a constant refrain that man is not the author, and consequently is never the master, of human life, which is entrusted to him as its administrator. Therefore, it is always wrong for him to dispose of it as though he were its owner. In particular it can never be justified to attack directly the life of any innocent human being" (Augustine Regan, *Thou Shalt Not Kill* [Dublin: Mercier Press, 1977], 29).

[39]In more contemporary teachings the same position is found. In the *Declaration on Euthanasia*, suicide like murder "is to be considered a rejection of God's sovereignty and loving plan" (Sacred Congregation for the Doctrine of the Faith, "Declaration on Euthanasia," in *Vatican Council II: More Post-Conciliar Documents*, ed. Austin Flannery [Northport, N.Y.: Costello Publishing, 1982], 510-17, at 512). Gerald Coleman sums up the tradition well, "Human persons, then, have only a right to the use of human life, not to dominion over human life. What makes killing forbidden is that it usurps a divine prerogative and violates divine rights" (Gerald Coleman, "Assisted Suicide: An Ethical Perspective," in *Euthanasia*, ed. Robert Baird and Stuart Rosenbaum [Buffalo, N.Y.: Prometheus Books, 1989], 103-9, at 108). Many of the above authors added two basic distinctions. First, only the direct taking of human life usurped God's authority; some indirect instances (indirect abortion, dangerous pain relief, etc.) were clearly considered permitted. Moreover, since there were sanctioned instances of self-defense and, in the history of capital punishment, similar instances of execution, the prohibition protected innocent human life. To directly take innocent human life was to violate God's prerogative and rights.

[40]Paragraph 194: "All must regard the life of man as sacred, since from its inception, it requires the action of God the Creator. Those who depart from this plan of God not only offend His divine majesty and dishonor themselves and the human race, but they also weaken the inner fibre of the commonwealth" (Pope John XXIII, *Mater et Magistra*, in *Gospel of Peace and Justice*, ed. Joseph Gremillion [Maryknoll, N.Y.: Orbis, 1976], 143-201, at 184-85). This phrase became key in *Humanae vitae* (13). There Pope Paul VI used it to affirm the limited dominion that the human has over human life and human generativity. Again, in its early use in papal encyclicals the phrase only emphasized divine prerogative.

[41]Richard Gula writes, "Closely related to the principles of sanctity and sovereignty is the divine law prohibiting killing as found in the fifth commandment" (*Euthanasia* [New York: Paulist Press, 1994], 26).

[42]See Joseph Boyle, "Sanctity of Life and Suicide: Tensions and Developments within Common Morality," in *Suicide and Euthanasia*, ed. Baruch Brody (Boston: Kluwer Academics, 1989), 221-50.

[43]Aquinas underlined this positivistic nature of "sanctity." In distinguishing one meaning of sanctity as purity, he wrote of the other, "it denotes firmness, where-

fore in older times the term *sancta* was applied to such things as were upheld by law and were not to be violated. Hence a thing is said to be sacred when it is ratified by law" (II-II 81, 8c).

[44]John Paul II, "Christifideles laici," *Origins* 18, no. 35 (1989): 561, 563-89, at 579.

[45]Congregation for the Doctrine of the Faith, *Instruction on the Respect for Human Life in Its Origin and on the Dignity of Procreation,* Introduction, para 5.

[46]See James F. Keenan, "The Moral Argumentation of *Evangelium vitae,*" in *Choosing Life: A Dialogue on Evangelium vitae,* ed. Kevin Wildes (Washington, D.C.: Georgetown University Press, 1997), 46-62; Keenan, "History, Roots and Innovations: A Response to the Engaging Protestants," in *Ecumenical Ventures in Ethics: Protestants Engage Pope John Paul II's Moral Encyclicals,* ed. Reinhard Hutter and Theodor Dieter (Grand Rapids: Eerdmans, 1997), 262-88.

[47]Pope John Paul II, *Evangelium vitae, Origins* 24, no. 42 (April 6, 1995): 689, 691-727. In the encyclical a certain tension between these two interests develops. On the one hand human life has something intrinsic to it that makes it in itself inviolable; on the other hand that which it has it derives from God the Creator who is Lord of life. Thus, a new argument for preserving life, the intrinsic worth of the human, is used to "bolster" the "Lord of life" argument, *and* as a result the Lord of life becomes less a declaration of God's sovereignty and prerogatives and more a description of the Creator. In *Evangelium vitae* (53), these two play in tandem: "God proclaims that he is absolute Lord of the life of man, who is formed in his image and likeness (cf. GN. 1:26-28). Human life is thus given a sacred and inviolable character, which reflects the inviolability of God." Here clearly human life has *in se* an inviolable character.

Moreover, while the "Lord of life" argument recurs repeatedly, it is always asserted in relationship to God's investment into human life: "Man's life comes from God; it is his gift, his image and imprint, a sharing in his breath of life. God therefore is the sole Lord of this life: Man cannot do with it as he wills" (39); "In the depths of his conscience, man is always reminded of the inviolability of life—his own life and that of others—as something that does not belong to him, because it is the property and gift of God the Creator and Father" (40); "To kill a human being, in whom the image of God is present, is a particularly serious sin. Only God is the master of life!" (55).

Still, the inviolability of life is never extrinsic to human nature as it was in the "traditional" position. Thus, "Life is indelibly marked by a truth of its own" (48). The Vatican summary highlights this: "The light of revelation, which reaches its fulness in Jesus Christ, confirms and completes all that human reason can grasp concerning the value of human life. Precious and fragile, full of promises and threatened by suffering and death, man's life bears within itself that seed of immortal life planted by the Creator in the human heart" ("The Vatican's Summary of *Evangelium vitae,*" *Origins* 24, no. 42 [1995]: 728-30, at 729).

[48]Early, in "Celebrate Life," the pope quoted from his address in Poland, "The Church defends the right to life, not only in regard to the majesty of the Creator, who is the first giver of this life, but also in respect of the essential good of the human person" (Pope John Paul II, "Celebrate Life," *The Pope Speaks* 24, no. 4 [1979]: 371-74, at 372). The essential good of the person emerges more clearly as the years of his pontificate advance. Often it appears in language regarding the sanctity of life.

[49]See para. 35. Of course, for John Paul II all of this must be understood by

locating not only the source of this initiative in God, but the end as well. "The plan of life given to the first Adam finds at last its fulfillment in Christ (35)." By Christ's blood (9, 25) we are both strengthened and given the ground of hope that God's plan will be victorious. In fact, in that piercing by which Christ gives up his spirit, he gives us his spirit; by his death he gives us life: "It is the very life of God which is now shared with man. (51)" Eternal life, the life that we are destined for, is "a sharing in the life of God himself, (52)" "therefore the life of God himself and at the same time the life of the children of God. (38)" Thus, though "this supernatural calling highlights the relative character of each individual's earthly life," our earthly lives "remain a sacred reality . . . (2)." Because of its origin and destiny, human life remains from its very beginning until its end sacred. For this reason, "The life which the Son of God came to give to human beings cannot be reduced to mere existence in time. (37, see 34)" Thus, the life which God bestows on us, through Creation, Redemption, and the Promise "is a drive toward fullness of life; it is the seed of an existence which transcends the very limits of time. (34)"

[50]"Vatican's Summary of *Evangelium vitae*," 729.

[51]On development in moral principles, see Thomas Kopfensteiner, "Science, Metaphor and Moral Casuistry," in *Context of Casuistry*, 207-20; John T. Noonan Jr., "Development in Moral Doctrine," in *Context of Casuistry*, 188-204; Marciano Vidal, "Progress in the Moral Tradition," in *Catholic Ethicists on HIV/AIDS Prevention*, ed. James Keenan, assisted by Lisa Sowle Cahill, Jon Fuller, and Kevin Kelly (New York: Continuum, 2000), 257-70; Raphael Gallagher, "Catholic Medical Ethics: A Tradition Which Progresses," in *Catholic Ethicists on HIV/AIDS Prevention*, 271-81.

[52]Despite my insistence that only those so disposed will seek the necessary consistency, the next question that arises is: what really is entailed by "consistency"? Answering that question is a very demanding challenge, as Patricia Beattie Jung demonstrates in chap. 5 of this volume.

[53]Bernardin showed considerable interest in the virtue of solidarity as a foundational virtue that helped define specific moral responsibility: "Solidarity implies a fabric of moral bonds that exists among humans because of a shared sense of personhood. . . . It also helps to define the moral responsibility of the state and its citizenry" (Bernardin, "Catholic Moral Vision," 153).

[54]James F. Keenan, *Moral Wisdom: Lessons and Texts from the Catholic Tradition* (Lanham, Md.: Sheed and Ward, 2004); Keenan, *The Works of Mercy: The Heart of Catholicism* (Lanham, Md.: Sheed and Ward, 2004).

[55]Margaret Farley, "Ethics, Ecclesiology, and the Grace of Self-Doubt," in *A Call to Fidelity: On the Moral Theology of Charles E. Curran*, ed. James J. Walter, Timothy E. O'Connell, and Thomas A. Shannon (Washington, D.C.: Georgetown University Press, 2002), 55-76.

[56]I want to thank Dan Daly and Stephen Pope, who helped me on several occasions to think through the relationship between virtues and norms.

5. Constructing a Consistent Ethic of Life: Feminist Contributions to Its Foundation
Patricia Beattie Jung

[1]Sidney Callahan, "Abortion and the Sexual Agenda: A Case for Pro-Life Feminism," *Commonweal*, April 25, 1986, 232-38.

[2]John Paul II, *The Gospel of Life,* 56. While the encyclical maintains the hypothetical justifiability of capital punishment, the Roman Catholic Church now teaches that executions can no longer be justified in modern societies virtually without exception.

[3]Susan L. Secker, "Human Experience and Women's Experience: Resources for Catholic Ethics," in *Readings in Moral Theology No. 8: Dialogue about Catholic Sexual Teaching,* ed. Charles E. Curran and Richard A. McCormick, S.J. (New York: Paulist Press, 1993), 577-99.

[4]John Paul II, "On the Dignity and Vocation of Women," 14.

[5]John Paul II, *The Gospel of Life,* 58-59.

[6]Ibid., 58 (italics in original).

[7]Secker, "Human Experience and Women's Experience," 587.

[8]Christine E. Gudorf, "To Make a Seamless Garment, Use a Single Piece of Cloth," in *Abortion and Catholicism: The American Debate,* ed. Patricia Beattie Jung and Thomas A. Shannon (New York: Crossroad, 1988), 279. Gudorf's essay was originally published in *Cross Currents* 34 (Winter 1984): 473-91.

[9]Gudorf, "To Make a Seamless Garment," 280.

[10]See chap. 3 of this volume.

[11]See chap. 10 of this volume.

[12]The notion of "group liability" in this regard is discussed by F. M. Kamm in "Terror and Collateral Damage: Are They Permissible?" *Journal of Ethics* 9 (2005): 381-401.

[13]Gudorf, "To Make a Seamless Garment," 282.

[14]Ibid., 286.

[15]For a discussion of this analogy, see Patricia Beattie Jung, "Abortion and Organ Donation: Christian Reflections on Bodily Life Support," in *Abortion and Catholicism,* 141-71.

[16]See Callahan's essay for a brief review of this debate.

[17]NB: The notion of freedom and reproductive choice affirmed here does not trump the careful consideration of and respect for other important values. Along with who decides, what is chosen is assumed to be of great moral significance.

[18]There is one rare exception to this rule. At least in the case of the coital activity associated with rape, the bishops teach that the morning after pill may be given in order to prevent conception. See United States Conference of Catholic Bishops, *Ethical and Religious Directives for Catholic Health Care Services,* 4th ed. (Washington, DC: USCCB, 2001)" § 36.

[19]In many parts of the world the Roman Catholic Church adamantly lobbies to outlaw both the dissemination of information about and distribution of contraceptive technologies.

[20]Indeed, in the 1980s many U.S. bishops held "listening sessions" with women in their diocese prior to developing the first draft of their pastoral letter on women, "Partners in the Mystery of Redemption," a project that was interrupted by the promulgation of John Paul II's letter of August 1988, *Mulieris dignatatum.* To my knowledge, only Archbishop Rembrandt Weakland held listening sessions with women in his diocese on the topic of abortion.

[21]Gudorf, "To Make a Seamless Garment," 283.

[22]Gudorf's analysis of the roots of this methodological inconsistency fell short, however, when she concluded that the separation of these spheres stemmed from

"the unconscious acceptance by the church at the end of the nineteenth century of the notion that religion's home is in the private realm" (ibid.). Even if that were to be established as historically true, the acceptance of the privatization of religion on the part of the Vatican could account for such a methodological inconsistency only if the approach to moral discernment Gudorf labeled "proportional consequentialism" were (wrongly) presumed incompatible with genuinely traditional accounts of natural law reasoning.

[23]Joseph A. Selling suggests that actually Louis Janssens began to explore the question of moral responsibility in the face of inevitable evil in two closely related articles. See "Time and Space in Morals" and "Acts with Several Effects," written in 1947. There Janssens suggested "that to be justified an evil did not have to be a remote effect of what we actually intend to do. It could be a middle term: we commit ourselves to some project that entails an evil but subsequently brings about a good." See Selling, "Proportionate Reasoning and the Concept of Ontic Evil: The Moral Theological Legacy of Louis Janssens," *Louvain Studies* 27, no. 1 (2002): 3-28, esp. 4, 13. Richard A. McCormick, S.J., tracked hints of this way of thinking back to arguments made by Gerald Kelly, S.J., as early as 1951. See McCormick, "Moral Theology 1940-1989: An Overview," in *The Historical Development of Fundamental Moral Theology in the United States*, ed. Charles E. Curran and Richard A. McCormick, S.J. (New York: Paulist, 1999), 53-54.

[24]Louis Janssens, "Ontic Evil and Moral Evil,"*Louvain Studies* 4 (1972-73): 115-56.

[25]Daniel C. Maguire, "The Vatican on Sex," *Commonweal* 103 (1976): 137-40.

[26]Richard A. McCormick, S.J., "Commentary on the *Declaration on Certain Questions Concerning Sexual Ethics,*" in *Readings in Moral Theology No. 8,* 563.

[27]Richard A. McCormick, S.J., "Proportionalism: Clarification through Dialogue," in *Historical Development of Fundamental Moral Theology in the United States,* 184.

[28]Ibid., 185.

[29]Ibid., 182.

[30]Ibid., 192.

[31]Ibid., 188.

[32]Charles E. Curran, "Moral Theology in the United States: An Analysis of the Last Twenty Years, 1965-1985," in *Historical Development of Fundamental Moral Theology in the United States,* 41.

[33]Charles E. Curran, "Official Catholic Social and Sexual Teachings: A Methodological Comparison," *Readings in Moral Theology No. 8,* 555-56.

[34]Todd A. Salzman, *What Are They Saying about Catholic Ethical Method?* (New York: Paulist, 2003). Salzman's fine text demonstrates that these methodological approaches can be distinguished on the basis of how they approach reason, experience, and tradition.

[35]Selling, "Proportionate Reasoning," 18.

[36]Jean Porter, "The Moral Act in *Veritatis Splendor* and Aquinas's *Summa Theologiae*: A Comparative Analysis," in *Historical Development of Fundamental Moral Theology in the United States,* 223.

[37]At most in such isolation the object of an act could be described as premorally good or evil. In this sense all instances of homicide could be described as onti-

cally evil, even if the consideration of intention and circumstances reveal a homicidal act to be morally justifiable.

[38]Porter, "The Moral Act in *Veritatis Splendor*," 223.

[39]Subjective culpability may be mitigated or aggravated by the distinct consideration of the circumstances surrounding the act and the agent's intention, but its objective evaluation is never *further* influenced by the consideration of such factors apart from its objective description.

[40]Jean Porter, *Nature as Reason: A Thomistic Theory of the Natural Law* (Grand Rapids: Eerdmans, 2005).

[41]Gudorf, "To Make a Seamless Garment," 291.

[42]In male sexual experience, male orgasm is nearly always associated with ejaculation. In female sexual experience, there is only a serendipitous monthly relationship between female orgasm, ovulation, fertilization, and implantation, and this only for the reproductive season of a women's life. The identification of male sexual experience with human sexual experience is androcentric and produced centuries of inadequate reproductive biology and sexology.

[43]It is interesting to note that Louis "Janssens already suggested in 1947 that 'we measure every act with the objective ruler of morality, i.e., *the human person adequately considered in regard to self and in relation with others*'" (Selling, "Proportionate Reasoning," 9).

[44]Lisa Sowle Cahill, *Sex, Gender and Christian Ethics* (New York: Cambridge University Press, 1996), 19.

[45]Ibid., 20.

[46]Jean Porter, "The Search for a Global Ethic," *Theological Studies* 62 (2001): 105-22, at 120.

[47]Jean Porter, "A Tradition of Civility: The Natural Law as a Tradition of Moral Inquiry," *Scottish Journal of Theology* 56 (2003): 27-48, at 29.

[48]Cahill, *Sex, Gender and Christian Ethics*, 55.

[49]Ivone Gebara, *Out of the Depths: Women's Experience of Evil and Salvation*, trans. Ann Patrick Ware (Minneapolis: Fortress, 2002). In a recent letter to *The New York Times Magazine*, a nurse midwife who has helped to deliver babies for twenty-one years (and who notes that she has never helped in an abortion) wrote: "the abortion option is a necessary moral choice in the messy quagmire of real life" (February 5, 2006, 12).

[50]Janssens, "Ontic Evil and Moral Evil," 134-38.

[51]Selling, "Proportionate Reasoning," 25-26.

[52]Thomas A. Shannon and James J. Walter, "Assisted Nutrition and Hydration and the Catholic Tradition," *Theological Studies* 66 (2005): 655.

[53]Shannon and Walter, "Assisted Nutrition," 661. The concern that the authors address continues to be exhibited in the Congregation for the Doctrine of the Faith's recent "Responses to Certain Questions concerning Artificial Nutrition and Hydration" and its official commentary. See *Origins* 37, no. 16 (September 27, 2007): 241-45.

[54]Cathleen Kaveny, "Either/Or? Catholicism Is More Complex," *Commonweal*, July 15, 2005, 7.

[55]Richard M. Gula, S.S., *Reason Informed by Faith: Foundations of Catholic Morality* (Mahweh, NJ: Paulist Press, 1989), 274.

[56]Ibid., 275-76.

6. Rhetoric and the Consistent Ethic of Life: Some Ethical Considerations
Elisabeth Brinkmann, R.S.C.J.

[1]David Fleming, "Rhetoric as a Course of Study," *College English* 61, no. 2 (November 1998): 171.

[2]Ibid., 172-73 (italics in original).

[3]Ibid., 178 (italics in original).

[4]Ibid., 179.

[5]Richard M. Weaver, *The Ethics of Rhetoric* (Chicago: H. Regnery, 1953), 18.

[6]John Courtney Murray, S.J., *We Hold These Truths: Catholic Reflections on the American Proposition* (Kansas City, MO: Sheed and Ward, 1988), 6-8. Murray quotes Thomas Gilby, O.P.: "Civilization is formed by men locked together in argument. From this dialogue the community becomes a political community" (6).

[7]See Keenan in chap. 4 of this volume.

[8]See SG, 102. The plan for pro-life activities states: "This focus [on abortion] and the Church's firm commitment to a consistent ethic of life complement each other. A consistent ethic, far from diminishing concern for abortion or equating all issues touching on the dignity of human life, recognizes the distinctive character of each issue while giving each its proper role within a coherent moral vision" (USCCB, *Pastoral Plan for Pro-Life Activities: A Reaffirmation*, Washington, D.C.: USCCB, November 14, 1985).

[9]See USCCB, "Political Responsibility: Choices for the Future," 1987; "Political Responsibility: Revitalizing American Democracy," 1991; "USCCB Statement on Political Responsibility," 1995; "Faithful Citizenship: Civic Responsibility for a New Millennium," 1999; "Faithful Citizenship: A Catholic Call to Political Responsibility," 2003; and "Forming Consciences for Faithful Citizenship: A Call to Political Responsibility from the Catholic Bishops of the United States," 2007.

[10]USCCB, "Faithful Citizenship: A Catholic Call to Political Responsibility."

[11]USCCB, "Forming Consciences for Faithful Citizenship: A Call to Political Responsibility from the Catholic Bishops of the United States," *Origins* 37, no. 25 (November 29, 2007): 389-401, at 395-400.

[12]"Reading between the Lines: Women's Poverty in the United States, 2006," Legal Momentum, New York, October 2004, www.legalmomentum.org (accessed February 1, 2008).

[13]USCCB, "Forming Consciences for Faithful Citizenship," 398.

[14]Ibid.

[15]"Editorial: Catholics and Politics 2004," *America*, May 24-31, 2004, 3.

[16]See, for example, Raymond L. Burke, "Prophecy for Justice: Catholic politicians and bishops," *America*, June 21-28, 2004, 11-15.

[17]Editorial, *America*, May 24-31, 2004, 3.

[18]Ibid.

[19]USCCB, "Faithful Citizenship: A Catholic Call to Political Responsibility."

[20]Editorial, *America*, May 24-31, 2004, 3.

[21]Robert Grant, "The Roman Catholic Hierarchy: Putting the Squeeze on Politicians," in *The Humanist* (March/April 2005): 18-22 (emphasis added).

[22]Bernardin, "The Catholic Church and U.S. Culture," in Spilly, vol. 2, 178.

[23]Ibid.

[24]Ibid., 179-80.

[25]Ibid., 181.

[26]Ibid., 181-82.

[27]Ibid., 184.

[28]Bernardin, "Faithful and Hopeful: The Catholic Common Ground Project," in Spilly, vol. 2, 331.

[29]Bernardin, "Catholic Identity: Resolving Conflicting Expectations," in Spilly, vol. 2, 167.

[30]Bernardin, "Faithful and Hopeful," in Spilly, vol. 2, 330.

[31]National Pastoral Life Center, "Catholic Common Ground Initiative: Principles of Dialogue," No. 1, www.nplc.org/commonground/PrinciplesOfDialogue(print). htm (accessed November 14, 2004).

[32]Bernardin, "Catholic Identity," 172.

[33]Bernardin, Homily, Mass Commemorating the 20th Anniversary of Episcopal Ordination, in Spilly, vol. 1, 518.

[34]Bernardin, "Changing Styles of Episcopal Leadership," in Spilly, vol. 2, 360-61 (emphasis added).

[35]Ibid., 361.

[36]Ibid., 359.

[37]Bernardin, "Catholic Church and U.S. Culture," 179.

[38]Ibid., 184.

[39]Bernardin, "Catholic Common Ground News Conference," in Spilly, vol. 2, 311.

[40]USCCB, "Forming Consciences for Faithful Citizenship," 395.

[41]See Keenan's remarks in chap. 4 of this volume.

7. Ministering in a Divided Church: Can the Consistent Ethic of Life Bridge the Contention?
Regina Wentzel Wolfe

[1]For discussions of American Catholics and public life, see the two-volume series *American Catholics in the Public Square*, ed. Margaret O'Brien Steinfels (New York: Sheed and Ward, 2004). Of particular note is the discussion of political party affiliation of American Catholics including surveys on Catholic voting patterns in part 4 of vol. 1, 211-78. For a somewhat different view and a historical perspective on the American bishops and public life, see Michael Warner, *Changing Witness: Catholic Bishops and Public Policy, 1917-1994* (Washington, D.C.: Ethics and Public Policy Center; Grand Rapids: Wm. B. Eerdmans, 1995).

[2]Introduction to the USCCB document "Forming Consciences for Faithful Citizenship," *Origins* 37, no. 25 (November 29, 2007): 389-401, at 390.

[3]Ibid., 395.

[4]Ibid.

[5]See chap. 10 of this volume.

[6]"Forming Consciences for Faithful Citizenship," 395.

[7]See chap. 9 of this volume, p. 151.

[8]Regina Wolfe, "Catholics at the Ballot Box," *The Tablet*, March 5, 1988, 264.

[9]Paul Perl and Jamie S. McClintock, "The Catholic 'Consistent Life Ethic' and Attitudes Toward Capital Punishment and Welfare Reform," *Sociology of Religion* 62, no. 3 (2001): 287.

[10]Ibid., 279.

[11]It is interesting to note that Perl and McClintock admit that their conclusion that "it is likely that the consistent life advocacy by the Catholic Bishops has successfully influenced the attitudes of some lay Catholics" is "contrary to most other scholars," who have "concluded that consistent life advocacy by the Catholic Bishops has been a failure, noting that there is little public support for the combination of principles they have preached" (ibid., 275-76).

[12]While the focus of this paper is on pastoral application of the consistent ethic of life in the United States, many of the same issues and concerns exist in the church in other areas of the world.

[13]Richard A. McCormick, "The Consistent Ethic of Life: Is There an Historical Soft Underbelly?" in *Consistent Ethic of Life*, ed. Thomas G. Fuechtman (Kansas City, MO: Sheed and Ward, 1988), 120. The six assumptions that McCormick identifies are: "1. biological givenness as normative . . . 2. sexism . . . 3. theological anthropomorphism . . . 4. the dominance of independence in Western (especially American) thought . . . 5. the interventionist mentality . . . 6. individualism." For a full discussion of these, see *Consistent Ethic of Life*, 97-109.

[14]Ibid., 109.

[15]Timothy E. O'Connell, *Principles for a Catholic Morality*, 2nd ed. (New York: Harper and Row, 1990), 195.

[16]Frans Jozef van Beeck, "Weaknesses in the Consistent Ethic of Life? Some Systematic-Theological Observations," in *Consistent Ethic of Life*, 130.

[17]See, for example, documents such as *Evangelium Vitae, Donum Vitae, Declaration on Euthanasia*; and United States Conference of Catholic Bishops, "Ethical and Religious Directives for Catholic Health Care Services," 4th ed. (Washington, D.C.: United States Catholic Conference, 2001), particularly §§ 45, 46, 48, 66, and 70. Also see *Choosing Life: A Dialogue on Evangelium Vitae*, ed. Kevin Wm. Wildes, SJ, and Alan C. Mitchell (Washington, D.C.: Georgetown University Press), 1997; and Daniel J. Wakin, "U.S. Catholic Bishops Move to Reinforce Ban on Birth Control," *The New York Times*, November 12, 2003.

[18]van Beeck, "Weaknesses in the Consistent Ethic of Life?" 133.

[19]See chap. 8 of this volume.

[20]See chap. 1 of this volume, 3.

[21]Ibid., 11.

[22]For a solid discussion of Christian discipleship, see Timothy E. O'Connell, *Making Disciples: A Handbook of Christian Moral Formation* (New York: Crossroad, 1998).

[23]See, for example, *Gaudium et spes*, particularly No. 62: "Let those who teach theology in seminaries and universities strive to collaborate with men versed in the other sciences through a sharing of their resources and points of view. Theological inquiry should pursue a profound understanding of revealed truth; at the same time it should not neglect close contact with its own time that it may be able to help these men skilled in various disciplines to attain to a better understanding of the faith." See also *Justitia in Mundo*, particularly No. 6: "Action on behalf of justice and participation in the transformation of the world fully appear to us as

a constitutive dimension of the preaching of the Gospel, or, in other words, of the Church's mission for the redemption of the human race and its liberation from every oppressive situation."

[24] For an in-depth view of Catholics in the United States today, see *American Catholics in the Public Square.*

[25] See Joseph Cardinal Bernardin and Oscar H. Lipscomb, *Catholic Common Ground Initiative: Foundational Documents* (New York: Crossroad, 1997). The principles—which can be accessed at the National Pastoral Life Center Web site, http://www.nplc.org/commonground/dialogue.htm—are as follows: "1) We should recognize that no single group or viewpoint in the church has a complete monopoly on the truth; 2) We should not envision ourselves or any one part of the church a saving remnant; 3) We should test all proposals for their pastoral realism and potential impact on living individuals as well as for their theological truth; 4) We should presume that those with whom we differ are acting in good faith; 5) We should put the best possible construction on differing positions; 6) We should be cautious in ascribing motives; 7) We should bring the church to engage the realities of contemporary culture."

[26] Charles E. Curran, *The Catholic Moral Tradition Today: A Synthesis* (Washington, D.C.: Georgetown University Press, 1999), xi.

[27] Ibid., 99.

[28] In a briefing paper prepared for the Religion Division of the Lilly Endowment, Kathleen Cahalan notes that, among other things, "Ministry requires pastoral sensitivity and capacity for working with individuals and families along a continuum that runs from more ordinary life events to extreme crisis." She reports that "many seminaries acknowledge that the three-year M.Div. degree as currently structured is inadequate for preparing congregational ministers, at least in terms of developing the practical skills of ministry. Further, many note that newly graduated pastors find the transition from seminary into full-time ministry quite difficult. When their graduates were asked what was lacking in their seminary education, the majority of pastors reported training in practical skills" (Kathleen A. Cahalan, "A Briefing Paper on the 1998 Theological School Competitive Grants Program" [unpublished paper presented at Capacity Building Program meeting, Louisville, Ky., 2000, photocopied], 7-8).

[29] For example, University of St. Mary of the Lake—Mundelein Seminary, the major seminary for the Archdiocese of Chicago—annually offers Marriage and Family Life as an elective in the pastoral life department. Over the past eight years, enrollment has averaged twelve students per year.

[30] Peter F. Drucker, "Knowledge Work and Knowledge Society: The Social Transformations of this Century," Edwin L. Godkin Lecture, John F. Kennedy School of Government, Harvard University, May 4, 1994. Accessed at http://www.ksg.harvard.edu/ifactory/ksgpress/www/ksg_news/transcripts/drucklec.htm.

[31] Ibid.

[32] Ibid.

[33] Ibid.

[34] National Conference of Catholic Bishops, *The Challenge of Peace: God's Promise and Our Response* (Washington, D.C.: United States Catholic Conference, 1983).

[35] Joseph Cardinal Bernardin, "Peace Is Possible, But Not Inevitable," interview by John M. Whiteley, Quest for Peace Video Series, transcript accessed at http://

sun3.lib.uci.edu/racyberlib/Quest/interview-joseph_cardinal_bernardin.html.

[36]Todd D. Whitmore, "Common Ground, Not Middle Ground: Crossing the Pro-Life, Pro-Choice Divide," *Christian Century* 113, no. 1 (January 3, 1996): 10-12.

[37]Ibid., 11.

[38]Ibid.

[39]Ibid., 12.

[40]William Bole, "Communitarian Lite: American Catholics and Their Politics," *Commonweal*, September 13, 2002, 16.

[41]"American Catholics in the Public Square: A Report to the Catholic Community," *Commonweal*, June 30, 2004, Special Supplement, 4.

[42]Ibid.

[43]Ibid., 8.

[44]Bole, "Communitarian Lite," 16.

[45]Ibid., 13.

[46]Ibid.

[47]Resources for adopting this strategy exist. See, for example, *When You Preach, Remember Me*, published by National Conference of Catholic Bishops, 13 min., 1993, videocassette.

8. From *The Challenge of Peace* to *The Gift of Peace*: Reading the Consistent Ethic of Life as an Ethic of Peacemaking
M. Therese Lysaught

[1]I would like to thank Father Michael Place for his very helpful comments on an earlier draft of this paper.

[2]National Council of Catholic Bishops, *The Challenge of Peace: God's Promise and Our Response* (Washington, D.C.: U.S. Catholic Conference, 1983).

[3]Joseph Cardinal Bernardin, *The Gift of Peace* (Chicago: Loyola Press, 1997).

[4]As he states in the Gannon Lecture: "The consistent ethic of life must be held by a constituency to be effective. The building of such a constituency is precisely the task before the church and the nation. These are two distinct challenges, but they are complementary" (SG, 13). See also 107.

[5]In other words, if I am right in arguing that the consistent ethic of life ought necessarily be read as an ethic of peacemaking and nonviolence, this will likely change how we think about it as a tool for shaping public policy. Additional work beyond the parameters of this essay will be necessary to explore what differences the peacemaking substance of the consistent ethic might make in how it is deployed in the public square, how that use is theologically justified, and what new possibilities might be opened up.

[6]I have culled this list from the spectrum of consistent ethic documents.

[7]Marvin L. Krier Mich, *Catholic Social Teaching and Movements* (Mystic, Conn.: Twenty-Third Publications, 1998), 210.

[8]Ibid.

[9]Thomas G. Fuechtmann, ed., *Consistent Ethic of Life* (Kansas City, MO: Sheed and Ward, 1988), v. Bernardin himself maintains that in naming the principle he was simply articulating the moral vision underlying the work of the National Council of Catholic Bishop's Respect Life Program. As he notes, when the bishops

inaugurated this program in 1972, "they invited the Catholic community to focus on the 'sanctity of human life and the many threats to human life in the modern world, including war, violence, hunger, and poverty'" (SG, 117).

[10]Paul VI, "World Day of Peace Message 1977."

[11]In the interest of space, I do not provide a detailed account of the pastoral here. Jim Castelli, in his book *The Bishops and the Bomb: Waging Peace in a Nuclear Age* (New York: Image, 1983), wonderfully details the behind-the-scenes story of the creation of the pastoral.

[12]*The Challenge of Peace* proceeds in four main sections, following an executive summary. The opening section is entitled "Peace in the Modern World: Religious Perspectives and Principles." Here the bishops outline the scriptural theology of peace outlined above. Part 2 is entitled "War and Peace in the Modern World: Principles and Problems." This presents the just-war principles and issues surrounding nuclear warfare and deterrence. Part 3 is entitled "The Promotion of Peace: Proposals and Policies," which details the bishops' policy recommendations. Part 4 is entitled "The Pastoral Challenge and Response," and includes the material being discussed here.

[13]As the document notes: "We believe the religious vision has an objective basis and is capable of progressive realization. Christ is our peace, for he has "made us both one, and has broken down the dividing wall of hostility . . . that he might create in himself one new man in place of the two, so making peace, and might reconcile us both to God" (Eph. 2:14-16) (§ 20). I think it is not coincidental that Bernardin likewise claims that behind his articulation of the consistent ethic is a "religious vision."

[14]Further, in the Old Testament "true peace implied a restoration of the right order not just among peoples, but within all of creation" (§ 32). Covenant fidelity notwithstanding, God was clearly understood to be the agent of peace, and the prophetic vision of peace cannot be understood absent its eschatological dimension.

[15]"Such a love does not seek revenge but rather is merciful in the face of threat and opposition (Mt 5:39-42; Lk 6:29-31)" (§ 47).

[16]This section references John Paul II's first encyclical *Redemptor Hominis*, 1979, also referenced by Bernardin in his Gannon Lecture.

[17]Building on this section, it would be interesting to examine the pastoral's ecclesiology, in particular its way of conceptualizing the church/state/society relationship and its attention to ecclesial formation. This same pairing of issues continues in Bernardin's work. It would be fruitful to more explicitly develop this aspect of his work, especially as we explore the difference his theological/peacemaking vision makes for the elaboration of the consistent ethic in the public realm.

[18]Castelli, *Bishops and the Bomb*, 91. My understanding is that Cardinal Bernardin located himself more firmly on the just-war side of the Catholic tradition than on the pacifist side. In his address in honor of Martin Luther King ("Memorial Service in Honor of the 55th Birthday of Dr. Martin Luther King, Jr.," January 14, 1984) he states clearly that "A nation has an obligation to defend itself against unjust aggressors and a certain military capacity is needed for this" (Spilly, vol. 2., 24). And in his commentary on *Rerum novarum* ("A Century of Social Teaching," February 25, 1991), he analyzes the Gulf War in just-war terms, staking out a somewhat ambiguous stance on whether or not the war satisfied the criteria. However, in the greater bulk of his work, he does not often put on his just-war hat. Even in his

treatment of the Gulf War, he seems deeply critical of the war. Earlier in the *Rerum novarum* commentary he states: "The very fact of the [Gulf] war sadly confirms that the challenge of peace still eludes us. While we were drafting the pastoral letter, we became convinced that the world cannot truly afford war today. The technology of modern weaponry, even so-called conventional weaponry, greatly multiplies death and destruction, as we have seen so vividly in news reports of the past five weeks. Moreover, the planet itself is wounded ecologically by modern warfare. Pope Paul VI's plea before the United Nations "No more war! War never again!" has more meaning today than in many a year" (Spilly, vol. 2, 73). Equally the greater bulk of his writing is devoted to the theological and practical importance of peacemaking. Interestingly in the account of the development of the pastoral provided by Castelli, it is difficult to identify the position Bernardin would have taken; Castelli certainly does not give the impression that Bernardin was deeply committed to the just war tradition.

[19]As Fr. Michael Place reminded me, fundamental moral theology was traditionally grounded in theology, but special moral theology never was.

[20]Castelli, *Bishops and the Bomb*, 113.

[21]J. Bryan Hehir, "From the Pastoral Constitution of Vatican II to *The Challenge of Peace*," in *Catholics and Nuclear War*, ed. Philip J. Murnion (New York: Crossroad, 1984), 5.

[22]Bernardin, "Dialogue as Universal Foundation of Peace," in Spilly, vol. 2, 55.

[23]He opens his very first homily to the presbyterate of Chicago prior to his installation as cardinal with the words: "Peace be with you," (" 'I am Joseph, Your Brother,' Evening Prayer with the Presbyterate, Archbishop-Designate of Chicago, Holy Name Cathedral, Chicago, Illinois" [August 24, 1982]); see Spilly, vol. 1, 281.

[24]Spilly, vol. 1, 105.

[25]Ibid., 107.

[26]Ibid., 108.

[27]Counsel to prayer is ubiquitous in his writings. In the second sermon he delivers in Chicago, he confesses: "Every good teacher knows that the best instruction begins in silence. The first and most profound silence is that of reflective prayer, listening to the word of God and responding to it in one's heart," (" 'It is a Spiritual Event,' Liturgy of the Solemn Installation of the Seventh Bishop of Chicago, Holy Name Cathedral, Chicago, Illinois," [August 25, 1982], Spilly, vol. 1, 291).

[28]Ibid., 134.

[29]Ibid., 138.

[30]Ibid., 111. The first reference to the consistent ethic of life in one of his sermons appears in 1984 ("Mass of the Holy Spirit, Saint Mary of the Lake Seminary, Mundelein, Illinois" [September 7, 1984]). It appears in the context of a brief reference situated in a broader commentary which constitutes the focus of this sermon to an audience of seminarians, namely, the cost of discipleship. Beginning with Dietrich Bonhoeffer, he counsels them on the costs (and later, joys) of discipleship. The costs may entail suffering, may entail martyrdom; they are not only private but public: "For I have faced keen opposition—in the form of innuendos, slanted or false interpretations of what I have proposed for the need for espousing a consistent ethic of life, as I have tried to witness to the values of the gospel and the teaching of the

Church in the face of indifference and hostility" (Spilly, vol. 1, 109). Of course, the grounds he gives for counseling them to such costly discipleship are Christological, givens that come with the territory when one follows Jesus.

[31]Bernardin, "Christ Calls Us Who Are Many to Be but One: Mass of Greeting and Thanksgiving for the People of the Archdiocese of Chicago," Grant Park, Chicago, Illinois (August 29, 1982), Spilly, vol. 1, 298.

[32]In his homily for "Passion (Palm) Sunday, Holy Name Cathedral, Chicago, Illinois" (March 27, 1983), in Spilly, vol. 1, 337-38.

[33]Ibid.

[34]Ibid., 11-26.

[35]Ibid., 21.

[36]Ibid., 22.

[37]Ibid., 68-69.

[38]Ibid., 69-73.

[39]"Thanksgiving Day Liturgy, SS Faith, Hope, and Charity Church, Winnetka, Illinois (November 24, 1983)," Spilly, vol. 1, 405-7.

[40]Ibid., 406. We see a similar resonance in his homily for the "Scouting Mass, Church of St. Dismas, Waukegan, Illinois (September 22, 1984)," in ibid., 412-14. Here he counsels the young Boy Scouts, Girl Scouts, Explorers, Webelos, Camp Fire Girls, and Junior Daughters of St. Peter Claver to build "campfires of God's kingdom" everywhere they can: "In building our 'kingdom campfires,' how do we find the right spots? Look for places where God's people are hurting. Build your campfires wherever there is loneliness, poverty, or need—places where people are excluded" (ibid., 413).

[41]Bernardin, "Thanksgiving Day Liturgy," ibid., 405.

[42]Joseph Cardinal Bernardin, *The Gift of Peace* (Chicago: Loyola Press, 1997), 5.

[43]Ibid., 6.

[44]Ibid., 15-16.

[45]Ibid., 47, emphasis in original.

[46]Ibid., 23.

[47]Ibid., 25.

[48]It is not unimportant that this reconciliation involves the sacraments of reconciliation and Eucharist.

[49]Ibid., 46.

[50]For those not familiar with the Prayer of St. Francis:
"O Lord, make me an instrument of your Peace!
Where there is hatred, let me sow love.
Where there is injury, pardon.
Where there is discord, harmony.
Where there is doubt, faith.
Where there is despair, hope.
Where there is darkness, light.
Where there is sorrow, joy.

Oh Divine Master, grant that I may not
so much seek to be consoled as to console;
to be understood as to understand;
to be loved as to love;

for it is in giving that we receive;
it is in pardoning that we are pardoned;
and it is in dying that we are born to Eternal Life."

[51]For example, what difference might it have made in the Terri Schiavo debacle had the pro-life lobby been shaped by the canons of gospel peacemaking—of kenotic, self-emptying love, of loving one's enemies, of forgiveness and reconciliation, of dialogue, of overcoming evil through redemptive suffering—rather than the language of hatred and enmity that we heard and witnessed? I explore this question at length in my essay, "Love Your Enemies: Toward a Christoform Bioethic," in *Gathered for the Journey: Moral Theology in Catholic Perspective*, ed. David M. McCarthy and M. Therese Lysaught (Grand Rapids: Eerdmans/SCM, 2007).

[52]He does offer a richer, Christological account in "Christ Lives within Me," where he ties concerns about biotechnology and sexuality (gnostic disregard for our bodiliness) rooted in the Incarnation (Spilly, vol. 1, 111) and the bodily resurrection.

[53]I thank Sheila McLaughlin and others at the Cardinal Bernardin Center for Theology and Ministry at Catholic Theological Union for making this draft available to me.

9. **From Ontology, Ecology, and Normativity to Mutuality: The Attitude and Principle Grounding the Ethic of Life**
Dawn M. Nothwehr, O.S.F.

[1]See Spilly, vol. 1, xix.

[2]For a thorough treatment of mutuality as a formal norm, see my *Mutuality: A Formal Norm for Christian Social Ethics* (San Francisco: Catholic Scholars Press, 1998; repr., Eugene, Ore.: Wipf & Stock Publishers, 2005), especially chap. 4.

[3]A basic definition of ontology is a particular theory about the nature of being and the kinds of existents. Ontology = Gk. *onta* = "the really existing things," "true reality" and *logos* = "the study of" or "the theory which accounts for" being. See in Peter A. Angeles, s.v. "ontology," *Dictionary of Philosophy* (New York: Barnes and Noble Books, 1981).

[4]Bernardin, "The Challenges We Face Together: Reflections on Selected Questions for Archdiocesan Religious Educators," in Spilly, vol. 1, 177.

[5]See in Karl Rahner and Herbert Vorgrimler, s.v. "ontology," *Theological Dictionary*, ed. Cornelius Ernst, trans. Richard Stachan (New York: Herder and Herder, 1965), 324. In contrast, Aristotle, for example, held that the world is eternal and the First Cause or Prime Mover is the most excellent and exalted being in the universe.

[6]Here it is important to distinguish pantheism from orthodox panentheism. See Rahner and Vorgrimler, s.v. "panentheism," *Theological Dictionary*, 333-34: "panentheism does not simply identify the world with God in a monistic fashion (God, the 'All') but sees the 'All' of the world 'within' God as an interior modification and manifestation of God, although God is not absorbed into the world. This doctrine of the 'immanence' of the world in God is false and heretical only if it denies creation and the distinction of the world from God (and not only of God from the world)."

[7]In contrast, Aristotle's ontology is grounded in accounting for the order of the world he perceived. He investigated different kinds of beings in the universe

(practice of ontology) and asserted what he discovered in order to account for the operations of the world.

[8]See, for example, the Apostles' Creed, the Nicene Creed of 325, the Nicene Creed of 381, or the Jerusalem Creed.

[9]Joseph Cardinal Bernardin, "Theology on Tap Mass," Homily 19th Sunday in Ordinary Time, Holy Name Cathedral, Chicago, Ill., August 11, 1996, in Spilly, vol. 1, 591.

[10]Joseph Cardinal Bernardin, "Religion Enrichment Day Homily," Chicago, Ill., March 5, 1985, in Spilly, vol. 1, 425.

[11]Here I follow the definition of ecology given by Ernest Haeckle in 1866 as "the interrelationships of living beings among themselves and with their environment," cited in Leonardo Boff, *Cry of the Earth, Cry of the Poor*, trans. Phillip Berryman (Maryknoll, N.Y.: Orbis Books, 1997), 104-5.

[12]See Bernardin, "Challenges We Face Together," in Spilly, vol. 1 , 177. In an e-mail to me dated September 27, 2005, Alphonse Spilly stated: "Cardinal Bernardin did not address environmental ethics or ecology in a major address. At one point Frank Kane indicated that the Cardinal had shown an interest in developing a pastoral letter or statement on the subject. The Cardinal's executive secretary had grown up as friends with the Director of the Brookfield Zoo, and I took her and her sister there one day and talked with George about environmental ethics. He recommended a number of books, but the press of turning out talks and columns on a daily basis did not allow me to pursue the research. I recall a brief conversation with the Cardinal about the topic, and he mentioned that Bryan Hehir didn't think that Joseph should apply the consistent ethic of life personally across too broad a spectrum of issues. It wasn't that it would not be fruitful; but for credibility's sake, Joseph couldn't be up on everything. (The Cardinal basically took the same position in regard to the U.S. Bishops' letter on the U.S. Economy. I recall a brief address on the topic when he made a pastoral visit to Chile and was asked to say something about the letter.)"

[13]United States Catholic Bishops, "Renewing the Earth," in *"And God Saw That It Was Good": Catholic Theology and the Environment*, ed. Drew Christiansen and Walter Glazier (Washington, D.C.: United States Catholic Conference, 1996), 223-43.

[14]Christine Firer Hinze, "Catholic Social Teaching and Ecological Ethics," in Christiansen and Glazier, *"And God Saw That It Was Good,"* 167.

[15]See Boff, *Cry of the Earth*, 104-5. Shortly after ecology was first defined by Ernest Haeckle in 1866 as "the interrelationships of living beings among themselves and with their environment," the science became conceptualized in three forms: environmental, social, and mental ecology. It is worth citing Leonardo Boff's explanation of these forms of ecology at length at 105: "*Environmental ecology* is concerned with the environment and relations that various societies have with it in history . . . and whether they integrate human beings into or distance them from nature. *Social ecology* is primarily concerned with social relations as belonging to ecological relations; that is, because human beings (who are personal and social) are part of the natural world their relationship with nature passes through the social relationship of exploitation, collaboration, or respect and reverence. Hence social justice—the right relationship with persons, roles, and institutions—implies some achievement of ecological justice, which is the right relationship with nature, easy access to its resources, and assurance of quality of life. *Mental ecology* starts from the recognition that nature is not outside human beings but within them, in their minds, in the form

of psychic energy, symbols, archetypes, and behavior patterns that embody attitudes of aggression or of respect and acceptance of nature." These three categories of ecological relations include all kinds of human relationships. There are no dominant hierarchies here. Rather, there are sets of profoundly related beings, each of which is affected by any change in any individual or community of beings.

[16]See SG, 117-24. See also Thomas A. Nairn, "The Tension between Moral Principles and Moral Attitudes: A Legacy of the Consistent Ethic of Life," The Erica and John Family Chair of Catholic Ethics Inaugural Lecture, Catholic Theological Union, November 17, 2002.

[17]Richard M. Gula, *What Are They Saying about Moral Norms?* (New York: Paulist Press, 1982), 1.

[18]See Karl Rahner, *The Dynamic Element in the Church* (New York: Herder and Herder, 1964), 63, and Richard M. Gula, *Reason Informed by Faith: Foundations of Catholic Morality* (New York: Paulist Press, 1989), 283-97, particularly 284-85.

[19]Daniel C. Maguire, *The Moral Choice* (Minneapolis: Winston Press, 1979), 220-21.

[20]See Gula, *Reason Informed by Faith*, 286-87.

[21]Timothy E. O'Connell, *Principles for a Catholic Morality*, rev. ed. (San Francisco: Harper, 1990), 180-84.

[22]See Gula, *Reason Informed by Faith*, 287-88.

[23]Joseph Cardinal Bernardin, "The Challenges We Face Together," in Spilly, vol. 1, 177.

[24]A word of caution is needed here. To specify the uniqueness of the God-human relationship is not to discount the gravity of the relationship of God with the rest of the cosmos. Distinctiveness does not necessarily mean inferior. There are, indeed, differences between humans and other creatures. But numerous considerations must be made (*ex objecto*) in making any one moral decision concerning competing claims between human claims and the well-being of other creatures.

[25]Joseph Cardinal Bernardin, "Promoting the Common Good through the Practice of Virtues," John Carroll Society, Cathedral of St. Matthew the Apostle, Washington, D.C., October 3, 1993, in Spilly, vol. 1, 573-74.

[26]See the Philippine Bishops, *What Is Happening to Our Beautiful Land?* (1988), in which they show that degradation of the environment is as urgent a life issue as nuclear war and other threats. See also Maguire's notion of the "foundational moral experience (FME)" as reverence for persons and their environment in his *Moral Choice*, 60-61, 72-99. Science has overwhelmingly shown the need for a clean environment for human well-being. See, for example, Dawn Nothwehr and Sylvia Hood Washington, *Struggles for Environmental Justice and Health in Chicago: An African American Perspective* (Chicago: DePaul University—The John J. Egan Urban Center, 2004).

[27]See in Rahner and Vorgrimler, s.v. "creation of man," *Theological Dictionary*, 109-10.

[28]For a thorough treatment of mutuality as a formal norm, see my *Mutuality*, esp. chap. 4.

[29]For a small sample of this huge literature, see, in the natural sciences, Thomas Berry, *Dream of the Earth* (San Francisco: Sierra Club Books, 1988); in law, Roderick F. Nash, *The Rights of Nature: A History of Environmental Ethics* (Madison: University of Wisconsin Press, 1989); in psychology, James Serpell, *In the Company*

of Animals: A Study of Human-Animal Relationships (London: Basil Blackwell, 1986); in philosophy, Erazim Kohak, The Embers and the Stars: A Philosophical Inquiry into the Moral Sense of Nature (Chicago: University of Chicago Press, 1984); in political science, Jeremy Rafkin, Biosphere Politics: A New Consciousness for a New Century (New York: Crown Publishing, 1991); in agriculture, Wes Jackson, New Roots for Agriculture (Lincoln: University of Nebraska, 1987).

[30]The definition of mutuality as a formal norm is only summarized here. For a thorough treatment of this topic, See my Mutuality. This reclamation of mutuality is grounded in biblical tradition and in the work of their intellectual ancestors—Irenaeus, Hugh of St. Victor, Thomas Aquinas, John Duns Scotus, H. Richard Niebuhr, and Martin Buber. Here the treatment and use of formal norms is situated within the context of post–Vatican II revisionist Roman Catholic moral theology. See Catherine Mowry LaCugna, "God in Communion with Us," in Freeing Theology: Essentials of Theology in Feminist Perspective, ed. Catherine Mowry LaCugna (New York: Harper San Francisco, 1993), 104-8. See also Elizabeth A. Johnson, She Who Is: The Mystery of God in Feminist Theological Discourse (New York: Crossroad, 1992), 124-49, especially 148.

[31]For a thorough discussion of Denis Edwards's theological contribution that supports the normativity of mutuality, see my "The Ecological Spirit and Cosmic Mutuality: Engaging the Work of Denis Edwards," in The Spirit in the Church and the World, ed. Bradford E. Hinze (College Theology Society Annual Vol. 49; Maryknoll, N.Y.: Orbis Books, 2004), 167-88.

[32]See Denis Edwards, "The Integrity of Creation: Catholic Social Teaching for an Ecological Age," Pacifica 5 (1992): 182-203.

[33]See Mary Parker Follett, Creative Experience (New York: Longman, Green & Company, 1924) and her Dynamic Administration (New York: Harper and Brothers, 1942). Also Carter Heyward, Touching Our Strength: The Erotic Love of God (San Francisco: Harper and Row, 1989), at 191: "Power is the ability to move, effect, make a difference; the energy to create or destroy, call forth or put down. Outside of a particular context, power bears neither positive or negative connotations. Power can be used for good or for ill. Using power-with others is good. Using power-over others is evil."

[34]See my Mutuality, esp. 233. There I define cosmic, gender, generative, and social mutuality in detail. This discussion of mutuality relies on that text.

[35]Denis Edwards, "For Your Immortal Spirit Is in All Things: The Role of the Spirit in Creation," in Earth Revealing, Earth Healing: Ecology and Christian Theology, ed. Denis Edwards (Collegeville, Minn.: Liturgical Press, 2001), 45-66, at 61. See also Gen. 1:1-2.

[36]Rosemary Radford Ruether, Gaia and God: An Ecofeminist Theology of Earth Healing (San Francisco: Harper, 1992), 2-3: "Ecofeminism brings together . . . ecology and feminism, in their full, or deep forms and explores how male domination of women and domination of nature are interconnected, both in cultural ideology and in social structures." See Beverly Wildung Harrison, "Politics of Energy Policy," in Energy Ethics, ed. Dieter Hessel (New York: Friendship Press, 1979), 56.

[37]Harrison, "Politics of Energy Policy," 57-59.

[38]This is the belief that all things are imbued with God's being in the same way that all things are in God. God is more than all that is and is a consciousness and the highest unity possible.

[39]Johnson, *She Who Is*, 232.

[40]Edwards, "Your Immortal Spirit Is in All Things," 57-62.

[41]Johnson, *Woman, Earth, Creator Spirit*, 1993 Madelava Lecture (New York: Paulist Press, 1993), 66-67.

[42]Johnson, *She Who Is*, 103.

[43]See for example, Harrison, "Sexism and the Language of Christian Ethics," in *Making the Connections: Essays in Feminist Social Ethics*, ed. Carol S. Robb (Boston: Beacon Press, 1985), 24-25.

[44]See Heyward, *Touching Our Strength*, 3, 4, 17, 22-23, and 34, and *The Redemption of God: A Theology of Mutual Relation* (New York: University Press of America, 1982), xxvi n17.

[45]See, for example, Heyward, *Touching Our Strength*, 91-92, and *Redemption of God*, 9.

[46]Johnson, *She Who Is*, 169.

[47]Edwards, "Your Immortal Spirit Is in All Things," 65.

[48]See Johnson, *She Who Is*, 217.

[49]Ibid., 50-51.

[50]Beverly Wildung Harrison, "The Power of Anger in the Works of Love: Christian Ethics for Women and Other Strangers," *Union Seminary Quarterly Review* 36 (1981, Supplement): 52 (emphasis in original).

[51]Edwards, "Making All Things New: An Ecological Theology of the Holy Spirit," unpublished paper, 3-4, presented at the Catholic Theological Society of America, New Orleans, La., June 8, 2002. Basil of Caesarea held that every event of Jesus's life and every event in the history of salvation was a Spirit event and in reciprocal relation with the events of salvation.

[52]Harrison, "Power of Anger in the Works of Love," 53. See also Carter Heyward, *Our Passion for Justice: Images of Power Sexuality and Liberation* (Cleveland: Pilgrim Press, 1984), 167.

[53]See Christine E. Gudorf, "Parenting, Mutual Love, and Sacrifice," in *Women's Consciousness, Women's Conscience: A Reader in Feminist Ethics*, ed. Barbara Hilkert Andolsen, Christine Gudorf, and Mary D. Pellauer (Minneapolis: Winston Press, 1985), 175-91.

[54]Here I can only summarize the case for mutuality as a formal norm. For the full argument see my *Mutuality*, esp. chap. 4.

[55]See Johnson, *She Who Is*, esp. 228-32. Also see her *Woman, Earth, Creator Spirit*, 66-67.

[56]For a case study that illustrates this, see my *Mutuality*, esp. chap. 5. See Edwards, "Integrity of Creation," 182-203.

[57]Edwards, "Making All Things New," 5.

[58]See Leonard Swidler, "Mutuality the Matrix for Mature Living: Some Philosophical and Christian Theological Reflections," *Religion and Intellectual Life* 3 (1985): 105-19.

[59]Ibid., 108.

[60]Ibid. Swidler cites the epistemological theories of Max Scheler and Karl Mannheim.

[61]See the reference to Laguna Pueblo/Sioux scholar Paula Gunn Allen in Johnson, *She Who Is*, 132-33.

[62]Swidler, "Mutuality the Matrix for Mature Living," 109.

[63]Ibid., 110.

[64]See Martin Buber, *I and Thou*, trans. Walter Kaufman (New York: Charles Scribner's Sons, 1970).

[65]See, for example, the closing section of his Dom Helder Camara Lecture, "The Consistent Ethic of Life," in the Archdiocese of Melbourne, February 23, 1995 (SG, 259-66) or his statement in his address to the First Friday Club, October 6, 1989: "To prevent deeper divisions, all those participating in the public debate about abortion should speak and act in an honest, mutually respectful manner that can seek and find common ground" (SG, 180-87).

[66]Edwards, "Your Immortal Spirit Is in All Things," 53.

[67]See Martin Buber, *Between Man and Man*, trans. Ronald Gregor Smith (New York: Macmillan, 1965), 22-23; Martin Buber, *I and Thou*, trans. Ronald Gregor Smith (New York: Charles Scribner's Sons, 1958), 96, 126; Robert E. Wood, *Martin Buber's Ontology*, Northwestern University Studies in Phenomenology and Existential Philosophy, ed. John Wild (Evanston, Ill.: Northwestern University Press, 1969), 70-71; and Martin Buber, "Interrogation of Martin Buber," by Maurice Friedman, in *Philosophical Investigations*, ed. Sydney Rome and Beatrice Rome (New York: Harper Torchbooks, 1970), 47.

[68]Swidler, "Mutuality the Matrix for Mature Living," 111. The danger of relativism can be cared for by identifying presuppositions, acknowledging biases, purposefully seeking out other voices and opinions, and probing them for the ways they challenge one, and holding modesty as the highest virtue. In the Christian community the focal coherence of scripture, traditions, and the *sensus fidelium* can provide additional safeguards.

[69]Edwards, "Making All Things New," 6.

[70]H. R. Niebuhr, *Responsible Self: An Essay in Christian Moral Philosophy*, paperback ed. (New York: Harper and Row, 1978), 70-71.

[71]Ruth L. Smith, "Morality and Perceptions of Society: The Limits of Self-Interest," *Journal for the Scientific Study of Religion* 26 (1987): 289.

[72]Edwards, "Making All Things New," 6.

[73]Smith, "Morality and Perceptions of Society," 288-91. It could be argued that mutuality actually disempowers one because human finitude prevents any person to *always* deal with *everything* and *everyone*. But, like the formal norms of love and justice, mutuality provides a standard and source of motivation, inspiration, vision, and instruction. To not consider mutuality, however, is to neglect a whole realm of moral responsibility and possibility.

[74]Margaret Catroneo, "A Contextual Catholic Ethics" (PhD diss., Temple University, 1983), 248.

[75]Edwards, "Making All Things New," 6-7.

[76]Daniel C. Maguire, "The Primacy of Justice in Moral Theology," *Horizons* 10 (1983): 77.

[77]Christine E. Gudorf, "Parenting," in *Women's Consciousness*, 175-91. See particularly 182n9 where Gudorf discusses a split in the dominant understanding of love by Catholic and Protestant theologians. Gudorf cites Anders Nygren, *Agape and Eros*, trans. Philip S. Watson (New York: Harper and Row, 1969), 712-13, in which he advances the idea that Luther considered love of neighbor to necessitate completely dispossessing and annihilating self-love. Gudorf indicates that Søren Kierkegaard, *Works of Love*, trans. Howard and Edna Hong (New York: Harper and Row, 1965), 68, is in full agreement with Nygren's reading of Luther. Prior to Luther

and in the patristic period Christian love was regularly referred to in terms such as *eros* or mutual love—see Aquinas's *ST* II-II 26.9-12. Contrary to Nygren's claim that his explication of *agape* was the normative New Testament understanding for all Christians, his interpretation was a phenomenon nearly exclusive to Protestant ethics. See Gerald Gilleman, *The Primacy of Love in the Moral Life* (New York: Newman Press, 1959).

[78]Gudorf, "Parenting," 182, 185. Most feminists see value in sacrificial love that is chosen freely, consciously, and with the full integrity of the lover intact, which moves the relationship toward greater mutuality or has mutuality as its goal.

[79]For a discussion of the relationship of love and justice see Gene Outka, *Agape: An Ethical Analysis* (New Haven, Conn.: Yale University Press, 1972), 73-92. He includes Rawls, Frankena, Fletcher, Brunner, Ramsey, and others in these remarks.

[80]See Josef Pieper, *Justice* (New York: Pantheon Books, 1955), 48-55, and *New American Justice* (Minneapolis, MN: Winston Press, 1980), 55-84, where Maguire defines "justice." See also Daniel C. Maguire and A. Nicholas Fargnoli, *On Moral Grounds: The Art/Science of Ethics* (New York: Crossroad, 1991), 27-32, 33-37.

[81]Maguire, *New American Justice*, 74. Several ethicists—for example, Daniel C. Maguire—clearly assume mutuality as part of their notion of justice. There is a burgeoning movement among feminist scholars, however, toward considering mutuality as an absolute criterion for Christian social ethical behavior. Increasingly, feminist ethicists are drawing mutuality to the foreground to stand as a distinct and normative consideration in the ethical process.

[82]Peter A. Angeles, s.v. "rationalism," *Dictionary of Philosophy*: "In general, the philosophic approach which emphasizes reason as the primary source of knowledge, prior or superior to, and independent of sense knowledge." Key rationalists are Plato, Aristotle, and Descartes.

Angeles, *Dictionary of Philosophy*, s.v. "law, natural": "The set of obligations or principles (laws, maxims, duties, codes, commands, etc.) binding upon one's conduct which are obtained by reason from examination of the universe (nature) in contrast to those obtained by revelation, intuition, innate moral conscience, authority, feelings, inclinations." Key figures are Thomas Aquinas, Cicero, Ulpian.

Angeles, *Dictionary of Philosophy*, s.v. "analytic philosophy": "A twentieth-century philosophic movement . . . that concentrates on language and the attempt to analyze statements (or concepts, or linguistic expressions, or logical forms) in order to find those with the best and most concise logical form which fits the facts or meaning to be presented. Central to analytic philosophy is the forming of definitions—linguistic or non-linguistic, real or contextual." Key figures are Bertrand Russell, G. E. Moore, Ludwig Wittgenstein.

Angeles, *Dictionary of Philosophy*, s.v. "positivism, logical": ". . . The acceptance of the verifiability principle, which is a criterion for determining that a statement has cognitive meaning. The cognitive meaning of a statement (as opposed to its emotive or other levels of meaning) is dependent upon its being verified. A statement is meaningful if-and-only-if it is, at least in principle, empirically verifiable. Some rock-bottom sense experience (positive knowledge) must be reached before a statement can have cognitive meaning." Two key figures are Thomas Hobbes and Chiam Perelman.

Angeles, *Dictionary of Philosophy*, s.v. "utilitarianism": ". . . One should act so as to promote the greatest happiness (pleasure) of the greatest number of people." Key figures are Jeremy Bentham, John Stuart Mill, and John Rawls.

[83]*Encyclopedia of Philosophy*, s.v. "justice." This article presents a discussion of major theories of justice.

[84]See my *Mutuality*, chap. 1, nn61-62.

[85]See Gudorf, "Parenting."

[86]Valerie Saiving Goldstein, "The Human Situation: A Feminine View," *Journal of Religion* 40 (1960): 108-11.

[87]See the discussion of Aristotle's and Thomas's understandings of these classical notions, see my *Mutuality*, chap. 2, after n62 and after n116. See also Gene Outka, s.v. "love," in *Encyclopedia of Ethics*, ed. Lawrence C. Becker and Charlotte B. Becker (New York: Garland, 1992). See also *Webster's Seventh New Collegiate Dictionary*, s.v. "love": "strong affection for another arising out of kinship or personal ties; attraction based on sexual desires; affection based on admiration, benevolence, or common interests."

[88]For a fine explication of biblical love, see Daniel C. Maguire, *The Moral Core of Judaism and Christianity* (Minneapolis: Fortress Press, 1993), 208-30.

[89]June Jordan, "Where is the Love?" in *Civil Wars* (Boston: Beacon Press, 1981), 142-44.

[90]A fine summary of biblical justice is Maguire, *Moral Core of Judaism and Christianity*, 126-65.

[91]See particularly Heyward's and Johnson's ideas concerning justice, in my *Mutuality*, chap. 1.

[92]José Miranda, *Marx and the Bible: A Critique of the Philosophy of Oppression* (Maryknoll, N.Y.: Orbis Books, 1974), 46-47. Miranda states, "In the Hebrew Bible, *hesed* appears together with justice (*sedakah*) and/or right (*mispat*) in synonymic parallelism or in hendiadys in the following instances: Jer. 9:23; Isa. 16:5; Mic. 6:8; Hos. 2:21-22; 6:6; 10:12; Zech. 7:9; Pss. 25:9-10; 33:5; 36:6-7; 36:11; 40:11; 85:11; 88:12-13; 89:15; 98:2-3; 103:17; 119:62-64." See *The Oxford Companion to the English Language*, s.v. "hendiadys": "A term in rhetoric for equal words joined by *and* instead of a one-word modifier (nice and warm rather than nicely warm), and similar words joined by *and* where one might have been enough, usually for emphasis . . ."

[93]See my *Mutuality*, chap. 1, n257, for references to Gilligan et al.

[94]See Reinhold Niebuhr, *Man's Nature and His Communities* (New York: Charles Scribner's Sons, 1965), 39; *The Self and the Dramas of History* (New York: Charles Scribner's Sons, 1955), 165; *The Children of the Light and Children of Darkness* (New York: Charles Scribner's Sons, 1944), 62.

[95]Cf. Abraham Edel and Elizabeth Flower, "Economic Justice: Notes and Queries," *Journal of Value Inquiry* 19 (1985): 257-58.

[96]Bernardin, "Theology on Tap Mass," Spilly, vol. 1, 591.

[97]See the contrast of character Jesus presents in Lk. 18:10-17.

[98]See Matt. 5:44-48.

[99]See Mk. 10:46-52; Lk. 8:22-26; Mk. 9:14-29.

[100]See John Rawls, *A Theory of Justice* (Cambridge, Mass.: Harvard University Press, 1971).

[101]Edwards, "Your Immortal Spirit Is in All Things," 61.

[102]Ibid.

[103]See, for example, Denis Edwards, "Ecology of the Holy Spirit: The 'Already' and the 'Not Yet,'" *Pacifica* 13 (June 2000): 142-59.

[104]See my *Mutuality*, esp. chap. 5.

[105]For data that supports this scenario, see Death Penalty Information Center, "Understanding Capital Punishment: A Guide through the Death Penalty Debate," available from Death Penalty Information Center, 1320 18th Street NW, 5th Floor, Washington, D.C. 20036.

10. The Consistent Ethic of Life and Developments in Genetics
Thomas A. Shannon

[1]Marv Mich, "The Consistent Ethic of Life and the 'Gospel of Life,'" in Marv Mich, *Catholic Social Teaching and Movements*, accessed at www.consistentlife.org/The %Consistent%%20Life%20Ethic.

[2]For a general overview of many of these issues, see "Notes on Moral Theology: Issues in Genetics," *Theological Studies* 60 (March 1999): 109-47: Thomas A. Shannon, "Ethical Issues in Genetics," 111-23; James J. Walter, "Theological Issues in Genetics," 124-34; M. Cathleen Kaveny, "Jurisprudence and Genetics," 135-47.

[3]For an important discussion of the scientific and religious dimensions of this problem, see John F. Haught, *Deeper Than Darwin: The Prospect for Religion in the Age of Evolution* (Boulder, Colo.: Westview Press, 2003), 13-26.

[4]"Biocultural Evolution and the Created Co-Creator," in *Science and Theology: The New Consonance*, ed. Ted Peters (Boulder, Colo.: Westview Press, 2000), 174-88.

[5]For a further discussion of this theme, see Thomas A. Shannon, "The Communitarian Perspective: Autonomy and the Common Good," in *Meta-Medical Ethics*, ed. M. A. Grodin (Dordrecht, Netherlands: Kluwer Academic Publishers, 1995), 61-76.

[6]For a discussion of this, see Peter Steinfels, *A People Adrift: The Crisis of the Roman Catholic Church in America* (New York: Simon and Schuster, 2003), chap. 1, but esp. 24-26.

[7]For an excellent, detailed chronology and analysis of these issues, see Thomas A. Massaro, S.J., "Catholic Bishops and Politicians: Concerns about Recent Developments," *Josephinum Journal of Theology* 12, no. 2 (Summer-Fall 2005): 268-87. This essay gives a detailed chronology of the role of various bishops in the 2004 presidential election and a very thoughtful analysis of how to think about the relation between religion and politics. See also Robert W. McElroy, "Prudence, Politics and the Eucharist," *America*, January 31, 2005, 8-11.

[8]Cathy Cleaver Ruse, "Election 2004: The Role of Moral Values," accessed at www.nccbuscc.org/prolife/publicat/lifeissues/110504.htm.

[9]USCCB, "Forming Consciences for Faithful Citizenship," *Origins* 37, no. 25 (November 29, 2007): 389-401.

[10]David D. Kirkpatrick, "Catholic Bishops, after a Divisive Debate, Choose a New Leader," *The New York Times*, November 16, 2004, A13.

[11]See in particular the important work by Lisa Sowle Cahill, *Bioethics and the Common Good* (Milwaukee: Marquette University Press, 2004).

[12]For an overview of the issues connected with human gene therapy, see LeRoy Walters and Julie Gage Palmer, *The Ethics of Human Gene Therapy* (New York: Oxford University Press, 1997).

[13]Thomas A. Shannon, "From the Micro to the Macro," In *The Human Embryonic Stem Cell Debate: Science, Ethics and Public Policy*, ed. Suzanne Holland, K. Lebacqz, and L. Zoloth (Cambridge, Mass.: MIT Press, 2001), 177-84. See also

Daniel Callahan, "Promises, Promises: Is Embryonic Stem-Cell Research Sound Public Policy?" *Commonweal*, January 14, 2005, 12-14.

[14]For example, see Laura Mansnerus, "New Jersey Faces Tough Competition for Stem Cell Scientists," *The New York Times*, January 17, 2005, A16.

[15]E. Richard Gould, *Body Parts: Property Rights and the Ownership of Human Biological Material* (Washington, D.C.: Georgetown University Press, 1996), 37.

[16]Karen Lebacqz, "Fair Shares: Is the Genome Project Just?" in *Genetics: Issues of Social Justice*, ed. Ted Peters (Cleveland: Pilgrim Press, 1998), 97.

[17]An older, but still excellent overview of general issues in this area is Barbara Katz Rothman, *The Tentative Pregnancy: Prenatal Diagnosis and the Future of Motherhood* (New York: Viking Press, 1986).

[18]Annette Patterson and Martha Satz, "Genetic Counseling and the Disabled: Feminism Examines the Stance of Those Who Stand at the Gate," *Hypatia* 17 (2002): 118-42.

[19]Dena Towner and Roberta Springer Loewy, "Ethics of Preimplantation Diagnosis for a Woman Destined to Develop Early-Onset Alzheimer Disease," *Journal of the American Medical Association* 287 (February 27, 2002): 1038-1040.

[20]For a fuller discussion, see Thomas A. Shannon, "Ethical Issues in Genetics," *Health Progress* 80 (September-October 1999): 34-37.

[21]For a helpful overview, see James F. Keenan, S.J., "History of Catholicism," in *Sex from Plato to Paglia: A Philosophical Encyclopedia*, ed. Alan Soble (Westport, Conn.: Greenwood Press, 2006), 143-53.

[22]Michael Novak, "Moral Clarity in the Nuclear Age," *National Review*, April 1, 1983, 354-92. This letter is the sole article in this issue.

[23]In his book *Why I Am a Catholic*, Garry Wills reveals that he is the source of this phrase. William F. Buckley asked Wills how he should respond to the recent encyclical and Wills replied, "Why not just say your position is 'Mater sí, Magistra no'?" This was evidently playing off a phrase then popular among the Cuban exiles in Florida: "Cuba sí, Castro no" (Garry Wills, *Why I Am a Catholic* [New York: Houghton Mifflin, 2000], 47).

[24]Note, for example, the call by Senator Hillary Rodham Clinton (D-NY) for opponents in the abortion debate to try to establish common ground to "help prevent unwanted pregnancies and ultimately reduce abortions, which she called a 'sad, even tragic choice to many, many women'" (Patrick D. Healy, "On Abortion, Mrs. Clinton Reaches Out," *The New York Times*, January 25, 2005, A1).

INDEX